Walking

with GOD

Colin Tinsley

Dedication

I would like to dedicate this daily devotional book to my parents, James and Elizabeth Tinsley from Dundrod, County Antrim. They gave birth to seven boys of which I was the fourth. All of us were brought up in the Christian faith together with its principles, foundations and standards. I often look back upon my childhood with very fond memories and for this I say thank you to my Mum and Dad. The Word of God was read and we were prayed for every day. The wonderful Christian blessings that were instilled upon me as a child, I now would like to pass them on to many other children who happen to use this book as their daily reading guide.

"Train up a child in the way he should go: and when he is old, he will not depart from it."
(Proverbs 22:6)

Walking with GOD

ISBN 978-1-905989-53-9 Walking with God

Published by

6 Hawthorn Hill, Kinallen, Dromore,
Co. Down, BT25 2HY, Northern Ireland.
www.hopeforyouthministries.org

If this book has been a blessing, help or encouragement to you,
both Colin and his wife Joanna would love to hear from you,
please contact them and tell them all about it.

Printed by JC Print Ltd E: info@jcprint.net

Designed by Stephanie Elliott and Philip K. Topping

Foreword

This daily devotional has been in the process for several years now and it is with great joy that as I write this foreword it will be a source of great blessing to you. When writing this book, I have started with creation in Genesis and from there tried to go systematically through the Old Testament covering the life story of eleven major characters.

I deeply love the Old Testament Scriptures and the lessons I sought to draw from them have blessed me so much. These were real people living real lives and worshipping and serving a real God, the same God as we worship today. "For I am the LORD, I change not" (Malachi 3:6). I trust as you use 'WALKING WITH GOD' as your daily reading guide, that it too will give you a deeper love and understanding for the Word of God. The Bible is the book that we read to learn about and hear from God.

This book is really to help tell the story of each Bible character in simple language and I pray you will enjoy reading it and that it truly will be a blessing to your soul. Also that you will be encouraged to read His Word and to live for God and to serve Him with all your heart, body, mind and soul. As you read, pray that God will use it to speak to you and encourage you to go on living for Him. Every blessing as you read.

Colin Tinsley

Contents

Creation
In the Beginning

Can you imagine what the world looked like before God made it? Everywhere we look there are trees and fields, lakes and ponds. Animals are in the fields and people are everywhere. We can see, feel warmth, and breathe the invisible air.

Before the very beginning of this world, there was God. He spoke and the world came into existence. God has always been from the very beginning of the world and will remain until the very end. In fact with God there is no beginning and there will be no end, for He is Eternal.

One day God spoke from heaven and said, "I'm going to make a world. I will create it out of nothing, all I have to do is speak and it will happen." That's exactly what God did. In literally six days God spoke this whole world into existence. In this chapter we will look at the six days of creation.

This book has been written to help you understand who God is and how you can have a daily relationship with Him. To know God as a believer is the best life ever and I wouldn't exchange it for anything; not even for all the money in the whole wide world!

What do you THINK about when you think about GOD?

Switch the Light on

In the very beginning there was nothing and it was completely dark. The Bible says the "Spirit of God moved." Then God spoke and said, "Let there be light," and immediately when God spoke there was light. The moment there was light the darkness disappeared. When God saw the light He liked it and He said "it was good."

The Bible tells us that God called the light 'day' and the darkness 'night'. Have you ever noticed the difference between night and day? Time had now begun. God in His awesome power was beginning to create the world. The world had begun, time had begun and I suppose you could say life on earth had begun.

Have you ever noticed how dark it is on a really dark night, then when morning comes everything changes as all the colours appear; we can see them because it is light.

When Jesus came to this world, the Bible called him the Light of the World. We can read this in John's gospel chapter 1. Light reveals everything that is hidden and shows us the way. When we see the light at the end of a tunnel it gives hope, and so it is with the Lord Jesus Christ. He is the light of my salvation. "The LORD is my light and my salvation." (Psalm 27:1)

Christ is the Christian's hope both now and forever. The opposite of light is darkness and the Bible tells us that if we do not have Christ in our lives, we walk in the darkness of our sin.

> Whenever it gets dark we can be afraid; REMEMBER JESUS said when you come to Him He will never leave you, He will comfort you and always be with you.
> (Hebrews 13:5)

The Big Blue Sky

On the second day of God's creation He made the air space between the sky and the sea. The air is divided into many different sections. The higher up the mountain you go the air will be thinner and also colder. If you are in an aeroplane, the air outside is so thin you probably couldn't breathe, also it would be freezing cold.

God made what He called a firmament. This is the atmosphere or air we breathe. It is between the clouds and the sea. The sea is full of water and the clouds are full of water. Can you imagine how perfectly He made the atmosphere? The clouds can float in it and birds can fly in it. The clouds don't fall and the sea doesn't float.

Even when we walk we keep our feet on the ground and we can breathe so naturally and normally. This is the firmament, the space between the sky and the sea. Below the firmament God covered the world with water and He called it sea, a beautiful big blue sky and a lovely clear blue sea.

Have you ever looked up into the sky and thought: "that is some sky?" I remember being on a mission trip to Poland and looking up at what was a beautiful clear blue sky, so blue and so beautiful. It reminded the team of God's handiwork in creation. That was some blue sky!

Where on Earth did the Earth come from?

We have now come to day number three of God's creation. On this day God made the earth, that is the dry land. God spoke and the land rose up out of the sea which He had made on the second day. Just in a moment the huge mountains were formed and all over the world, land appeared; flat land and hilly land. On this day God called the dry land earth. It was at first empty and barren. Then God spoke and said, "Let there be trees and grass to fill the earth." Every tree and flower was to produce seed so they would keep on producing exactly the same type of trees and flowers.

Grass appeared in the fields and trees were everywhere; huge oak, pine, fir, beech and walnut trees. There were hedges and bushes of all sorts of colours and all shades of green. There were fruit trees; banana, pear, orange, every fruit you can imagine were all there.

Everywhere there were beautiful flowers; every flower you could imagine. The smell would have been incredible as they bloomed. Have you ever looked all around you, especially in the countryside, a park or even in a garden? I have a garden and there must be over 100 shades of green, with trees, shrubs, bushes and flowers. It is so pleasing just to see and appreciate God's perfect design; His handiwork in creation.

When you look around OUTSIDE, what can you SEE that God has MADE?

The Sun, Moon and Stars

We have now come to day number four of God's wonderful creation. On this day God made the sun, moon and stars. God made two huge lights called the sun and the moon, the sun to show light during the day and the moon to show light at night time. God placed them in the sky to light up the whole world.

Have you ever wondered how far away the sun is? It is ninety-three million miles away. If it was any closer we would melt and if it was any further away we would freeze. God knows everything and has perfect wisdom and is so powerful in every possible way.

Have you ever wondered what holds the moon in the sky? It just hangs on nothing. Isn't it amazing to think how God placed the sun, moon and the stars and they don't fall to the ground? The sky is so big there is room for millions and billions of stars, all sorts of colours and all sorts of sizes. Some of these stars are even bigger than the whole world. We could never count them, yet God has a name for every one of them. The sun, moon and stars were to indicate times and seasons.

Sometimes we sing, "Our God is a great big God." So He is; He is all-powerful. He is so big and we are so small, yet He loves us and cares for us so much. Even when a little bird falls to the ground He knows all about it. How much more does He care for you?

How much do you think God cares for you?

"For God SO LOVED THE WORLD, that he gave his only begotten Son, that whosoever BELIEVETH IN HIM should not perish, but have everlasting life." (John 3:16)

Fish and Birds,
all sorts of Colours

Everything was now beginning to take place. The earth was made as well as all the sea. The sky was there with the sun, moon and stars, but there was no movement. The sea was full of water and the air was completely empty.

Then God spoke and said, "Let the sea be filled with fish and the air with birds." Suddenly there was all sorts of movement and beautiful sounds. In the sea there were fish of all shapes and sizes and all sorts of beautiful colours. There were huge sharks and whales. Alongside them were little fish, long fish and flat fish. God spoke and told them to swim and fill the sea with lots of baby fish.

The air was filled with every kind of bird, from huge eagles to little robins, each making their own whistling and chirping sounds. God spoke to them and told them to go forth and multiply and fill the earth. This then ended the fifth day. When God looked at what He had created, He said it was good.

As you look around at God's beautiful creation, do you agree that it is good? If you were able to make an animal, tree or even a fish, could you do a better job? Would you agree with me that God has done a perfect job?

Here come the Animals

We have now come to the sixth and final day of creation. The air was filled with birds and the sea was filled with fish, but on the earth there was no life at all; everything seemed so quiet.

Then God spoke again and said, "Let the earth be filled with animals." As He spoke, all sorts of animals appeared everywhere; there were tall giraffes, massive elephants and big buffalos. As well as this there were little squirrels, hamsters and rabbits running everywhere.

There were two of every kind of animal, both male and female. God told them to go forth and multiply and fill the earth. The animals were to breed after their own kind. Donkeys had baby donkeys and elephants had baby elephants and monkeys had baby monkeys.

Can you imagine a horse having a baby lion or a lion having a baby zebra? Of course not! God had it planned out perfectly. Each animal was to breed with their own kind. Some people think we came from monkeys, but this is impossible! Monkeys have baby monkeys and human beings have baby human beings, every animal had baby animals after their own kind.

There was only one thing missing, there was something absent in the world. Do you know what it was? People of course! People were also made on the same day as the animals, the sixth day. Tomorrow we will find out how that happened. Sometimes it's good just to sit back and thank God for who you are and everything He has given to you.

"In everything give thanks: for this is the will of God in Christ Jesus concerning you."
(1 Thessalonians 5:18)

Adam the first Man

After God made all the animals He was very pleased. As they scattered all over the earth there was lots of food for them to eat. Then the best and most exciting part of God's creation was about to come, for even though God had made all the fish and animals, the birds and the trees, none of them could talk to Him or even love Him.

So God then decided to make man. He wanted man to be made in His own image; to be like Him so they could talk to each other and so that man could love God and live for Him. He took some dust from the ground and from the dust He made a man. Then He breathed into that man and man became a living soul. Man was different from all the animals, they all had bodies but no soul but man had a soul which would live forever.

Our bodies are just like houses that we live in. Although our bodies will not last forever, our soul will live on forever and ever and ever. Man now could talk with God, think about Him, pray to Him, sing about Him and obey Him. After God made man He was very pleased. The first man in the whole world was called Adam, which means red clay.

Creation had now ended, everything was made and God was very happy with how it all looked. This was now the sixth day, the day when God made all the animals and Adam the first man. There were lots of different birds, fish and animals but only one human being and he was made in the image of God.

Eve the first Woman

As God looked upon the whole earth He was very pleased with what He saw. Then He noticed that all the animals had mates but Adam was all alone. He thought it was not good that Adam should be alone. Adam needed someone, a suitable helper, someone with whom he could walk and talk and share life with.

God then decided that He would make a woman. Adam was made from the dust of the ground but this time it would be different. God caused Adam to fall into a deep sleep and while Adam was sleeping, God took a rib bone from his side and from that bone God made a woman and called her Eve.

Just like Adam, Eve had a body and a soul. Her soul would never die. When Adam awoke he was delighted to see Eve who became his wife. She was part of his flesh and bones. She was made from a rib close to his heart, so that he would be reminded to love her, care for her and look after her. Now they could worship and talk to God together.

Adam and Eve were made perfectly. They never argued, fought, or got angry. They were never afraid, tired, sad or even worried. The world was perfect and everywhere they looked it was peaceful and beautiful.

God takes a Rest

As God looked upon the whole world which He had just created He was very happy. It was very, very good. The work of creation had been completed in just six days. In six days God made the whole world.

Then, on the seventh day God rested. You might think God rested because He was tired, but this is not the reason. God wanted this day to be a holy day. A day that is different from all the rest. God rested the seventh day because the work of creation was now finished, it was perfect and there was nothing more God needed to do.

This day was called the Sabbath day, when special emphasis should be put on worshipping God and giving thanks to Him. The day we use to worship God and go to church is called The Lord's Day. When Jesus rose again from the dead on the third day, it was the first day of the week or The Lord's Day. This is when the Christian calendar begins.

Another reason God wants us to keep the Sabbath Day holy is because our bodies need to have physical rest. God in His perfect design knew that our bodies would get tired if we worked every day without stopping. On this day we can rest and worship God.

The Garden of Eden

God made a home for Adam and Eve; it was not a big house but rather a beautiful garden. It was called Eden. In it were all sorts of trees, flowers and wild life. God had given Adam the responsibility of naming all the animals. The animals were all given names before Eve was created. When a massive grey animal walked past Adam, he called it an elephant. Then when a tiny little grey animal walked past he called it a mouse and so on until every animal was named.

Here in the garden Adam and Eve had all the food they could possibly eat. God was very pleased with His creation. He told Adam and Eve to go and multiply and fill the earth. God wanted them to have children and grandchildren and great grandchildren.

Every evening God would come into the garden to visit with Adam and Eve to see how they were. This was their favourite part of the day, when God came to visit them. God gave Adam and Eve a free will. He didn't force them to obey Him, rather He gave them a choice either to obey or disobey Him. They were humans and not robots, so even today, He doesn't make us read the Bible and talk to Him in prayer or witness for Him. We have that choice; we choose to worship, follow and obey God or we choose not to.

What would your choice be?

The Special Tree

The Lord then gave Adam and Eve a test. In the middle of the garden He placed a tree. It was called the "tree of the knowledge of good and evil." He told them to eat of any fruit tree but never to eat of that one. God told them that if they ate of that tree, they would surely die. When God made them they were to live forever, but now because of their freewill they had that choice.

Adam and Eve knew how serious it was to disobey the Lord and also of the consequences of eating of that tree. There were hundreds of fruit trees to eat from. They could eat from any of them apart from this one. We are now coming to one of the most important events in history; if Adam or Eve touched that tree and took anything from it then they would die. If not, they would remain perfect and would live forever.

Adam and Eve loved God and really wanted to obey Him so they decided it was best not to touch the tree. Sin had not come into the world yet. Something was going to happen, very, very soon that would change the world for ever. Do you know what it was? It was something to do with the tree in the middle of the garden, the special tree that God told Adam and Eve not to touch.

GOD has given us rules for our lives TODAY. He has given us the 10 COMMANDMENTS. Do we obey these?

13 January　　　　　　　　　　　 Genesis 3:1-13

The Devil arrives on Earth

Have you ever wondered where the devil came from? Away before God ever made this world He lived in Heaven. God had thousands of angels who worshipped him. The leader of all the angels was called Lucifer, also called Son of the Morning. He was the most beautiful of all the angels in Heaven.

As Lucifer watched all the angels bowing down and worshipping God, he began to get jealous, for he wanted all the angels to bow down and worship him. He wanted to be like God and eventually he wanted to be God. He wanted to sit on a throne higher than God's throne. He was determined to replace God in Heaven.

Of course this could and would never happen. Lucifer was not God and could never replace God. But one third of all the angels believed Lucifer and followed him in a great rebellion against God. As a result God cast Lucifer and all his followers out of Heaven.

Lucifer then became Satan or the Devil. His fallen angels became demons or evil spirits. Satan still hates God. He hates the Bible. He hates everything that is good and right; he is also a liar. Tomorrow we are going to see how he tricked Eve into disobeying God, just at the moment when she least expected it. What was about to happen would change the world forever.

CREATION 21

Satan tricks Eve

One day Eve was standing near the tree of knowledge of good and evil in the middle of the garden. She knew that she was not to take from the tree of knowledge of good and evil. She had no intention of ever touching this tree; to do so was not only wrong, but it would be disobeying God.

Satan was now in the earth and he made his way to the home of Adam and Eve to their garden, the garden of Eden. Satan was not a little red devil with horns as some people think he is. Rather he disguised himself as a serpent. A serpent was probably one of the most beautiful animals in the garden. One day the serpent came over and asked Eve why she was not taking the fruit from the tree of knowledge.

Eve then told the serpent what God had told her and that if they were to eat of the tree, they would die. The serpent then laughed at Eve and told her that this was not true. In fact he told Eve, if she ate of this tree then she would become as wise as a god. He also told her that they wouldn't die, but that they would know the difference between good and bad, and right and wrong.

"You will become just like God," Satan said. He then told Eve how nice the fruit would taste and what it would be like to be like God. Satan hated God and knew exactly what he was doing, he was tempting Eve to disobey and ultimately sin. Every day we are like Eve; we are tempted. The question is do we resist the temptation or give in to it? What did Eve do? Did she listen to the Devil and eat the fruit or obey God and not touch the fruit? Tomorrow we will find out!

Adam and Eve sin against God

Eve was now face to face with the biggest decision of her life. God had told her not to touch the fruit from the tree in the middle of the garden, and now the devil, in the form of a serpent, is telling her it's ok to eat the fruit.

Eve then made the decision to disobey God and believe the lie of the devil. She lifted up her hand and took fruit from the tree and ate it. Adam wasn't very far away and he came along and he also took the fruit from Eve that also came from the tree.

Isn't it amazing that when we see a sign 'wet paint, do not touch', we put our finger on the paint to see if it is dry. Why is it if we pass a window that says, 'please don't look through the window', we look through the window! If we came to a door with a notice saying this door is locked please don't try to open, how many people would try to open the door?

The moment Eve took of the forbidden fruit she sinned against God. Adam and Eve were supposed to live forever but because of what they did they would have to die. As a result every person in the whole world born after Adam and Eve is born with original sin and will all die. All of us will die one day, but we have a soul that will live on forever either with God in Heaven or with the devil in hell.

This is the most important message in the Bible. The Bible tells us that; God loved us so much that He sent the Lord Jesus into this world to die for us so our sins can be forgiven. (John 3:16)

CREATION 23

The First Clothes

As soon as Adam and Eve had taken fruit from the forbidden tree they realised they had done wrong. They realised they were naked and began to make clothes out of fig leaves to cover themselves.

This is the first time in the Bible we read about people making clothes. Before this Adam and Eve didn't even realise they were naked as they were clothed in God's perfect righteousness. Now everything was different. Sin had come into the world and as we continue reading the Bible we will soon see the consequences of sin.

Every evening God would come walking into the garden to visit Adam and Eve. Being made in His image, God had a special love towards them. When God called their names, they were afraid and hid themselves in the garden because they knew they had sinned against God. Is it possible to hide from God? No, it is not, because God can see everything and He knows everything too.

Adam and Eve had to answer to God, so Adam blamed Eve and even blamed God for making her and Eve blamed the serpent. Even today no-one likes to be blamed. We always seem to blame someone else. God cursed the serpent, probably one of the most beautiful animals in the garden that could walk upright. From that moment on it would crawl on its belly and eat the dust of the ground. He told the snake that it would be hated by man. That is why most people today don't like snakes and cringe at the sight of them. God then spoke to Adam and Eve and he had some startling news for them.

Sin must be Punished

God had now met Adam and Eve in the garden of Eden for the last time. All because of their sin, they could not remain in Eden. Adam and Eve would have to leave the beautiful garden that they called home.

God had some startling news for Adam and Eve. Sin always has its consequences and God told Adam that he would have to work now and earn a living. He told Adam that, "you will have to work hard and you will now sweat from the brow of your head in the heat of the day because the ground will no longer be perfect, it will be cursed with thorns, thistles and weeds."

God told Eve that she would suffer pain in childbirth. Leaving the garden of Eden would mean pain, suffering, sadness, sickness, sorrow and eventually death. But worst of all, Adam and Eve were separated from God and never again would they see Him face to face on earth.

God still loved Adam and Eve just as much as before, but God hated sin and could never allow sin to come before Him again. Everyone born since Adam and Eve is born with sin in their hearts. Sin must be punished and we all deserve to die because of it, but the message of the Bible is God's gift of forgiveness to the world.

His Son Jesus came into the world to save us from our sin so we must believe in Jesus Christ in order to be saved from everlasting death.

CREATION 25

A Lamb is killed

Now that Adam and Eve had eaten of the forbidden fruit, God decided they would have to leave the garden of Eden in case they would also eat of the tree of life. Before they left the garden God killed an innocent lamb, first of all to make clothes for Adam and Eve and also as a sin offering.

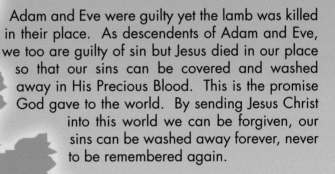

The lamb was killed and its blood was shed as a sacrifice because of the sin they committed in the garden. The lamb was a picture of the Lord Jesus Christ. The Lamb was innocent just as Jesus Christ was. Jesus was perfectly harmless and sinless yet He was put to death and His blood was shed to take away our sin. God gave Adam and Eve the promise of a Saviour through the image of the sacrificed lamb.

Adam and Eve were guilty yet the lamb was killed in their place. As descendents of Adam and Eve, we too are guilty of sin but Jesus died in our place so that our sins can be covered and washed away in His Precious Blood. This is the promise God gave to the world. By sending Jesus Christ into this world we can be forgiven, our sins can be washed away forever, never to be remembered again.

God promises that whoever believes in Jesus Christ, confessing and turning away from their sin, is forgiven and will be saved forever.

Adam and Eve leave the Garden of Eden

Full of remorse and regret Adam and Eve had to leave the garden of Eden, never to return again. How they wished they had never listened to Satan. Today millions of people are deceived by the deceitfulness and lies of Satan. Temptation is so strong that most people are not able to resist it.

The Lord has promised to help His people to overcome temptation. "There hath no temptation taken you but such as is common to man: but God is faithful, who will not suffer you to be tempted above that ye are able; but will with the temptation also make a way to escape, that ye may be able to bear it." (1 Corinthians 10:13)

Full of sadness, and probably tears, they walked out of the garden with their lamb skin clothes on. They were leaving perfection and paradise and all around them was evidence of sin and corruption. The fact that they would never see God face to face again would have been the most difficult thing to accept. How they missed the fellowship with God every night.

Because of sinful disobedience they would live in regret forever. There would be pain and sorrow and eventually death for them, all because of sin. As they left the garden God placed two angels over the entrance of the garden with flaming swords guarding the entrance to the tree of life. This was to ensure that sinful man could never come near it again. All because of a tree, sin came into the world. But Jesus died on a tree at Calvary to take away the sin of the world; Christ was the second Adam.

"For since by man came death, by man came also the resurrection of the dead." (1 Corinthians 15:21)

Cain and Abel are born

Even though Adam and Eve were out of the garden of Eden they were happy because they knew that one day they would see God again. God promised that He would send a sacrifice to take away the sins of the world. When they sacrificed a lamb, by building an altar of stones, it was a picture of the Lamb of God, the Lord Jesus Christ who would come into the world to die for their sins. Just as we look back to Jesus dying, Adam and Eve looked forward to His coming.

One day God gave Adam and Eve a baby; the first baby in the world. His name was Cain. Soon after this Cain had a baby brother called Abel. No doubt as Cain and Abel were growing up they would learn all about God and the garden of Eden. They would also learn the story of Satan and the tree and how they had to leave the garden because of their disobedience. As a result they would learn all about sin and how they were born with a sinful nature.

This sinful nature was soon evident in the lives of the two boys. They would fight, argue, tell lies and do all sorts of wrong things. No doubt it broke their parents' hearts. All because of sin the world would no longer be perfect. Adam and Eve would also explain to the boys about the 'blood sacrifice' this was an offering to God to have their sins forgiven. Cain and Abel would have also brought joy to their parents as they watched them grow up.

Cain kills Abel

As Cain and Abel grew up they soon found what type of work they liked to do. Abel became a shepherd looking after sheep and Cain became a farmer working the land. They would soon know all about hard work. With so many weeds, thorns and thistles they could not forget how the ground was cursed because of sin.

The time came for the boys to prepare a sacrifice. Abel built an altar and brought his best lamb to be sacrificed. He really was sorry for his sin and prayed to God to forgive him. God saw Abel's heart and accepted his offering. God sent fire from heaven to consume his sacrifice.

Cain on the other hand brought vegetables to be offered. God had made it clear that an animal must be sacrificed so that blood can be shed for sins to be forgiven so He rejected Cain's sacrifice. Cain thought he could come to God his own way on his own terms. But there was only one way to God, the way of the sacrifice of the lamb. Today there is still only one way to God; the way of the sacrificed Lamb of God, the Lord Jesus Christ.

Cain was so angry that God accepted Abel's sacrifice and had rejected his. He was full of jealousy and anger. His temper, anger and frustration became worse and worse until it exploded. One day when he was out in the field with his brother Abel, they got into a fight and Cain killed his brother Abel. This was the first murder in the Bible.

Sometimes we can get so angry, we say we hate someone so much we could kill them. The Bible says this is like actual murder. How God hates it when we hate someone else.

The Lamb of God

Perhaps Cain had no intention of killing his brother Abel, but that is what sin does to us; it takes us further than we want to go. Cain was so afraid he decided to run away and hide just as his parents had done in the garden of Eden. They too wanted to run away and hide. Can we hide from God? Of course not, God knows everything. (Psalm 139:1-4)

As Cain was running away God called out to him and asked him where his brother Abel was. He told God he didn't know. "Am I my brother's keeper?" he asked God. He was lying and trying to cover up his sin. Can you see how one sin can lead to another? Not only this, he was also being disrespectful to God. Instead of bowing down with complete sorrow he was trying to be smart as if he didn't care. Do we ever try to cover up our wrong doing? We must take responsibility for our actions and not blame others.

Cain spent the rest of his life running from God, trying to please God in his own way but he must come to God His way.

Sin left a terrible mark on the world; how terrible Adam and Eve must have felt. To cover their sin, a lamb had to be sacrificed and its blood shed. This lamb was a picture of the Perfect Lamb of God the Lord Jesus Christ who would one day pay the ultimate sacrifice by dying on the cross to take away our sins. Only by looking to this Lamb and by believing in this Lamb who is the Lamb of God, God's Son, the Lord Jesus Christ, can we be forgiven and saved forever and ever!

More and more People

Adam and Eve had lots and lots of children, grandchildren and great-grandchildren. In fact more and more babies were born until eventually there were millions of people on the earth.

Adam lived until he was 930 years old. It was normal at the very beginning of the world for people to live for hundreds of years. There weren't as many sicknesses and diseases as we have today to weaken people; this was God's plan to populate the whole earth.

The average age for a person to live today is well over 70, although the Bible mentions 70 as the average age of death. Due to Adam and Eve sinning in the Garden of Eden they would eventually die, in fact so would everyone. Everyone eventually died apart from Enoch and Elijah who both went straight to heaven without ever dying.

The Bible tells us that sadly the people forgot about God and lived their lives without Him. It grieves the Lord when we leave Him out of our everyday lives. The hearts of the people were full of sin, hatred, envy and all sorts of wrong things. God told Adam and Eve that every generation must bring an animal as a sacrifice for sin. Soon the people never bothered, they forgot all about God and didn't worship Him anymore. God was not pleased. Soon He would have to judge this sinful world so that He could preserve the human race and eventually send the promised Saviour.

Does God like it when we try to live OUR LIVES without Him?

Enoch walks with God

Every once in a while the Bible singles out an individual for one reason or another. We can learn so much from these Bible characters. While the world was full of so much sin and falling away from God, we read about a man called Enoch.

The Bible says Enoch loved God and that he obeyed and worshipped Him. Enoch lived a pure and separated life unto the Lord. Even though he lived in the world he was not part of the world, because he lived a life pleasing to the Lord.

Enoch was a preacher, who warned the people to come back to God. He warned the people of the danger of blocking God out of their lives but the people didn't listen to him. You may think it is difficult to be a Christian today. How much more difficult would it have been in Enoch's day?

The Bible says, "Enoch walked with God." This is a lovely statement. When we walk with our best friend we can talk about everything and Jesus is a "friend that sticketh closer than a brother." (Proverbs 18:24) We can share anything and everything with Him. Enoch knew God in a special way and today we can also have that intimate walk with God.

Enoch had this testimony that he pleased God. Is God pleased with your life?

A strange name for a Baby

Enoch and his wife had a little baby boy named Methuselah. After Methuselah was born Enoch walked with God for another 300 years. Methuselah lived to be the oldest person in the whole world for he lived until he was 969 years old.

Maybe when Methuselah was born it caused Enoch to think more about God. Sometimes God uses little babies to make their parents think about Him. This is possibly why Enoch spent the rest of his life walking with God.

The name Methuselah has a very strange meaning, it means, 'When he is gone, judgment will come.' Why would anyone call their baby such a name? Soon we will be reading all about the flood that destroyed the whole world. The flood came exactly 969 years after Methuselah was born. When he was gone, God sent His judgment upon the whole world, so Methuselah's name was prophetic, as the meaning of his name came true.

All over the world there were fewer and fewer people following God and something had to be done about it. People were created to glorify and enjoy God; now they didn't even care about Him.

Does God like it when we forget about Him and leave Him out of our LIVES?

Straight to Heaven without dying

So far everyone who had been born had died, but with Enoch it was different. Enoch walked so closely with God, that one day while he was out walking, God took him straight to heaven without dying. Isn't that amazing? Wouldn't that be wonderful to go straight to heaven without having to die? However, unless the Lord Jesus comes back before we die, we will all one day die. How our heart is with God when we die is a very important issue because we do not know how, when or where we will die.

However, there is one thing we can know and that is where we will go when we die. Christians are sure of eternal life with God in heaven. Once our sins are truly forgiven and we have received Jesus Christ by faith into our hearts, we are promised eternal life in heaven with the Lord. (Romans 6:23)

On the other hand, if a person is not saved, if they have never trusted in Christ for Salvation then they will never be in heaven, no matter how good they are. The sin we are born with separates us from God forever, because there can never be sin in heaven. That is why the Lord Jesus Christ is our only hope; Christ Jesus came into the world to save sinners (1 Timothy 1:15). Jesus died on the cross to take away our sin and forgive us. This is something we must accept if we are to be saved, and have our sins forgiven.

Why not ask God to forgive you and save you if you have not already done so.

The World forgets about God

As God looked down from heaven at the world, he was deeply saddened. He had made a perfect world and in it He made man to worship, glorify and enjoy Him forever. Now the world had completely forsaken and forgotten all about God.

God had almost regretted making the world when He saw sin everywhere. When God saw the state of man and how sinful man had become, He decided to destroy the world and start all over again. How it must have grieved the Lord at the thought of destroying something that once was so beautiful. Life without God is not worth living.

God was gracious and kind because He wanted to give everybody an opportunity to be saved before He destroyed the world. God decided to send a flood into this world to destroy it, so He scanned His eyes over the whole world looking for someone who loved Him. He found another man, whose name was Noah. God was going to use Noah to build an ark to survive the flood. Noah was a faithful man who lived a life pleasing to God.

Sin is a SERIOUS thing. When God looks down from HEAVEN and sees you, are you someone who pleases the Lord?

Mr. Noah builds an Ark

When God saw Noah He was very pleased with his life. Noah was a righteous man and a man whom God could trust to obey Him. When God explained how to build the ark and why He wanted an ark, Noah immediately agreed to build it.

Building the ark would take 120 years. It was going to be a massive ship; as big as an ocean liner. The main reason for building the ark was that it was to be a place of safety and shelter for anyone who wished to be saved from the flood; two of every kind of animal were to be brought into the ark.

The ark was to be 137 metres long, 23 metres wide and 14 metres high. It had three decks, a window and only one door. As the people watched with excitement and disbelief at this ark being built they thought Noah was mad, but God had said He would destroy the whole earth with a flood and that only people inside the ark would be safe.

It took great faith for Noah to build this ark because it had never rained upon the earth before. When Noah told the people he was building an ark as a shelter from the flood they laughed him to scorn. They laughed at what was to be their only hope. The ark of course is a lovely picture of the Lord Jesus Christ. He came to rescue and save us, just as the ark was to rescue and save the people in Noah's day.

Today many people laugh at the message of the gospel, just as they laughed at the offer of safety in the ark in Noah's day. Do you laugh at the message of the gospel?

In come the Animals

Noah worked at the ark for 120 years, labouring day and night. He took every opportunity to tell the people why he was building the ark. There was so much sin everywhere that God was going to destroy the whole world and start all over again. Noah told the people that if they were sorry and repented of their sin then they would be saved, then they could come into the ark and would not have to perish. The people just laughed and made fun of Noah.

God continued to direct Noah every step of the way. Even though it never rained the entire time, Noah kept working. Finally the job was finished and the ark was completed. Noah had to then store enough food to last an entire year for all the animals that would be inside the ark.

God then told Noah to bring two of every kind of animal into the ark, both male and female. God helped Noah make all this happen for He caused two of every kind of animal to go into the ark. After the flood they would then breed and populate the whole earth again. Of course, it was not necessary to bring the sea creatures like the fish and whales because they already lived in the water.

In came the animals; monkeys, donkeys, horses, cows, sheep, lions, tigers, dogs, cats, giraffes, buffalos and so on. Two of every kind of animal both male and female walked side by side into the ark. Can you imagine the beautiful sight of all the large and small animals, from the smallest mouse to the largest elephant walking into the ark?

The ark became like a big zoo full of every sort of animal that was found on the earth, from birds to insects. God had caused two of every animal to go into the ark. Watching this alone should have caused the people to realise that God is in control and what He says He will do.

How do you feel when people mock you for something you believe in?

CREATION 37

Please come in

The ark was now built and the animals were all safely inside the ark. Noah had faithfully obeyed all the Lord's instructions as to how to build the ark and how to put pitch on it; a tar-like substance to help make it waterproof.

At every opportunity Noah would have pleaded with the people to come into the ark. It was a very serious matter, but everyone just laughed at Noah and called him a fool. It had never rained before, therefore they could not imagine a flood, but Noah continually warned them, time and time again to come into the ark.

Now the final opportunity had come and all the animals were now aboard. The only people to believe were Noah, his wife, his three sons, Shem, Ham, and Japheth; and their wives. Out of all the people in the whole world only eight were saved from the flood.

"Please come into the ark and be saved from the flood," Noah begged the people. The more he pleaded, the more the people laughed at him. How foolish the people were not to listen to the advice of Noah. The ark of course was a reminder of Salvation, for those who came into the ark were saved from the flood. Likewise for those who come and put their faith and trust in Jesus Christ they too will be saved. For those who mock and delay and do not get saved they will be like those outside the ark, lost forever.

Why do you think many people don't want to get saved TODAY?

God shuts the Door

Noah invited the people to come into the ark for the final time. "This is your last opportunity to come into the ark. If you do not come in, you will perish in the flood that will soon come," he told them. The people were so angry. It had never rained before and the sky was always blue. The people thought Noah was out of his mind.

Maybe some people wanted to come into the ark but because of peer pressure from their friends they would not take the step. Many people, I feel would love to get saved and follow Christ, but because of peer pressure they don't take the step.

This is like so many today. Many people know they should be saved, even want to be saved but sometimes because of fear of what their friends might think or say they remain outside of Christ, lost forever. Please learn from the story of the ark; don't be like the crowd staying outside of security and safety, rather come to Christ and be sure of your salvation.

The last opportunity was over. Noah together with his wife, their three sons and their wives were now inside the ark, together with two of every kind of animal. Then God shut the door and because God shut the door it could never be opened unless God opened it. Even when the floods would come and the people would beg Noah to let them in, it would be too late to get saved as God had shut the door.

> God calls people to Himself and they keep saying NO. Then God shuts the door of opportunity for the final time. This could be your FINAL OPPORTUNITY! (Genesis 6:3)

Down comes the Rain

After God shut the door and Noah and his family were safely inside the ark, they waited and waited. Out of all the people on the earth only eight were saved from the flood. Nothing happened the first day or the second day. Can you imagine the yells and screams of the people as they would have mocked and made fun of Noah?

How hot it must have been as they waited three, four, five, six days inside the ark. It had never rained on the earth before. The people thought Noah was completely mad but Noah however remained calm and his faith was strong. God had told him to build an ark and to bring the animals in two by two. He also told Noah to warn the people that they must get inside the ark or they would perish forever. Noah warned the people and not one person outside of his family heeded the warning.

Then early on the seventh morning, the sky was different. Suddenly there were clouds in the sky, it was colder than normal and in the distance was the sound of thunder and the strikes of lightning. Then came the rain. It rained and rained and rained. In fact it continued to rain for forty days and nights without stopping.

The people screamed in vain for Noah to open the door. How sorry they must have felt. Perhaps Noah yelled back, "I cannot open the door." "Why not?" they screamed. "Because God himself has shut the door!"

The rain came down and the floods came up. The houses were soon covered. The people fled to the mountains but soon they were covered also. Every person and every animal outside the ark perished in the flood. How devastating it must have been. Did you know that the year the flood came the oldest man in the world, Methuselah died. Do you remember what his name means? 'When he is gone judgment will come.' God judged the world with a worldwide flood, all because of the people's sin and disobedience.

Safe in the Ark

For forty days and nights the rain beat down upon the ark. Even though the storm was unbelievable outside the ark, everyone was completely safe inside the ark.

The Bible says that, "all the fountains of the great deep were broken up and the windows of heaven were opened." (Genesis 7:11) This means that all the rivers, seas and underground water systems all burst open and completely flooded the earth together with all the rain that fell. Such was the power, force and magnitude of the great flood.

The storm was gigantic, never before had the people seen anything like it. The people outside would have done anything to get into the ark but now it was too late; they had missed their opportunity. The ark was built exactly as God had told Noah to build it; therefore it sailed safely through the storms, right on top of the whole world. Everything was now completely covered right up to and over the highest mountain in the world.

Just as Noah and his family were safe in the flood, we too can be safe with Jesus Christ. The ark was the only way they could be saved. Likewise today, the only way we can be saved is by believing in the Lord Jesus Christ and by putting our trust in Him alone to have our sins forgiven.

> Just as Noah put his TRUST in God and obediently built the ARK, are you trusting in Jesus Christ today to be your Saviour?

The Flood ends

After forty days and forty nights, the rain eventually stopped. Everything on the earth had died. God had judged the world and now it was to start all over again. Noah didn't leave the ark immediately. In fact he was in the ark for a year and ten days. This means that after the rain stopped it took another 11 months for the water to seep away. Can you imagine how much water that was and how long it would take to seep away?

The ark landed on top of Mount Ararat in the land of Turkey, and it took five months for it to land here after it stopped raining. Noah then sent out a raven to see what would happen, but it didn't come back because it was a scavenger and lived off the dead carcasses.

After that, Noah sent out a dove. Soon it came back because it had nowhere to land, as the waters were still covering all the land. Seven days later he sent out the dove again and this time it came back with an olive leaf plucked off in its mouth. Now the flood was down to the level of the trees and seven days later the dove was released again, but it did not return.

At this stage God again spoke to Noah and told him the earth was now dry and it was time to leave the ark and to send the animals out and let them spread over all the earth and multiply greatly. What a lovely feeling to come to the end of such a long journey.

Noah probably had no idea how long he would be in the ark. We may find God placing us in a job, school or church to be a witness for Him. We should be PATIENT until it is God's time for us to move on.

The promise of the Rainbow

The first thing Noah and his family did when they came out of the ark was to make a sacrifice and by doing this they were putting the Lord first. They were acknowledging God in their lives for His safe keeping and protection, as well as being obedient to God, as this is what God had told them to do.

God promised to send His Son Jesus Christ into this world to be the final sacrifice for sins. God told Noah that Jesus would be born in the line of Shem, Noah's oldest son. This sacrifice was also a way of saying that Noah believed that God would send a Saviour into the world for the sins of mankind.

Then Noah and all his family looked up to the sky and there was one of the most beautiful things they had ever seen. It was a rainbow made up of all sorts of beautiful colours and this was a promise from God that He would never again destroy this world by a flood. Sometimes when it rains you can find a rainbow in the sky, reminding us of the great flood that came upon the earth. Although God does tell us that the world will be destroyed again, He promised that He would never send another flood. The next time the world is destroyed it will be by fire and brimstone from heaven.

God was pleased with Noah because he put the LORD first in his life. How important do you think it is to put the Lord first in your LIFE?

The Tower of Babel

The flood was now over and everything was back to normal. God had told Noah and his family to have lots of children and repopulate the whole earth.

Many changes had now taken place. For the first time ever people were allowed to eat meat. Before the flood there had been no law and order and everyone did what was right in their own eyes. The world had been full of wickedness but the people were now to respect law and order.

But again the people did not listen to God. The Lord had told them to spread across the earth, but they refused to do so. After many generations and thousands of people they now had built a huge city where the whole world lived. This city was called Babylon or Babel. Everyone spoke the same language and could understand one another.

Then the people began to build a tower that they hoped would reach all the way to heaven. They had soon forgotten about God and began to worship the sun, moon and stars. They thought when they built the tower high enough they could step out of the tower into heaven to meet with God.

How foolish the people were. This was an impossible thing to do. We can only get to heaven by trusting in the Lord to take us there. Only faith in Jesus Christ will secure us a home in heaven. (John 14:6)

If someone were to ask you, HOW DO YOU GET TO HEAVEN, would you be able to tell them?

CREATION 44

Where did all the Languages come from?

The Bible says when the people were building the tower of Babel that God came down amongst them. God was grieved in his heart to see what the people were trying to do. This building would have to be stopped and God had the perfect solution.

Up until this time, everyone spoke the same language and could understand one another but suddenly God confused their language and they all started talking in completely different languages. While someone would have asked for bricks, the person he was talking to had no idea what he was saying and suddenly the place was filled with frustration and confusion.

Everyone then came down off the building and started to get into groups where they could understand each other. Then they all began to scatter across the country and throughout the world. Have you ever wondered where all the different languages came from? Have you ever wondered why people speak Chinese, Japanese, Italian, Russian, and Polish etc? Well, you can trace all these languages and people right back to the day when God confused the language in Babylon.

Not all the countries and languages of the world were formed at this time. Many of our modern languages developed over a long period of time from more ancient languages.

Isn't it an amazing thing that out of all the languages in the world, when someone talks to God in their own language, God immediately understands them!

CREATION 45

Walking all over the World

We have now come to the end of Creation and it is such a vast and amazing subject. Creation shows us that the Hand of Almighty God is everywhere.

Now that God had confused their language the people were gradually spreading all over the world. This is what God had planned to happen, after the flood God told Noah and his family to multiply and spread across the earth.

Simply because the people had refused to obey God, they were now all mixed up and confused. Sin brings confusion to people where life is supposed to be simple, sweet and enjoyable. Now it is full of sin, frustration and confusion. When we are told to do one thing we do another. That is confusion.

God has given us only Ten Commandments and they are broken every day. This causes confusion! The problem with all this is sin and sin has always been the root of the problem. Remember in the Garden of Eden when God told Adam and Eve not to touch the middle tree. They disobeyed God and sin came into the world.

All the problems in the world ever since are a result of sin. Yet God loved us so much He sent His only begotten Son, the Lord Jesus Christ, into the world to die for us to take away our sin. What we do with Jesus Christ will change our lives and destiny forever. Will you believe in Him and accept Him or will you reject Him? We are separated from God because of the sin we are born with. The only way back to God is Jesus Christ. He is the bridge between heaven and earth.

Abraham

God speaks to Abraham

The earth now had a completely new start and after the flood the people eventually spread throughout the earth. After the Lord confused the language of the people they still worshipped false gods. It was in the people's nature to worship, but God wanted the people to worship Him only. Perhaps we should ask ourselves, what is it in my life that I spend the most time with and maybe even worship? It might not be a god of wood but you can worship things like sport or maybe people. If there is something which keeps you from spending time with God then you need to ask God to help you deal with it.

All across the earth the people multiplied and built towns and cities to live in. The people did not worship God, but rather nature; things that God had made. They would make images of wood and stone and bow down to them.

Just as there was Enoch and Noah, God would choose someone who would be faithful to Him. In every generation God would have someone who would be faithful to Him; someone who did not bow down to false gods or go with the crowd, a person who would stay true to God. The Lord was going to choose someone to teach the nation and lead the people in the ways of God. Maybe that's why the Lord has you exactly where you are at the present time.

Not far from the city of Babel was a family with three sons; Terah was a Shepherd and had three sons, Abram, Nahor and Haran. Haron died young and left a son called Lot whom Abram would look after and raise as his own son. All these people worshipped the moon god, Ur, except for Abram and his wife Sarai.

Abram worshipped the true Jehovah God of Heaven and he offered sacrifices to the Lord. God loved Abram who later was called Abraham. One day God spoke to Abraham and told him he must be prepared to leave his home and family and go to a land which would be his new home. Immediately Abraham prepared himself to leave all and follow God.

God had a plan for Abraham's life; it meant leaving all his comforts, family and friends to follow Gods will and plan for his life.

> God has a plan for every one of His children. Do you love the Lord more than anything? Is He more important to you than all those other things you love?

A Promise, Decision and a Challenge

When God spoke to Abraham he listened intently to what the Lord had to say to him. God was asking Abraham to leave his home, family and country to go to a far away land. The Lord promised Abraham that if he did what He said, then the Lord would bless him. He promised Abraham that He would make him a great nation, make his name famous and that the whole world would be blessed because of him.

As Abraham listened to God and His great promise, how thrilled he was. Of course through Abraham's lineage the promised Messiah would be born, the Lord Jesus Christ. This is how we are blessed today as our sins can be forgiven by trusting in Jesus Christ. Have you ever thanked the Lord for this blessing?

Abraham had to make the biggest decision of his life as he had many luxuries he would have to give up. Would he step out in faith and follow the Lord in complete obedience? If this was your choice what would you do? Is it still possible to live a life of faith? I say, "Yes it is." By this I mean completely trusting in God to help you and provide for you everyday of your life, not really knowing what the future holds but knowing who holds the future. God never changes and just as He looked after Abraham He can look after you.

The place Abraham would go to was called Canaan, the Promised Land, which today is Israel. The descendants of Abraham are the Israelites or the Jews; God's chosen people. The challenge Abraham faced of course was that he didn't know where the Lord would lead him. He would have to entrust his life completely into the hands of the Lord to guide and protect him.

What a challenge this is. May the Lord give us the faith of Abraham to live for and follow Him.

ABRAHAM 48

Abraham worships God

Abraham wasted no time and when the Lord called him to go, he never made excuses. Do we make excuses when God wants us to do something? He packed his bags and his tents and together with his wife they made their way to where God wanted them to go. Together with his father and his wife and nephew Lot, they made their way across the land. They also took their herds of cattle, camels, sheep and goats and all their servants and herdsmen.

Abraham made his journey in faith. He had no idea where he was going. "By faith Abraham, when he was called to go out into a place which he should after receive for an inheritance, obeyed; and he went out, not knowing whither he went."(Hebrews 11:8) He depended completely on God to guide him.

Abraham eventually arrived in the land of promise. When he got there the Lord told him that this was his land for him and his children. The first thing Abraham did was to build an altar, make a sacrifice and worship the Lord. The first place they went to was called Bethel meaning 'house of God'; here Abraham pitched his tent and made another sacrifice to God.

In Canaan where Abraham now was, the people were called Canaanites; they were heathen people who did not know God. They worshipped idols of wood and stone, they were a very wicked and sinful people. God brought Abraham here to be a witness to the people and every time Abraham sacrificed a lamb, he had a great opportunity to witness to the people of the True God. Every time he made a sacrifice and built an altar he was worshipping God.

Am I depending completely on God in my life? For example, in school when things get tough, when I have to make decisions about my future, my friends etc.

God brings people into our lives and sends us to places which may seem strange to us. Maybe this is because God is using you to be a witness to others.

ABRAHAM 49

Trusting God in days of trouble

Abraham had left all to follow the Lord; this of course didn't mean life would be all sunshine and free from trouble for him. The Lord will still send us little trials and tests along the way to really test our faith.

Soon after Abraham arrived in Canaan a famine came upon the land and soon there was little food and the crops were failing. God had promised to supply Abraham's every need, but when the famine came Abraham gathered all his possessions together and went down to Egypt.

This was a great test for Abraham and he failed. Whenever the going gets tough this is when we must really call upon the Lord to help us. God had called Abraham into the land of promise; this was for his family and his inheritance. While all the heathen people moved down into Egypt Abraham just followed them, forgetting God's promises to him.

We are not to follow the ways of the world, maybe this was God's way of cleansing the land from idol worship by bringing a famine. What an opportunity Abraham had to prove God in times of difficulty, but he didn't take the opportunity to stand up for God.

Sometimes when trials and difficulties come our way we take the easy option and give in. God wants us to really come close to Him and not to follow the ways of the world. Even though we live in this world we are only here for a short time and while we are travelling through this world we must be focused on the one to come, Heaven. While we are journeying through this world the Lord has promised to lead, protect, guide and never to leave us. He is true to His promise, but like Abraham, we often make the mistake of walking away from God, right out of His will and doing what we think is best. When trouble comes my way do I immediately ask God for help?

ABRAHAM 50

1st Corinthians 10:13 says…. "But God is faithful, who will not suffer you to be tempted above that ye are able; but will with the temptation also make a way to escape, that ye may be able to bear it."

A terrible Lie

As Abraham was approaching Egypt he began to think about his wife Sarah. Sarah was very beautiful and he was worried the king of Egypt might find her attractive and take her for his own wife.

He then told Sarah, his wife, that if Pharaoh inquired who she was that she was to tell the king she was Abraham's sister. Abraham thought that if the king liked Sarah and wanted to marry her then he might kill Abraham so he could marry Sarah.

This was a terrible thing to do. I can imagine if I asked my wife to do this she would put me in the dog kennel! Even though Sarah was Abraham's half sister, a half truth is a whole lie in the eyes of God. The Lord hates liars. Always tell the truth no matter the cost! Abraham should not have advised Sarah to deny she was his wife.

Sarah was then taken by the king and told the king she was Abraham's sister. He thought she would make another lovely wife to add to his collection. Then God sent great plagues to the palace of Pharaoh and Pharaoh soon realised she was already married to Abraham and in anger he let them go.

Abraham returned to Canaan and at the altar he made a sacrifice to the Lord pleading for the Lord's forgiveness. Whenever we do wrong we must immediately confess it to the Lord and ask for His forgiveness. Abraham could have lost his life for telling lies but the hand of the Lord was upon him and rescued him from danger, the good thing however was that he asked the Lord to forgive him.

Telling lies is a terrible sin and the Lord tells us that liars will not be in the Kingdom of Heaven. Even God's chosen man, Abraham, needed to learn that it is important to trust God completely and not try to sort out difficulties in a way that seems to be clever, without asking help from God. Proverbs 3:5-6

ABRAHAM 51

Lot makes a choice

Abraham was a very wealthy man and had lots of servants and herdsmen to look after his thousands of animals. Lot his nephew also had lots of herdsmen to look after his animals but soon the herdsmen began to quarrel with each other and fight over the land where their animals were.

Abraham said to Lot that they had better separate from each other as he did not want any bitterness to come between them. This was very wise of Abraham to notice potential problems and as a result he tried to mend the situation. It is always good to stop potential quarrels and problems before they get completely out of hand, especially if two people are Christians. What a bad testimony it is for people to see two Christians quarrelling or a Christian arguing with someone else and maybe even losing their temper.

Abraham gave Lot the choice of where he wanted to live; it was best they go their separate ways. Out of all the land, Abraham gave Lot the first choice. He did not choose the best and give the rest to Lot, rather he gave Lot the first choice. This was so thoughtful, generous and kind of Abraham.

Lot had a good look around him; he had a choice of all the lovely fertile land surrounding the cities of Sodom and Gomorrah. These were wicked cities where the people sinned against the Lord greatly. Lot made this choice to go towards Sodom and Gomorrah. We do not read of him praying about the matter, he was only interested in earthly riches and the enjoyment of living close to the wicked cities. He only thought of the present. He did not think of the future and the problems it might cause living so close to such wicked cities.

When we make choices we must think of the present and the future and pray to God for guidance. What is the most important for you, the present or the future?

Genesis 13:14-18 & 15:3-6

A Son promised to Abraham

Abraham and his nephew Lot had now gone their separate ways. Lot chose to go toward the cities of Sodom and Gomorrah while Abraham stayed in the mountains. The Lord again spoke to him and promised him that as far as he could see in every direction, the land was his. God also promised Abraham that he would have many children; far more than the sand on the seashore. The Bible is full of promises for us; every day we should find a promise in the Bible just for us.

How could this possibly be, since Abraham had no children? The Lord was going to give Abraham a son and through him and every generation after him, eventually the Lord Jesus would be born. Every one who trusts in the Lord for salvation will become a child of God. In the world there are millions of Christians, as many as the sand on the shore. Are you one of those children the Lord was talking about?

Abraham then moved his tent to Mamre, near Hebron which means Fellowship. Here he built another altar for worship and fellowship with God. One night, late in the evening, God took Abraham outside his tent and spoke with him. The Lord told Abraham to look up into the sky. He told Abraham his descendants would be as impossible to count as the stars in the sky. What a promise this was from God to Abraham.

Although Abraham and Sarah were getting very old and it seemed impossible that they would have a son, God had promised Abraham they would. Abraham loved the Lord and believed what He said would come to pass. This should also teach us to take the Lord at His Word. What He says will come to pass.

ABRAHAM 53

A little boy called Ishmael

After God promised Abraham a son, it was a long time before anything happened and both Abraham and Sarah were very old. Abraham was eighty-five and Sarah was seventy-five and Sarah began to get impatient as she desperately wanted a child. There is only one thing more difficult than having a child and that's not having a child. The pain and the frustration must have been unbearable at times and no doubt it would have caused many tears.

Sarah became so impatient that she came up with an idea; she had given up on the idea of having a child and desperately wanted Abraham to be a father. Sarah had a handmaid called Hagar who had lived with them for many years. She had become a believer and follower of God. Abraham and Sarah had been good witnesses for the Lord and what a good example this is for us to be an example everywhere we go.

Sarah then suggested that Abraham have a baby with Hagar. This was sin and was not God's will for Sarah and Abraham. Abraham was trying to take control of this area of his life instead of believing the promise God had given to him. Sadly, Abraham agreed and in less than a year a baby boy called Ishmael was born to Abraham and Hagar. This was not the son that God was talking about. Even though Abraham was a great man of faith, he still failed God many times.

Abraham loved his son Ishmael. He was his pride and joy. Many years passed and soon Ishmael grew up to be a teenager. After this God changed Abram's name to Abraham and Sarai's name to Sarah. Abraham means 'father of many nations' and Sarah means 'a Princess'. The son that God was talking about had not yet been born but would be one day soon, this son was called Isaac.

When God makes a promise, He will keep it. We need to trust Him no matter how long it takes. He will carry out that promise in His perfect timing.

ABRAHAM 54

The Power of Persuasion

One of the great points in Abraham's life is God's promise to him that he would have a son and through his son the world would be blessed. This was a promise from God. Around fifteen years after Ishmael was born, God again reminded Abraham that Sarah would have a child and he was to call his name Isaac.

Sarah became impatient and acted rashly by involving Hagar in their desire to have a son. How often, we too can become impatient and try to do things our own way. I have no doubt both Abraham and Sarah regretted what they had done as we read on in the story in the Bible of how all sorts of problems developed between Hagar and Sarah, problems like jealousy and bitterness.

It is never right to do wrong even if we think it will eventually work out for the good. By telling a lie you may escape punishment for the present, but eventually the truth will come out and you will be found out. At times our friends can tempt us to do wrong, things like smoking, drinking, or going to places where we know we shouldn't go. They make us feel stupid if we say "no"; their arguments are often very persuasive and very often we say "ok." Remember it's always harder to say "no" but God will help you to say no at the right time.

Watch out for those who will try to PERSUADE you to do wrong. If you give in to them, you may live to REGRET IT for the rest of your life.

ABRAHAM 55

Entertaining Angels

God had consistently blessed and helped Abraham despite all his failures. Abraham's name meant, 'father of many nations' and Sarah's name meant 'Princess.' No doubt Abraham would spend a lot of time thinking about God's plan and will for his life. It is very good to take time out from the busy lives we all live and talk to God about His plans for our lives.

Living up in the mountains in their tent, Sarah and Abraham would not normally have had many visitors. One day three men came to visit Abraham and he was so delighted to see them he immediately offered them hospitality, by offering them food, water and somewhere to sit down. Sometimes when strangers come to us we can be very hostile and suspicious of them. Not all strangers are bad people. Did you know that God sometimes sends angels into our lives as people to see how we react to them?

These three men were angels sent from God. They knew all about Abraham and Sarah. One of the angels told Abraham that a miracle was going to happen to Sarah. Even though she was ninety years old God would make it possible for her to have a child. No doubt Sarah had given up on the idea, even though she longed for a son more than anything else in the whole world. What wonderful and exciting news this was. There is always so much bad news; it is good to bring good and positive news to people.

Sometimes when we meet strangers we can be cold towards them and maybe ignore them. God tells us in His Word that we must be careful how we treat strangers because they may be especially brought along our pathway of life for a reason. "Be not forgetful to entertain strangers: for thereby some have entertained angels unawares." (Hebrews 13:2)

ABRAHAM 56

Sarah laughs in unbelief

Three angels had come to visit Abraham. While Sarah was in another part of the home the angels brought news to Abraham. They told him that Sarah would definitely have a son. Even though this seemed impossible, God was going to make it possible.

Sarah was not in the company of the angels and Abraham when they told Abraham she would have a son, but when she overheard one of the angels say that she was going to have a baby, she laughed to herself. When she laughed to herself one of the angels said to Abraham, "Why did Sarah just laugh?" When Sarah came into the room she denied it and said she didn't laugh.

Have you ever done that? Denied you have said or done something? Telling lies is the easiest thing in the world to do and yet it is one of the sins God hates the most. One lesson we can learn from Sarah is that we can never cover up our sin. We can never hide anything from God; He sees everything, hears everything and He knows everything. It is always best to tell the truth at all times, no matter the cost.

Sarah laughed because of her unbelief; to her it was impossible for her to have a baby because she was so old. For God nothing is impossible; God was about to work a miracle in her life as God can do anything. Maybe someone you know is not a Christian and you think they will never get saved. No one is too hard, complicated or difficult for the Lord. In fact, the message of the angels was true and in less than a year from that time Sarah did have a baby boy called Isaac.

Isn't it great that in spite of our lack of FAITH at times, God still blesses us.

ABRAHAM 57

Abraham pleads with God for the People

After the three angels had finished talking with Abraham, they rose to leave his house and two of them walked on towards Sodom and Gomorrah. One of them, believed to be the Lord himself, stayed behind to talk with Abraham. The Lord told Abraham that He was His friend; what a privilege to be called the friend of God!

Then the Lord began to tell Abraham His plans; He told him that because Sodom and Gomorrah were very wicked cities they would both be destroyed. In fact, the other two angels were on their way to begin the destruction. The Lord told Abraham that the people were so wicked and vile and utterly full of evil that they must be destroyed.

Abraham began to think of his nephew Lot and his family. He then asked the Lord if fifty righteous people could be found in the city, would God save them from being destroyed? The Lord told Abraham if he could find fifty, forty, thirty, twenty even ten righteous people then He would not destroy the city. Sadly, out of all the people in those two huge cities there were less than ten followers of the true God.

"Ten people," Abraham thought, Lot had four daughters, two of whom were married. He no doubt thought in all the time Lot was in this city of Sodom, surely some of its citizens had become followers of the Lord. This reminds me of the judgement day when the Lord Jesus comes back to earth. It will be too late to witness and win our family and friends. We must tell them today that they need to be saved and become true followers of the Lord today.

ABRAHAM 58

Laughing at the Warning

The reason the angels came to the cities of Sodom and Gomorrah was to destroy them because of their wickedness. They walked into the city to rescue Lot and any other believers who wanted to escape death. Whenever the angels arrived at Lot's house and went inside, suddenly there came knocking and banging at his door.

Outside there were men both young and old, who wanted the angels whom they thought were men to come out to them. They weren't interested in their message; all they wanted was to engage in behaviour which the Bible describes as gross sin, terrible in the eyes of the Lord.

The angels quickly warned Lot to go and get his daughters and their husbands. When Lot went to them they just laughed at him. They didn't believe the city was going to be destroyed; they were so content living in the world. What a poor testimony Lot had even with his own family that they didn't even listen to him as he warned them about the judgment. Even the wicked people of the city seemed to notice no difference about him as they brought their sin right to his front door.

God very graciously calls Lot "righteous Lot" in the New Testament and tells us that Lot was vexed, or upset, by the sin all around him. It is sad that he had no influence for God on any of the people around him. Do others know that I belong to Jesus Christ?

Lot had the choice of the land and he chose what seemed good to his eyes but brought death and destruction to his own family. Do we make an impact for God with our family? Do we try with God's help to show them how wonderful it is to be a Christian?

Is my behaviour different from people who are not Christians? What about my language and the places I go?

ABRAHAM 59

Sodom and Gomorrah are Destroyed

The two angels told Lot that he must leave the city of Sodom now but he was reluctant to leave. Lot had become so settled in the wicked and immoral city of Sodom that he was almost sorry to leave it. All his friends and family were there, all his wealth and possessions were in the city as well.

The Lord promised Abraham that He would rescue Lot. When Lot's two married daughters and their husbands refused to come with them the angels grabbed Lot, his wife and his two other daughters and they began to flee from the city.

As they ran out of the city towards the mountains the angels warned them not to look back. If they looked back they would not escape. Once they made it up into the mountains they kept running. God then poured out His anger and wrath upon the city of Sodom and the cities of Sodom and Gomorrah were completely destroyed with fire and brimstone from Heaven.

All the buildings, people and animals were completely destroyed. They were destroyed because of their sinfulness and immoral lifestyles. God is pure and holy, He made us in His image that we may worship and adore Him. The people in Sodom and Gomorrah hated God and everything that was righteous.

It is interesting to note that for the final time this world will be destroyed by the same means. God will destroy it with fire and brimstone after the great Judgment Day. That is why it is so important to put our trust in the Lord and follow Him all the days of our lives.

Changed into a Pillar of Salt

As Lot and his family were fleeing Sodom, Lot's wife began to think of her other two daughters, her lovely home and everything else she owned down in the city, her heart was still in the worldly city of Sodom. The angels had warned them not to look back.

Lot's wife could no longer resist the temptation, as she ran she looked back and something terrible happened. The moment she looked back she became a pillar of salt; she literally became a body made of salt. How shocked and distressed poor old Lot must have felt.

There is a similarity here between Eve and Lot's wife. They were both told not to do something and because of their disobedience, death came into the world. As a result of Eve's sinning we all die because of our sin and with Lot's wife her disobedience brought about her death, as she was turned into a pillar of salt.

God calls us to a life of obedience; obedience to Him. That is why we have the Bible as the rule book of our faith. It helps us to live our lives obediently before the Lord.

Lot and his two daughters continued running until they came to a place called Zoar and how sad he must have felt. He followed the world so closely and was trapped by it. Many years ago when he had left Abraham he had everything. Now he had failed the Lord and the sin of the world surrounded him everywhere. Lot was once a friend of God, who then became a friend of sin; he was a saved soul with a wasted life.

When the Lord saves you, use your life WISELY in a way that will please the Lord.

ABRAHAM 61

Lessons from Sodom and Gomorrah

God destroyed both these cities of Sodom and Gomorrah because of the terrible wickedness that was in them. We must never lose sight of the teachings and the warnings found in the Bible. The people in these cities were living in very sinful relationships. This is an attack on the family, the secret to any country's greatness and strength are strong family values.

God's only and most natural way is for man and woman to get married and create families, anything else is an attack on the family, on society, on the Bible and most of all on God Himself.

Today in newspapers, television, the internet and many other forms of media the family is being undermined and attacked. Marriage between man and woman seems to be less and less common. We must be strong and must not support such programmes that promote such sinful activity.

The Christian life is not always easy, there are times when we must stand up and be strong. When things are wrong we must say they are wrong. Tell the people who say there is nothing wrong with it that they are wrong because the Bible says so. God is the author of the Bible, a God of love, He loves the sinner but hates sin and He will forgive those who come to Him with repentance and ask for forgiveness.

Isaac is Born

After the angel of the Lord appeared to Abraham and Sarah to promise them that the time had come for them to have a baby they were ecstatic. Abraham was one hundred years old and Sarah his wife was ninety.

The day came when little Isaac was born; Isaac means laughter or joy. Maybe he was called Isaac because both his parents laughed with unbelief at the prospect of them being parents at such an old age. Nevertheless, God promised them they would have a son together and through his seed the Lord Jesus, the Saviour of the world would eventually come. All of us should have a little bit of Isaac in us. It is good to laugh and we should certainly have the joy of the Lord in us. We need to be careful though, not to laugh in disbelief at the promises of God.

Abraham loved Isaac and he was overjoyed at having this little boy, as all fathers and grandfathers naturally are. Abraham spent lots of time with his little boy Isaac; he would have told him all about God and how the Lord had led him through life, all about leaving Egypt and following the will of God to the Promised Land.

Problems however, were not far away as Ishmael, the older son of Abraham, was now getting jealous of the attention that Isaac was getting. While Abraham naturally loved both his sons, he had a special love for Isaac as he was the son that God had promised him. Sometimes we can become jealous of our brothers or sisters because of the attention they often receive. God hates it when we become jealous.

We should be happy for our brothers and sisters and LOVE THEM as we love ourselves and treat them as we like to be treated.

Forced to leave Home

The time came when problems between little Isaac and his older half brother Ishmael grew and grew. This caused friction between Sarah and Hagar, Sarah's maid. Abraham was stuck in the middle as he was the father of both boys.

When Sarah told Abraham to send Hagar and Ishmael back to Egypt, he had no choice but to do as Sarah had asked. Hagar was just a maid in their home and when she was asked to leave she had no choice but to pack her bags and go.

Now she was forced to leave her home with her son and no man to help her. God promised Abraham that He would look after Hagar and Ishmael and that He would bless Ishmael and make of him a great nation. It was a difficult thing for Abraham to send them both away. By faith Abraham obeyed God, as this is what he was supposed to do.

Sometimes in life we have to make difficult choices, as sometimes we have to let go of our friends in order to do and fulfil God's will. It is not always an easy thing to do but sometimes it must be done. When you know it is the thing to do, it is best to do it quickly.

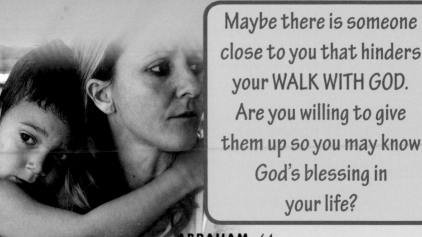

Maybe there is someone close to you that hinders your WALK WITH GOD. Are you willing to give them up so you may know God's blessing in your life?

Finding God in desperation

Both Hagar and her son were now without a home and a place to live. They were on their way back to her homeland but had no idea where it was. There was no public transport or telephones in those days; it was a lonely journey. They were in the desert walking, the weather was hot, and without food or water they thought they were going to die.

Soon Ishmael felt ill from the heat of the day and was now hungry and thirsty. Things were becoming very serious. If they didn't get water soon they would dehydrate. They probably took water and food with them but soon it was all used up. They were so far into the desert they didn't know which way to go. Do you ever feel like this, wandering about from day to day not really knowing where to go or what to do? Don't wait until you are in complete desperation to talk to the Lord. Get into the practice of talking to Him every day.

Hagar then put her son under a sage bush in the desert. She began to cry at the thought of her son dying in the desert. Hagar began to pray and cry to God for help; she was in complete desperation as she was lonely, thirsty and thought they were both going to die. The moment she prayed, she heard a voice from heaven saying "Hagar, don't be afraid" it was the angel of the Lord. "God has got great plans for Ishmael your son, open your eyes to see what God has done."

As she opened her eyes, right in front of her was a well of cool refreshing water. God provided for them in their desperate need. He continued to look after them as they journeyed across the desert and eventually made a new home. He blessed Ishmael and he grew up to be a fine young man who believed in his mother's God.

Just as God provided for and blessed Hagar, He can do the same for us too. You may say, "He never helps me," then I ask you, "Have you ever asked the Lord to help you?"

The Ultimate test

In the meantime Abraham and Sarah were enjoying spending time with their son Isaac. Probably Abraham spent every spare moment he had with Isaac. Now that Ishmael was gone, Isaac was Abraham's only son. Abraham would often think of the promise God gave him, that through his son Isaac the promised Messiah, the Lord Jesus Christ, the Saviour of the world would be born.

Abraham brought Isaac up and taught him the things of God. Every time he made a sacrifice he would explain the meaning of it and how one day God would send the perfect sacrifice into this world, the Lord Jesus. Every time a lamb was killed and its blood was shed for sins to be forgiven, Abraham would explain the meaning of this to Isaac.

Abraham loved Isaac but did he love him more than he loved God? As God looked down from heaven He decided to put Abraham's faith to the test. Late one evening the Lord called out to Abraham and asked him to do something that would rock his faith to its core. The Lord asked Abraham to take his son Isaac up into the mountain and prepare him for a sacrifice. Abraham couldn't believe his ears. To clarify what he just heard, he said, "Do you mean my son Isaac?" "Yes Abraham," the Lord said, "your only son Isaac." Abraham still couldn't believe his ears. This was the greatest challenge of his life and the greatest decision he would have to make. Now he must decide between his love for his son and his love for God!

Sometimes if things come between us and God, or if we spend more time with things or people than God, then He may have to put our love for Him to the test. Is there anything or anyone you love more in this world than God?

An Obedient Boy

Early the next morning God spoke to Abraham. Abraham wakened Isaac from his sleep and told him they were going on a journey. Two servants also went with them. This was a fifty mile journey to Mount Moriah that would take three days to complete.

Isaac would have been excited at the thought of going on a trip; he loved his father and he especially loved it when they were going somewhere. As they walked they carried wood for the sacrifice. Then Isaac asked his father where the sacrifice was. How could Abraham possibly explain to Isaac that he was the sacrifice? "God Himself will provide a sacrifice," he told Isaac.

When they got to the bottom of the mountain, Abraham told his servants to wait until both he and Isaac would return. Abraham's faith was so strong that he believed that when Isaac died God would bring him back to life again and they would both return again to the bottom of the mountain. (Hebrews 11v17-19)

When they got to the top, they started building an altar for the sacrifice. Then Abraham set Isaac down and told him how God had spoken to him a few nights before. "God has asked me to prepare you for a sacrifice Isaac," Abraham said with tears in his eyes. Isaac was much younger than Abraham; he could have run away down the mountain but he didn't. Isaac loved his father and he loved God; he willingly agreed to obey his father and climbed up onto the altar, willing to give up his life as a sacrifice.

This is one of the greatest tests in the entire Bible. We can learn so much about obedience from Isaac with such a big test. Are we obedient to our parents in the little things in life?

ABRAHAM 67

Throw your Knife down

Abraham and Isaac built an altar on top of Mount Moriah. It was then that Abraham explained to Isaac that he was to be the sacrifice, so Isaac willingly climbed up unto the altar and Abraham bound him hand and foot.

Isaac understood that this was the will of God for his life and he was obedient to God's will. Abraham knew God was testing his faith, the question is would he pass the test? God will never ask you to do such a thing, however He will test you from time to time to see how great your love is for Him.

As Isaac lay on top of the altar as still as the night air, Abraham with tears in his eyes lifted up his knife, raised it to the sky and was just about to plunge it right into the heart of his child. As he did so, he suddenly heard a voice shouting, "Abraham, Abraham." It was the voice of the Lord. God told him to throw down his knife, and let Isaac go free. The Lord now knew that God was first in Abraham's life. Abraham passed the greatest test of all proving that he loved God more than any other. God had told Abraham to prepare Isaac and offer him as a burnt offering, not to kill him; Isaac was freed and didn't have to die. Now Abraham could clearly understand what it would cost God to give up His only begotten Son, Jesus Christ, for us.

This is a wonderful picture of the Lord Jesus Christ, except Jesus went all the way to the cross and did die; He died as the ultimate sacrifice for sinners and for sin. Not only did Jesus die, praise God He rose again the third day. The number three is quite significant in the Bible as Abraham and Isaac came back down the mountain on the third day.

ABRAHAM 68

A substitute provided

Abraham was so relieved to hear the voice of God. He dropped his knife and freed Isaac from the ropes that bound him to the altar. Over in the bushes behind the altar was a ram, a male sheep with its horns caught in the bush. God had caused the ram to get stuck in the bush so it could be used as a substitute instead of Isaac, Abraham caught the ram and tied it upon the altar. The ram was sacrificed and its blood was shed that day upon the altar.

What happened that day was a very clear picture and brilliant illustration of God's love for us. Isaac reminds us so much of Jesus Christ, as He went all the way to the cross in full obedience to God, His father. Abraham reminds us of God the father as He sent His only Begotten Son into this world to die for us. This story perfectly illustrates God's wonderful plan of salvation.

The altar reminds us of the cross where Jesus bled and died to take away our sins. Throughout the Old Testament, time and time again there are clear pictures reminding us of God's promises and they pave the way for the ultimate sacrifice on Calvary's cross.

Just as the ram became a substitute for Isaac, the Lord Jesus became a substitute for us. We deserve to die because of our sin. Yet, God so loved the world that He sent the Lord Jesus into this world to be our substitute. He came to die that we might live. Only by trusting in Jesus Christ alone as the perfect substitute, can our sins be forgiven.

Find my Son a Wife

Many years had now passed since Abraham and Isaac went on that three day journey to Mount Moriah. Isaac was now a grown man; his mother Sarah had passed away and Abraham was very concerned about him because he was not married. Abraham was now very old and he would often remember God's promise that he would have a son and through him his seed would be blessed.

Abraham lived in Canaan and most of the people here worshipped idols and false gods. Abraham didn't want Isaac to marry one of these heathen women, so he called his servant Eliezer and told him he had a job for him to do. Eliezer was a very faithful servant.

Abraham explained to Eliezer his concern for Isaac as he was not married; he then told Eliezer to go to Mesopotamia where Abraham's relatives lived. Here he was hoping to find a good and godly girl for Isaac to marry; he was to look out for his brother Nahor so that he could help him.

What a challenge Eliezer was faced with, to find a wife for Abraham's son Isaac; a man who would inherit all the wealth and riches of Abraham. A man from whom eventually would come the Saviour of the world, the Lord Jesus Christ. What a job and responsibility Eliezer faced. He also was a man of God and he prayed really hard that the Lord would guide him.

Eliezer prepared ten camels, some servants and gifts of gold and silver to take with him. Off he went on a journey that would take him many weeks to seek a wife for the son of Abraham his boss. This may sound like a strange task, yet it reveals one of the most beautiful and romantic stories in all the Bible of how God brought two people together.

Providence is a wonderful thing, it is when God makes something happen like when two people meet and the timing is just perfect, God's perfect timing.

ABRAHAM 70

A remarkable Answer to Prayer

Abraham's servant eventually arrived at the town he planned to travel to. Outside the town was a water well. He noticed many women coming towards the well to draw up water for their families.

Eliezer began to pray to God for help in finding a wife for Isaac. There were hundreds of women in this town but as he prayed to the Lord, he told the Lord that he would ask a woman for a drink of water from the well. If she offered him a drink of water and then offered to give water to all his camels as well, then he would know this was the girl that was to become Isaac's wife. This seemed like an impossible request, as camels were big thirsty animals that drink gallons of water.

When the first woman came along, Eliezer asked her for a drink of water. "Certainly," she replied, "and while you enjoy a drink of refreshing water I will water your camels also." This is one of the most remarkable answers to prayer in the entire Bible. Eliezer could hardly believe it. Immediately he wanted to meet her parents and explain why he had made such a journey. Her name was Rebekah.

God promises to answer our prayers, no matter how impossible they seem to us. All God asks is that we believe He is the God of the impossible. Sometimes we come to impossible situations in our lives, have you ever prayed and really believed that God will answer your prayer? Sometimes we may want something badly but God knows this is not what is best for us. This does not mean He has not heard your prayer. Learn to trust God to work all things for your good when making requests to Him.

ABRAHAM 71

Here comes the Bride

Rebekah then took Eliezer and his servants to meet her family. Here he was offered a lovely meal by Rebekah's parents but he could not eat until he explained the reason for his visit. Everyone stood speechless as he told them the story about praying to God concerning watering the camels.

Rebekah's parents asked her what she wanted to do. Rebekah also loved the Lord; she was willing to leave her family, friends and her country to marry a man whom she had never met. Sometimes when we pray we expect to wait years for God to answer, God can answer our prayers the moment we pray. Make sure when we pray about something, that we really want it to happen, then the Lord will answer according to His will.

This was an exciting time for everyone and Rebekah was willing to follow God, completely relying on Him to look after her. After her family received many gifts from Abraham, Rebekah then left with Eliezer and all the camels to make the long journey back to Isaac who was patiently waiting for a girl sent from God to marry him. The bride-to-be was now on her way to meet and marry Isaac. Each day he would walk in the fields waiting and waiting to see if Eliezer had found the girl for him.

Just like Rebekah, are you trusting and completely relying on God for everything in your life? Having a future partner in life is something we should pray about as we get older, someone whom God will bring into our lives at the right and proper time.

The Wedding Day

After many days of journeying, Rebekah made it to Abraham's home. Before she got there she noticed someone walking in the fields. Eliezer told her it was Isaac, Abraham's son, the man to whom she would be married. Can you imagine how she felt as she got closer and closer to Isaac or how Isaac felt? They had never met before and God had brought them together to get married.

This surely is one of the most romantic stories in the Bible of how God brought two people together. Both Isaac and Rebekah believed in God and they both wanted to live their lives pleasing to Him.

When they married, Abraham was very happy. God had promised to bless him and through his children eventually the Saviour of the world would come the Lord Jesus Christ. Eliezer proved himself a very faithful messenger; he never talked about himself, just about his master and his master's son.

What a lesson that is for us; to talk about God more and the Son of God, the Lord Jesus, even more. To think less about ourselves and more about God and less about what we want and more about what God wants. Sometimes in life we can become selfish and only focus on ourselves. It is good to consider other people and everything we do in life should be pleasing to the Lord.

ABRAHAM 73

JACOB
The story of two Twins

Isaac and Rebekah were married for many years before they had any children. They knew they would have children one day as God had promised them they would. God said He would send the Saviour of the world, the Lord Jesus Christ, through Isaac's family.

After being married for twenty-five years Rebekah gave birth to twins. The eldest was Esau and the youngest Jacob. God told Rebekah that the oldest son would serve the younger. Normally in Bible times the eldest son would be the one to inherit the birthright of his father.

Even before they were born, Jacob and Esau were wrestling in their mother's womb. Just before Esau was born, Jacob held onto Esau's heel as if to say, "I want to be born first." Esau, the firstborn child was red and hairy, while Jacob looked like any other newborn baby.

Isn't it an amazing thing that when God made you, He made you unique? No one else is exactly like you; this is what makes us all special, especially in the eyes of God.

HAVE YOU EVER taken a moment just to THANK GOD for making you, you?

Genesis 25:27-28

Two different Boys

When Jacob grew up he was slimmer and smaller than Esau his brother. Esau grew up to be a big, strong, hairy man. Both boys were very different. Esau loved to be outdoors all the time, and he especially loved hunting.

Jacob preferred to be around the house helping his mother with the cooking. Perhaps because of this, Rebekah loved Jacob more than Esau, and as we will see, this was to cause many problems in their household later on.

God loves all His children in exactly the same way; no matter how we look or how we are doing in school, He loves us all. Maybe you are jealous of your brother or sister, or even a friend at school. God doesn't like it when we are jealous of each other, rather we should learn to love, respect and appreciate others as they are.

Many people have hidden sins in their hearts; sins like hatred, jealousy, envy, anger. We need to be honest with God and ask Him to help us with these hidden sins.

Everything for a Bowl of Soup

One day Esau came home from a long day's hunting. He was very hungry and he could smell the most delicious smell ever; it was Jacob making soup. He asked Jacob for a bowl of soup and Jacob agreed upon one condition; that he would swap his birthright as the firstborn son. Esau was so hungry that at that moment he cared for nothing else in the world. He must have thought he was going to die unless he tasted some soup.

Esau agreed and before God he promised Jacob the rights of the eldest son; his birthright and the promise that God would bless him. Esau quickly gulped down the homemade soup and felt very content, then off he went on his way again.

What a price he paid! He gave up everything he could have inherited, just for a bowl of soup.

In Bible times, it was a very special custom for the eldest son to inherit two kinds of blessings. The first was a material blessing; such as land and cattle. With this blessing, he would receive twice as much as the other children and he would become the new leader of the tribe or family. The second was a spiritual blessing, which could not be seen; this was the most important for it was the promise that God would bless him.

Always be careful when you make rash decisions. You could live to regret them for the rest of your life.

The wrong Son is Blessed

At this time Isaac and Rebekah were very old. God had blessed Isaac greatly during his life time with long life and increased wealth and riches. Now he was at the end of his life and would soon die, so he asked to see Esau, his eldest son, so that he could give him his birthright blessing.

God had already said that Jacob would inherit this blessing. When Isaac called for Esau, his eldest son, he asked him to go hunting and prepare a fresh meal from the animal he would kill. Rebekah had overheard the conversation and she immediately prepared a lovely meal that she knew Isaac would like. She then told Jacob that Esau was away to hunt and she dressed Jacob up in Esau's clothes. She took the skin of a goat and tied it around his arms, neck and shoulders, so that Isaac would think Jacob was the very hairy Esau!

Isaac was very old now, and blind, and when he called for Esau, the cleverly disguised Jacob brought him in the freshly made meal. Isaac held his son by the arm and neck. He believed it was Esau and gave him the special blessing.

As a result of this deceit, Jacob's family was divided and was never close again. Esau was so angry that all this had happened while he was away hunting; so much so that he promised to kill Jacob the moment his father died. Jacob wanted a blessing in his life, but he went about it the wrong way.

> Family life is very important and special, try not to do anything that causes strife and bitterness that will last for years.

JACOB

What about my Blessings?

Have you ever thought about how much God has blessed you? Esau never really cared for the blessings which God had prepared for him and because of this he lived in regret. Sometimes we are blessed so much we often take it for granted. Blessings from God, such as living in a comfortable home, having friends and family who love us, having enough food to eat and a school to go to are often the blessings that we take for granted.

Sometimes we only enjoy God's blessings if we can see them, but God promises us so much more. When we walk with Him, He promises us that He will supply everything we need. The Bible is full of promises and tells us how the Lord will bless His people.

God says He will always be with His people and never leave them. He will keep them from worry and fear and has promised to give His people strength in times of temptation, comfort when they are sad and help in every time of need.

When the Lord saves us He gives us a birthright; a right to enter heaven when we die. When we prefer the things of this world to the offer of salvation through Christ Jesus, it is like selling our birthright. God has promised to bless you so much.   Don't lose out by giving it all away just because of some temporary pleasure. In the Christian life there are things which are right and things which are wrong. Ask God to help you know the difference.

Lord, thank you for all the blessings you have given to me, there are so many that I can't even count them.

A hard Pillow

With so much confusion in the family home, Rebekah came up with an idea. She persuaded Isaac that Jacob should travel to another country to find a wife. However the women in the other country didn't believe in God. Jacob was to go where his mother's people lived. He was to stay with his uncle Laban.

It is very important if you love the Lord Jesus Christ that you marry a Christian person when you grow up; someone who believes as you do, and wants to live for God.

Before Jacob left home, Isaac blessed him with the covenant blessing. God would bless him, as He had his grandfather Abraham and his father Isaac. When Jacob left he didn't realise he would be gone for 20 years and would never see his mother again. It is always good to hug your mother and tell her how much you love her. You never know when you might see her for the last time.

As Jacob began to make the long journey to his uncle's house he soon became very tired. He didn't have a hotel to stay in, or even a tent to sleep in. He was so tired he found a big stone and used it for a pillow. Soon he fell asleep and while he slept he had the most beautiful dream ever. Do you dream? Dreams are wonderful, although most times we can never remember what we have dreamt about.

Jacob had much to think about. The quarrel with his brother, his ageing parents, but best of all the blessing of God and how the Lord would bless him.

A beautiful Dream

Jacob was on a long journey and after finding a stone for a pillow he soon fell asleep. As he slept he had the most beautiful dream ever. In his dream he dreamed that beside him was a long ladder reaching all the way from the ground up to Heaven.

It was the longest ladder he had ever seen and on the ladder were many angels running up and down. At the very top of the ladder was God. God spoke to Jacob in his dream; He said "I am the God of your grandfather Abraham and of your father Isaac. I will bless you as I have blessed them. All this land around you is yours; you will have more children than the sand on the sea shore."

What God was saying was that through Jacob and his descendants the Lord Jesus Christ would be born. Those who believe in the Lord Jesus Christ will be saved, and counted as the children of God. Are you a Christian? Are you one of those children that God spoke about? Sometimes Christians are known as Children of the Covenant, because of God's covenant with Abraham, Isaac and Jacob!

This ladder reminds me of the Lord Jesus Christ. He is the way that reaches to heaven, He is the only way to God, and He came to this earth to make it possible for us to go to heaven. By dying on the cross, Jesus made it possible for us to come to God. On the cross He took away our sin and by trusting in Him alone we can be forgiven.

When Jacob woke up he called the place Bethel, which means, 'House of God.' "Surely the Lord is in this place and I knew it not," he thought.

Have you ever sensed the presence and power of God as Jacob did? It really is a wonderful experience.

Jacob falls in Love

Jacob had left his mother and father's house because it was not safe for him to stay there after he tricked his brother by taking his father's blessing. His mother advised him to go to a different country where Jacob had an uncle. Maybe he could live with him and find some work to do.

No doubt one of the things in Jacob's mind was finding a wife. It is every girl's dream and every boy's natural desire to grow up and meet someone with whom they can share their life.

It is a natural thing to fall in love; in fact, it is one of life's most beautiful experiences. When you truly fall in love with someone, you will go on loving them for ever and ever. This is true love coming from the heart; your whole world will be turned upside down. You will not stop thinking about this person and you will want to be with them for ever.

Rebekah, Jacobs's mother wanted Jacob to find a wife. She had looked after him until now and she knew he needed someone to care for him. The Bible clearly teaches that this is a good and natural thing to do. It doesn't happen to everyone, but it is a natural desire to want to get married and spend the rest of your life with someone you love. Jacob was about to meet someone with whom he would instantly fall in love.

When you grow up what type of person would you like to get married to?

Jacob finds the wrong Bride

Jacob continued to travel for many days. He was heading for Haran, his mother's home place. Once he arrived there he stopped at a well to talk with some shepherds and there he noticed a woman coming to water her father's sheep.

Jacob fell in love with her at first sight. This girl was his cousin and it was the first time they had met; in fact he was so excited, he kissed her. Jacob then met Laban his uncle and told him he wanted to marry his beautiful daughter Rachel, whom he had just met. In Bible times it was very common for cousins to marry.

Laban agreed, on condition that Jacob would stay and work for him for seven years. Jacob loved Rachel so much he agreed to do so. At the end of seven years the wedding was arranged. After Jacob had made his vows on his wedding day to his new wife, he lifted up her veil to kiss her but to his horror, under the veil was Leah, Rachel's older sister. He had been tricked.

When Jacob angrily asked Laban why he had tricked him, Laban told him in his country it was not a good custom for a girl to get married before an older sister. Jacob loved Rachel so much that he worked for another seven years so that he could marry Rachel too. He also kept Leah as his wife.

Jacob now knew what it was like be tricked and he was paying the price for what he had done to his brother all those years before. There is a saying that you reap what you sow, "Be not deceived; God is not mocked: for whatsoever a man soweth, that shall he also reap." (Galatians 6:7)

Working fourteen years for a Wife

After working for a total of fourteen years, Jacob was finally given permission to marry Rachel. He loved Rachel very much and wanted to marry her so badly. This meant that he now had two wives, Rachel and her older sister Leah.

In Bible times it was often the custom for men to have more than one wife. This often resulted in difficulties in the home when the wives were jealous of each other. Sometimes they argued and teased each other. For a long time Rachel could not have any children which made her very sad. The situation worsened as Leah would often tease her. Eventually, Rachel had a son whom she called Joseph. We will learn more about him later.

Jacob had now lived in Haran for twenty years; he had two wives, eleven sons and lots of cattle, sheep and camels. He felt ready to return home to his birthplace. Laban was, in many ways unkind to Jacob and was always trying to cheat him out of money. Laban's sons were also jealous of Jacob as everything he did seemed to go well for him.

Finally the Lord told Jacob to get up and return home again. Laban wasn't happy about this idea, but Jacob had made up his mind that he was returning home with his wives, children, servants and thousands of animals.

Sometimes in life it is good to move on to a new chapter. We may need to let go of old things so that our lives may take on a new course, for example, changing schools. We encounter new friends, new subjects and new teachers. Our lives change, but God never changes; He is always the same.

14 years

Genesis 32:24-32

Jacob wrestles with an Angel

As Jacob was heading back to his homeland, he was really worried about what his brother might do to him. He wondered if his brother would forgive him or still be angry with him; after all, his brother Esau had every right to be angry and had vowed to kill him.

While Jacob was making his way back, they came to a river named Jabbok. He sent all the animals and his family across the river to the other side, but he did not cross the river.

Suddenly, in the middle of the night, an angel started wrestling with Jacob; it was the angel of the Lord. This continued for hours and neither of them gave in. Jacob finally cried, "I will not let you go until you bless me."

As a result of this wrestling match, the angel of the Lord knocked Jacobs's hip bone out of joint. For years Jacob had been wrestling within himself and he had always wanted his own way. Now the angel of the Lord was saying to Jacob, will you submit and give up and let God rule in your heart and life? Finally, before morning, Jacob gave up and the angel won the wrestling match.

That night Jacob's name was changed from Jacob which meant 'twister' to Israel, meaning, 'Prince with God'. He was now a changed man and was determined more than ever, to live his life for God.

Maybe you are wrestling with yourself over many things. God wants to get your attention,- are you willing to stop wrestling with your worries, fears and pride and let God take complete control of your life? Maybe you are just being twisted, God wants to help you, why not let Him? Ask Him to help you, right now!

JACOB 84

Jacob meets up with his Brother

After more than twenty years in exile, Jacob headed home. He was afraid to meet his older brother Esau again for he recalled how he had cheated his brother by taking the birthright from him.

However, after meeting the Angel of the Lord, he was much more at ease. In the distance he saw his brother coming with four hundred men. Jacob then went alone and bowed down to meet his brother. He was truly sorry for the way he had treated him.

To his surprise his brother threw his big arms around him, hugged him and they both wept for joy. Esau also was a changed man, for he too had met the Lord. When the Lord enters a person's heart and life, he changes them forever.

Jacobs's wife, Rachel died not long after this, giving birth to another son Benjamin. He was the youngest of Jacob's sons and a full brother to Joseph. Jacob's father, Isaac died after this; he was buried with his grandfather, Abraham.

What a wonderful thing it is when brothers and sisters can live together in harmony, forgiving each other when necessary. This is what the Christian life is all about, not holding grudges against each other. Jacob never forgot the night he met the Angel of the Lord, it changed his life forever.

Can you remember the time you met the Lord. HAS HE CHANGED YOU YET?

JOSEPH
Joseph the little boy

Joseph is probably one of the most familiar names in the Bible. It is the remarkable story of a young boy who had much, lost much and gained even more in the end.

It is a story of adventure, sadness and happiness, and one which everyone at some point can relate to. As we study the life of Joseph we will see many types and pictures of the Lord Jesus Christ. That is what the Bible is all about; finding Jesus, trusting in Him and walking the Christian life with Him.

Joseph was born into a large family with eleven brothers and one sister. Ten of his older brothers were much older than he and were in fact grown men when he was just a boy. His older brothers were wicked, living very sinful lives. How it broke their father's heart to see the way they lived. Joseph's younger brother was called Benjamin and sadly his mother had died the same day Benjamin was born.

Joseph always tried to do what was right even though his brothers hated him. They were so jealous of Joseph in every way, but Jacob, Joseph's father, loved him more than any of his other sons.

Maybe we try to do what's right and every time we do it, it makes others mad or even jealous. Jealousy is a terrible sin; we all get jealous of different things and different people. We should ask the Lord to help us not to be jealous of other people but rather to be happy for them.

What is it that makes me jealous? We should pray and ask the Lord to help us with this problem.

JOSEPH 86

The Rainbow Coat

No matter how small the gift, it is a wonderful feeling to receive a present. The fact that someone took the time to think about me and get something for me was so thoughtful.

One day Joseph received a lovely new coat from his father; it was very special, for it was made of many different colours, just like the rainbow. When Joseph tried on his new coat it fitted perfectly. How kind it was of his father Jacob to give this to Joseph.

Joseph had ten older brothers and instead of being proud of their little brother Joseph, they began to hate him. They became so jealous of him that they despised him with their very hearts. Perhaps they thought Joseph was only trying to please Jacob his father so he would be remembered when it was time for Jacob to leave his inheritance. How terrible Joseph must have felt. Even if he tried to explain, they would mock and make fun of him even more.

When people become jealous of you they will often try to make you look small and feel bad. This is why it is so important to stay close to the Lord, for He will strengthen you and keep you strong. Maybe we have a problem of being jealous of other people. If this is the case we have to remember that jealousy is sin and God hates sin.

Is there ever anything I do that makes other PEOPLE jealous?

Genesis 37:5-8

Dreamer Boy

Most people who are familiar with the story of Joseph know about the dreams he had which made his brothers hate him even more. In Joseph's dreams he dreamt that together, with all his brothers, he was out gathering the wheat into sheaves, when suddenly all their sheaves bowed down to his.

The next morning Joseph was so excited that he told his brothers all about his dream. They looked at him with anger. "Do you think that one day we will bow down to you," they said. "We will never do that."

Today God speaks to us through reading His Word the Bible. In Joseph's times God would often speak to people through prophets, dreams and visions. He would frequently send angels down to deliver messages and on rare occasions He even spoke through animals. Old Testament people did not have the complete written Word of God that we have today in the form of the Old and New Testaments.

Once when Jacob, Joseph's father, was a young man God spoke to him through a dream. He dreamt there was a ladder going the whole way up to heaven and back down again and on it were angels going up and down. Now God was teaching Joseph through these dreams that he had a perfect plan for Joseph's life.

Most of the time dreams are a mixture of the thoughts that go on in our head during the day. In the Old Testament there are many examples of dreams that were specially sent from God.

JOSEPH 88

Anger and Jealousy
of Brothers

Joseph's first dream made his brothers really angry. Then he had another dream. This time he dreamt that the sun, moon and the stars were all bowing down to him.

Joseph was so excited that again he got all his brothers together again and began to tell them all about the sun, moon and the stars bowing down to him. It seemed to say the sun and moon were his parents and the stars were all his brothers. They had had enough! "We will never bow down to you, we don't even like you; in fact we hate you." Every passing day, Joseph's brothers became more and more jealous of him. They were angry with him and jealous of him for being their father's favourite son.

Jacob was disappointed with his older sons, they turned out to be quite wicked in many things that they did. On the other hand, Joseph was pure and honest; he was a hard worker, kind, well mannered and pleasant to be around.

Even though Joseph's brothers hated him so much, he loved them and treated them all as friends. In all his ways he behaved himself wisely.

To hate someone is a TERRIBLE THING. Are there any people I really hate?

JOSEPH 89

Genesis 37:12-17

The fifty mile Journey

For a young person to walk five miles today would be quite a challenge. In Bible times there were no cars, trains, planes or even bikes so most people travelled by foot.

Jacob owned lots of camels, cattle and sheep and his sons would often spend weeks at a time away from home, looking after their father's livestock. One day Jacob asked Joseph to go and find his brothers, to see how they were all doing. They were some fifty miles away looking after their father's sheep.

Joseph took some food for himself on the journey and of course some for his brothers as well. No doubt he would have taken his new coat with him; how warm it would be and how brightly it would shine with all its different colours.

The journey went along roads, through forests, maybe even across rivers and finally he came to Shechem. Looking lost, Joseph asked someone if they had seen his brothers. He then realised he had another fifteen miles to travel to Dothan. There, in the distance, he could see all the sheep and his brothers standing watch over them.

Many times we are asked to do something or go somewhere. Do we respond by being grumpy or do we willingly obey our parents? God blesses obedient children.

When **ASKED** to do something for our parents do we moan and groan?

Cast into a Pit with no hope

As Joseph went running eagerly towards his brothers, little did he realise what was ahead of him. As his brothers saw him coming towards them, they thought of a plan to kill Joseph. They hated Joseph so much they wanted to kill him; they wanted to teach him a lesson for having all those dreams and to make sure they would never come true.

Thankfully, Joseph's eldest brother, Reuben, was more soft-hearted. He told his brothers not to kill him, but rather to throw him into a pit. Reuben secretly hoped to release Joseph when they were not looking and return him safely to his father again.

As Joseph approached his brothers his happiness soon changed. Quickly they grabbed him and ripped off his coat. Before he knew it, he was staring into a dark pit. Without a moment's warning he found himself at the bottom of the dark and lonely pit. At any moment the face of a bear or lion might put its head over the entrance. How lonely Joseph must have felt.

As we read the story of Joseph in the Bible we read many times, "and the Lord was with Joseph." How comforting this must have been to know, that even though his brothers hated him, God loved and cared for him. Sadly, although Reuben knew they were wrong to hate Joseph and mistreat him, he didn't have the courage to stand up for what was right. Christians never have to be lonely, because God is always with them.

What do we do when the crowd we're with want to do SOMETHING WRONG?

JOSEPH 91

Sold as a Slave

Joseph was lying in the bottom of a pit waiting to die. His brothers, having hated him for so long, were now happy that he was gone.

Sometime later they saw people coming in the distance. They soon realised they were Ishmaelite merchants on their way to Egypt. They were travelling to Egypt to sell their rich spices and herbs. Then the brothers had an idea. Why not sell Joseph as a slave? Together they could get money for him and he would be gone forever.

Joseph was sold by his brothers for twenty pieces of silver and then he was tied up and taken away to Egypt, to be sold as a slave. How low and lonely Joseph must have felt, to be hated and treated in such a way. How would you have felt if you were Joseph?

As we read of the Lord Jesus Christ in the New Testament we learn that he too was hated. Even his friends wanted to kill him and one of his own disciples sold him for thirty pieces of silver. Then within days Jesus Christ was crucified on the cross for the sins of the whole world.

Throughout Joseph's troubles, the Bible says that the 'Lord was with Joseph.' This is the secret to life, having the Lord Jesus with you every day of your life. He will guide and guard you and keep you from danger, both day and night.

Can you honestly say you know that the Lord is with you?

Telling lies to deceive Dad

Joseph was now gone and his brothers were so happy but how were they to break the news to Jacob, their dad? Again, not short of wicked ideas, they came up with a plan. They killed a goat and put the blood of the goat on Joseph's lovely coloured coat.

When they got home they took the coat to Jacob, their father. When Jacob saw the coat he began to weep. He told all his sons that he sent Joseph out to see them and he believed their tale that a wild animal had attacked Joseph and killed him. For days and weeks Jacob mourned for his son and could not be comforted. Not one of Jacobs's sons spoke up and told the truth; they deceived their father. In a similar way, many years earlier Jacob had deceived his own father Isaac when he tricked him by pretending to be Esau. The Bible says that we will reap what we sow.

This was a terrible thing to do and maybe you would never dream of doing such a wicked thing. However, telling one lie is as bad as many lies. Also, to tell a small lie is as bad as telling a big lie. If you have told lies to your parents, maybe now is the time to speak up and tell the truth. Go now and apologise to them for telling lies. Then tell the Lord you are sorry. He will bless you for doing this and help you not to do it again.

HOW DO I FEEL

whenever I tell

a lie?

The Lord was with Joseph

After a long journey on a camel, bound and unable to talk with anyone, Joseph was all alone. Finally, they arrived in Egypt; a huge country with many cities, lots of people and huge temples used for idol worship.

Soon Joseph was standing with many other young people at Egypt's slave market. It would be easy for the Ishmaelites to sell Joseph as he was a strong, healthy young man. Many people were walking around looking for slaves to come and work for them. How frightened Joseph must have felt. Many times we read in the Bible that the Lord was with Joseph.

Then an important Egyptian officer called Potiphar came along and had a good look at Joseph. He liked him, so he paid the price for him and off Joseph went, not knowing where he was going. Everything and everyone were strangers to him. No doubt he would have thought of his family, his father and especially his little brother Benjamin.

All this time God was watching over Joseph for He had planned his life out perfectly. Sometimes we cannot see the future and things seem to be getting worse and worse. Just as the Lord was with Joseph, be assured, if you are a Christian, the Lord is with you too. He will be with you when you rest your head at night and when you wake up in the morning.

Sometimes when everything seems to be going wrong for you, remember Joseph.

JOSEPH 94

Joseph finds a new Home

After being sold as a slave, Joseph found himself in the home of Potiphar. Potiphar was a captain in the king's army; he was a very important and well respected man as well as being very wealthy. Potiphar had many other slaves working for him, some in the house and others to keep the grounds around the house.

Potiphar was kind to Joseph who no doubt felt homesick and was missing his family. He had to learn a new language and new customs as he now lived in a different country. All this time the Lord was with Joseph. Even though there were idols all around him, Joseph never forgot his father's God. Joseph's difficulties made him rely more and more upon God.

Sometimes in life we have to move house, which can be very upsetting and extremely stressful. Maybe we don't want to move and we don't want to leave our friends behind and the idea of going to a new school is daunting. Ask God to help you, wherever you go.

One day all the Christians in the world will be moving home but it won't be stressful. It will be the most exciting journey ever, for this new home will be Heaven. There we will meet millions of new friends; it will be the last journey we will ever have to make.

Are you ready to make that JOURNEY?

Genesis 39:5-6

Promoted for being faithful

It is good to be rewarded for being faithful. Most people who are promoted in their jobs are promoted because of their hard work and faithfulness. Here today, in our study of Joseph, we find something very encouraging happening to him.

As Joseph went about his chores from day to day, Potiphar soon noticed that there was something different about him. Joseph was different than all the other slaves. The Lord was with Joseph and He encouraged him to work hard and to be diligent in everything he did.

One day while Joseph was getting on with his daily duties Potiphar came over to him with a reward. Joseph was promoted to oversee Potiphar's entire household. He was in charge over all the other slaves and all the affairs of Potiphar's house; Potiphar was able to trust completely in Joseph. The Bible says, "The Lord blessed all the Egyptian's house for Joseph's sake; and the blessing of the Lord was upon all that he had."

Not only was the Lord with Joseph, but the Lord was now truly blessing him for being faithful to Him. At school, there are always people taking notice of you in everything you do. Wouldn't it be wonderful if they came to you and said, "There is something different about you. You stand out from all the rest." Deep down in your heart you would know it isn't you but rather the person God has made you to be.

Pray that God would make you to be the person that He wants you to be.

Accused of wrong doing

Everything seemed to be going perfectly for Joseph; he loved his new job and home, and his boss was very kind to him. Joseph was in charge of everything in his house; he was even in charge of all of Potiphar's riches. No doubt people would ask Joseph what his secret of success was and then Joseph would be able to testify of the Lord in his life.

Remember, as a Christian, when everything seems to be going well, then someone isn't very happy. That is the devil of course; he loves to ruin everything that is good, pure, decent and honest.

The one person that Joseph had no control over was Potiphar's wife; even though she had everything in this world that she could ever want, there was something missing in her life. As she watched this handsome young man going about her house she took a fancy to him.

Joseph never paid any attention to her, as many times she would come close and make suggestions to him. She would smile to him and try to gain his attention. Joseph would stand firm on his beliefs not to touch another man's wife.

One day Potiphar's wife grabbed hold of Joseph and told him to come and lie down beside her, but he told her that he would do no such thing and ran for his life. In the process she grabbed hold of Joseph's coat and began screaming out loud. When her husband came home, she lied to him and told him that Joseph had tried to lie beside her. Potiphar was very angry and without even giving Joseph a chance to explain himself, sent him immediately to prison.

> Young person, be wise like Joseph. If you ever find yourself in a similar situation, run for your life.

Genesis 39:20-21

Joseph ends up in Prison

After Joseph was wrongly accused he was sent to prison. One moment he seemed to have everything and the next he was in prison. Naturally, Potiphar would believe his wife when she accused Joseph of wrong doing, even though he really liked Joseph and was much better off for having Joseph around. The Bible tells us that the Lord prospered Potiphar because of Joseph.

This didn't seem to matter now, for Joseph went straight to prison without a trial. Prisons were not like they are today, often they were cold and damp. The whole time Joseph was in prison we do not read of him complaining. He knew God had a plan for his life and this must be part of it.

How easy it would have been to complain to God and continually ask, "Why me Lord?" One thing we do know is that the whole time Joseph was in the prison, the Lord was with him. How encouraging that must have been to have the presence of the Lord with him every day and night. Joseph had to learn to completely trust in the Lord with every aspect of his life.

This is exactly what God wants us to do, no matter where we end up or what we end up doing, we must say with total assurance, "I am exactly where God wants me to be."

Have you ever been in a SITUATION when something has gone wrong and you ask, "WHY ME LORD?"

I can translate Dreams

Joseph was now in prison and while there, an amazing thing happened. One day the prison guards came to Joseph and told him that he was going to get promoted; they had watched his life and realised there was something different about him.

Joseph was put in charge of all the other prisoners as the prison keeper completely trusted Joseph. He was handed the keys of the entire prison, so he could visit all the other prisoners. Isn't it amazing how God completely turned everything around? He made Joseph a happy prisoner; even in the prison, the Lord was with Joseph.

One day, while talking to two of the other prisoners, they told Joseph about two dreams they had. One was a baker and the other a butler and they were troubled about their dreams and couldn't understand them. In his dream the butler was pressing grapes into Pharaoh's cup. Joseph said that the dream meant in three days he would get out of prison and get his job back. Joseph asked the butler, when he got out of prison to mention his name to the king so he would get out of prison too. He promised to do this but never did.

When Joseph heard the second dream it was not so good. The baker was carrying bread to the king and the birds came and ate it. Joseph told him that in three days he would be taken from prison and executed. This is exactly what happened.

Sometimes when things go well for us we promise all sorts of things to people. Do we keep our promises? How important and honest it is to do so.

Group's
EGYPT™
Joseph's Journey
from prison to palace

The King cannot sleep

Poor Joseph! As he sat there in prison, no doubt he might have thought how unfair life must have been. Here he was in prison, hated, and totally rejected by his brothers at home. Potiphar thought evil of Joseph and the butler hadn't even mentioned his name to the king to get him released.

Two years had passed since the butler got out of jail and never once did he remember Joseph. Then one night Pharaoh had two dreams which troubled him so much he could not sleep. He was so anxious to know what they meant that he called for all the wise men and magicians of Egypt. As the king explained his dreams, not one of them could help him.

Then the butler heard about the king and his dreams and he remembered a young Hebrew prisoner who had been able to explain what his dreams meant and how they had come true exactly as he said.

Can you imagine how Joseph felt once the message came filtering through that he was wanted by the king? Before he went, he washed himself and put on some nice fresh clothes because he was going before the king.

It had taken the butler two years to remember what Joseph had done for him. Sometimes we can say "thank you" to people and promise to do this and that but very often we are like the butler and we forget all about our promises.

When you promise to do something, make sure you remember your promise.

JOSEPH 100

Brought before the King

Can you imagine how Joseph must have felt after spending quite a few years in a dirty old prison? Now he was allowed out of prison to go and see the king. As Joseph stood before the king, the king told him that he had had two dreams and he didn't know what they meant. The king had already asked all the magicians and wise men to translate the dream but they couldn't. Pharaoh told Joseph that he had heard Joseph could do such things. Joseph replied, "This wisdom does not belong unto me, but to the God whom I love and serve. Tell me your dreams and the Lord will tell me the meaning of them."

Joseph listened intently as the king explained his first dream. "As I stood by the river Nile there were seven fat cows that came out of the river and were standing eating grass. Then another seven skinny cows came out of the river and ate the seven fat cows and they were just as skinny as before."

"In my other dream I was in a corn field and there was a stalk with seven good ears of corn growing from it. While I was looking at this stalk with seven good ears, there appeared seven withered ears and ate up the seven good ears of corn."

Joseph began to tell the king what his dreams meant and how both these dreams had the same meaning. The seven fat cows and the seven good ears of corn represent seven good years of harvest. The seven thin cows and seven withered ears of corn represent a famine. Joseph explained to the king that there would be seven years of plentiful harvest and then there would be a famine such as Egypt had never seen. He advised Pharaoh to prepare for the famine and get the best man in all of Egypt to oversee the whole project. Who do you think got this job? Joseph of course!

Sometimes when everything is going wrong for us, it can be God's way of preparing us for something better in the future.

JOSEPH 101

From Slave to Prime Minister

As Pharaoh listened to the meaning of his two dreams, he was impressed with Joseph's answer. As Pharaoh thought who would be wise enough to lead Egypt through the famine he realised Joseph was the man for the job. Pharaoh said to all his assistants, "Who could do this job better than Joseph? He is a man filled with the spirit of God."

Joseph was then made a ruler over all of Egypt; in fact he was made second in command to the king. Now he wore beautiful robes; people were bowing down to him as the prince and ruler of Egypt. Joseph now had a lovely palace as a home and God provided Joseph with a beautiful wife.

In all of this change in Joseph's life he never once forgot who he was. God was always number one in his life, it was God who had now prospered Joseph and in everything Joseph did he gave God the glory and honour. God was with him in the pit, God was with him in the prison and now the Lord was with him in the palace.

One of the greatest truths in the entire Bible is that when you give your heart to Jesus Christ and get saved, truly born again, then God promises to be with you every single day. Even when you have bad days, He will be with you. In life many things don't always go the way we want them to. However, one thing we can be sure of is, that if you ever suffer for being a Christian, God knows all about it and will be with you to help you.

When something goes well for you, DON'T FORGET to acknowledge God and THANK HIM.

A Famine is coming

Joseph was now the Prime Minister of Egypt. Isn't it amazing how the Lord turned everything around for Joseph? Joseph straightaway began to prepare for the famine that was to come; he travelled the country instructing the people to build huge store houses to store the grain. Every year for seven years they were to keep some back to last through the famine.

During the seven years of plenty, Joseph and his wife had two sons, Manasseh and Ephraim. Manasseh's name meant 'to forget'. God helped Joseph to forget all his difficult years so when the child was born he called him Manasseh. The other son was called Ephraim meaning fruitful. Even while in affliction God caused Joseph to be fruitful.

After seven years of plenty, just as Joseph had said, the crops failed. Now for seven years a mighty famine swept over the land, the rain stopped and the crops failed. Soon the people began to get hungry and they had to use the food stored during the years of plenty.

Everyone who came to Pharaoh for food was sent to Joseph. Not only was the famine spread throughout Egypt but also the surrounding countries like Canaan, Syria and Arabia. The word was spreading quickly that in Egypt there was a huge storage of food. Joseph's father Jacob and all his brothers were now getting hungry. All those years ago they hated Joseph and swore they would never bow down to him. They were about to sow what they reaped. Tomorrow is a new day!

The Word of God says "all things work together for good to them that love God." (Romans 8:28)

Unbelievable but true

Many years ago Joseph had a dream that his brothers would bow down to him. How jealous they were, and how they hated him! Over in Canaan there was a serious shortage of food, so Jacob sent Joseph's ten older brothers to make the journey to Egypt to buy grain. When they arrived in Egypt they were sent to the ruler to buy the grain.

On meeting Joseph, the ruler, they bowed down to him hoping to get some food. Joseph recognised them immediately but did not tell them. They had no idea this was Joseph. Joseph spoke roughly to them and almost accused them of being spies to test them. "Who are you and where do you come from?" he asked. As soon as they told him about his father Jacob and their brother Benjamin, Joseph had to tell all the attendants to leave.

After they left he burst into tears and was overcome with emotion, then he revealed himself to them. "Brothers, I am Joseph." At once they all bowed with shock and begged Joseph not to kill them. "Brothers," he said "you meant it for evil but God meant it for good." Joseph then kissed and hugged all his brothers.

No doubt they would have thought back on all those years earlier, when Joseph had dreamt they would bow down to him twice. Now they realised, they had just bowed down twice to their brother, Joseph.

Joseph's life was full of trials and testing. God had a plan and a purpose for his life and now it was all coming into place. Joseph forgave his brothers, just as Jesus forgives us for all the sins we have committed.

If your friends did to you what Joseph's brothers did to him, would you forgive them?

Moving House

After Joseph revealed himself to his brothers, it was quite an emotional time for them all. Joseph was especially happy to see his younger brother, Benjamin, and after he heard all about his father Jacob, he sent his brothers home to Canaan to bring Jacob his father to him.

On their way back they took many gifts from Joseph and also from Pharaoh. When the brothers got home they ran with excitement to see Jacob, "Joseph is alive!" they cried. "He is the ruler over all of Egypt and he lives in the palace with the king." Jacob, overcome with emotion, told his sons to take him to Joseph. He wanted to see his son before he died, as he was now an old man.

It was a big step for Jacob to leave his country and take his whole family to Egypt. They took with them men, women, children, sheep, camels, donkeys and all their belongings. Nothing was left behind in Canaan for the famine had swept through the land and their only hope was to go to Egypt.

Jacob was a man of God, the Lord comforted Jacob assuring him that He was doing the right thing and reminded him how He would be with him and would make of him a great nation. It was not easy to leave the land he loved, but Jacobs' love for his son was greater. How he wanted to see his son!

Imagine if our motivation in everything we did was to see the Son of God. To see Jesus in everything we do. Our motivation for living should be Jesus Christ.

What stresses you out the most? What difficulties has God helped you through?

JOSEPH 105

Is it really you Son?

Excitement filled Joseph's heart as he made his way to the Egyptian border to meet his father Jacob! He hadn't seen his father in years. This would have been a very emotional time for them both. As they hugged and kissed each other it was a very joyous occasion.

Jacob was now 130 years old and after he saw Joseph he said he was ready to die. Joseph then took his father to meet Pharaoh. Pharaoh was delighted to meet Jacob; after all, it was Joseph who saved the Egyptians from starvation.

Pharaoh then invited Joseph's entire family to come and live in Egypt. He gave them the best of land on which to feed their animals and everyone was very happy. It was especially nice for Jacob to meet his two grandsons, Ephraim and Manasseh.

After Jacob was in Egypt for about seventeen years the time had come for him to die. He called all his family around him and gave them a special blessing. The promises that God had given to Abraham, Isaac and Jacob would now be passed on to his sons and Joseph's two sons as well. Joseph's brothers and two sons would be leaders in the twelve tribes of Israel, God's chosen people, the Jews.

Sometimes when children are growing up they can have disagreements with their families. We should always love, honour, respect and obey our parents. If we have any ill feeling towards them we should immediately make up or the Lord may punish us for treating them badly.

Have you ever spoken back angrily to your parents without saying sorry? Now is the time to say sorry and God will bless you for doing so.

Joseph reminds me of Jesus

We have now come to the end of this part of Joseph's life. Joseph had had a wonderful reunion with his family, his father had died and life continued for them in Egypt.

The account of Joseph is a wonderful picture of the Lord Jesus Christ. Joseph was hated, despised, and rejected by his own people, just like Jesus. Joseph had a loving, caring heart, just like Jesus and he cared for and provided for his people. Doesn't the Lord Jesus do this for us?

Just as God had a plan for Joseph's life, He also had a plan and purpose for sending His dear Son the Lord Jesus Christ into this world. That reason was to die for our sins; God has a plan and purpose for your life. Put your life completely into His hands. He cares for you, loves you and He will look after you. That is a promise from God.

"Christ Jesus came into the world to save sinners." (I Timothy 1:15)

"All that the Father giveth me shall come to me; and him that cometh to me I will in no wise cast out."
(John 6:37)

Moses

A promise from God

Throughout the Old Testament we find God continually reminding His people of a promise He gave to Abraham, Isaac and Jacob. God told these men that their descendants would be as numerous as the stars of Heaven and the sand on the seashore.

God continually taught Abraham, Isaac, Jacob, their families and the Hebrew people to love, obey and follow Him. The Lord patiently guided and helped His people every time they got into trouble, to show them the importance of putting their trust in Him.

God allowed Jacob's son, Joseph to become a slave in Egypt and the Lord was with Joseph and continually blessed Joseph right throughout his life. Then Pharaoh, the king of Egypt invited Joseph to bring his entire family over to live in Egypt. At the beginning, there were about seventy people in total but as time went by these families began to grow, until there were thousands of Hebrews living in Egypt.

Eventually a new Pharaoh came to the throne of Egypt and he did not remember Joseph. As he looked upon the land of Goshen and saw thousands of Hebrews; he began to feel threatened. These were God's people however and the Lord had promised to bless and look after them. Even though life was great for the Hebrews now, trouble was just around the corner and their faith and reliance in God would be tested to the limit, but God would not fail them.

This is a brilliant picture of the Christian life. No matter what we are going through or will go through, we can be sure the Lord is with us.

Slaves in Egypt

When Pharaoh noticed the growth in the Hebrew population he felt threatened. He thought that the Hebrews would soon outnumber the Egyptians and might even join with his enemies to fight against Egypt. Pharaoh sent soldiers and armed Egyptians to Goshen to threaten the Hebrews and force them to work as slaves.

The Hebrew people were no longer allowed to work for themselves but instead, were forced to work as slaves. Brutal taskmasters wore them down under heavy burdens and made them build cities. Day after day, the Hebrews worked in the hot sunshine, making bricks, mixing mortar, building walls and carrying out all sorts of manual labour. The taskmasters stood by with whips to punish anyone who rested or slowed down in their work. Day after day God's people suffered severely under the cruel rule of Pharaoh.

Even though the Hebrews were bullied and severely mistreated, they never lost their faith in God. Pharaoh never succeeded in breaking the spirit of their faith in God. No doubt the Hebrews were often sad and discouraged, but God allowed this to happen for His own reasons. Pharaoh forced them to work harder and harder, making more and more bricks than the day before. Their bondage and exhausting work became almost unbearable.

Maybe in your Christian life, you are finding things difficult and almost unbearable at times. Always remember there are others who suffer much worse than you. Quite often we can be full of self pity thinking that the whole world is against us, when all we need is to realise how blessed we really are.

Baby Moses

Things became worse and worse for the Hebrews and no doubt they wondered why the Lord was allowing them to remain as slaves. Their workload seemed to become impossible as they worked from day to day under the brutal taskmasters.

Despite this, Pharaoh noticed the population seemed to be growing even faster, so he proclaimed a most shocking and cruel law, that all the baby boys under two years old would have to die. Pharaoh was afraid of all the males who might grow up to fight against him, so he tried to stop the population from growing.

The Hebrew mothers would never harm their little sons, so Pharaoh ordered his soldiers to find all the baby boys under two years. They were to throw them into the river and drown them. What a terrible man Pharaoh must have been. At this time there was a baby boy called Moses, born into a Hebrew family. His parents were called Amram and Jochebed. Moses had a big brother called Aaron who was three, and an older sister called Miriam who was seven when Moses was born.

Moses was a strong, healthy and beautiful little baby. When news came that he would be drowned in the river, his parents began to cry unto the Lord for help. They loved their little boy but what could they do to save his life? They needed to hide him so they came up with an idea to hide Moses in a basket. This would be the beginning of one of the most adventurous life stories ever.

MOSES 110

A baby in a Basket floating down the River

When baby Moses was just three months old, his parents decided they had to carry out their plan to hide him. If the Egyptians heard Moses crying he would surely be put to death as all baby boys had to be killed to stop the population growing.

Jochebed made a basket of bulrushes (strong reeds) and covered it with pitch (tar) to make it waterproof. She then put three month old Moses in the basket and gently placed it in the river Nile among the plants. Jochebed watched with tears, as it gently floated in the river. Miriam watched with curiosity as the little basket with her little brother floated in the river.

The same day the Princess of Egypt, Pharaoh's daughter, came along with her maids to wash in the river. As she was bathing, she noticed the basket floating in the river and immediately she sent for it to find out what was inside. To her great surprise she found a beautiful little baby. Her heart melted as she looked down at the tiny baby. This is where Moses got his name from, as it means 'drawn out of the water.'

Miriam was terrified to see that Pharaoh's own daughter had found Moses but then she noticed that the Princess had compassion on him. Losing no time, the seven year old girl ran quickly over to the Princess and suggested getting a Hebrew woman to help look after the child. Having no experience in looking after such a little baby, the Princess thought this was a great idea. Miriam ran like the wind and got her mother to come to the Princess. When the Princess saw Jochebed she asked her to help look after the baby and for doing this she would also pay her wages for doing so. So the Princess paid Moses' own mother to look after him!

Isn't it amazing how God has turned everything around in an almost unbelievable direction? This is what the Lord does, He surprises us in the most unexpected ways.

MOSES 111

Childhood privileges

Little three month old baby Moses, who, like so many others had been doomed to death, now found himself in the palace with all the privileges of a Prince. His own mother was bringing him up and anything he needed, he was sure to get.

As Moses was growing up, his mother took every opportunity to teach him about God. He learned about Abraham, Isaac, Jacob, Joseph and how they now came to live in Egypt. Moses loved this history and would have been curious about what the future held for his people.
At the same time, Moses was being taught in mathematics, geography, law, medicine, history and many other important subjects by the best teachers in Egypt. Moses became well educated in the knowledge and wisdom the Egyptians could supply. Moses also realised that, being a Prince, he was next in line to the throne of Egypt. Someday he could become the next ruler of Egypt.

In the meantime the Hebrews continued to suffer at the cruel hands of Pharaoh. There were two extremes; the Egyptians were trouble free and the Hebrews continued to suffer. Through it all, God had not forgotten His people and one day they would be freed.

Sometimes we take our childhood for granted. Many children around the world have no home and no-one to love them. They may have no school, only hard work and no pay. Try to do your best in school and love and appreciate your parents and family more than anyone else in the world.

Moses on the run

Moses had everything a young person could ever dream of. Lots of money, new clothes, servants, horses, whatever he wanted, he was sure to get. However, he never forgot his childhood and how time and time again his mother would teach him about the Lord and the history of God's people right up to the time when he was drawn out of the water.

As the years went by, Moses became less comfortable in the palace and really wanted to be with his own people, the Hebrews. Every day he would hear how life was becoming more and more difficult for them. The cruel taskmasters were worse than ever, continually beating the men and making them work under very difficult conditions.

Then Moses decided he was willing to suffer with the people of God, his people, rather than have the luxuries and pleasures of a wicked, sinful, heathen country. One day when he was forty years old he went over to visit the slaves. When he arrived he was shocked to see how his people were mistreated by the Egyptian taskmasters. As he was watching, he noticed an Egyptian beating a Hebrew slave. Moses, full of anger, went over to him and with one blow killed the Egyptian. As the slave ran off, Moses quickly buried the Egyptian in the sand.

The next day he went to visit his people again and noticed two Hebrews arguing with each other. When he tried to stop them, they turned around to him and said, "Are you going to kill us, as you did the Egyptian yesterday?" Moses realised he had been found out and began to fear for his life. If Pharaoh found out he would kill him, so Moses ran for his own safety. Moses could not run forever, because God had a big plan for him and soon he would have to return to Egypt.

Can you control your anger and frustration?
Asking God to help you is a good thing to do.

MOSES 113

The Burning Bush

Moses fled to the land of Midian to escape punishment. Little did he know that he would be on the run for the next forty years. Up until now Moses had lived a comfortable life, but after he committed the terrible sin of murder he was very miserable. No doubt he regretted his actions. Sin always brings misery and makes us very uncomfortable and it is always best to acknowledge our sin before God.

Moses came to a well where he sat down to rest. He noticed several women coming to the well for water, but was shocked to see how they were chased away by some rough shepherds. Standing to his feet he went over to help the girls get their water. Jethro was the father of these girls and when he heard how Moses had helped his daughters, he offered Moses a job as a shepherd. Moses eventually married one of Jethro's daughters.

Moses had spent forty years in the palace learning to be Prince, now in the desert he had to learn humility. When he reached this stage in his life, no longer full of pride but rather, realising how important God was in his life, the Lord began to speak to him. In the meantime, the old Pharaoh had died and a new, much harsher Pharaoh had succeeded him. The Hebrews were being slaughtered every day and began to cry to God for help and deliverance. God heard their cry and was going to help them.

One day when Moses was looking after the sheep all by himself, he noticed that a bush beside him was on fire. As he got closer he noticed the bush continued to burn, but never burned away, it was burning but was not being consumed. As he got really close to investigate this strange yet interesting bush, a voice spoke from the bush, "Take off your shoes, for you are standing on holy ground." The Lord was speaking to Moses through the burning bush. In the most unusual and unexpected of places, the Lord spoke to Moses.

> We should live our lives like this; at any moment expecting to hear from God about His will for our lives.

MOSES 114

Making excuses

As Moses stood before the Burning Bush, the Lord continued to speak to him. God reminded Moses that He was the God of Abraham, Isaac, Jacob and of the Hebrews as well. The Lord then told Moses that he was going to set his people free. Moses was so glad to hear this; how he longed to be with his people again.

God then told Moses that he was the one who was to go to Pharaoh and tell him to let the Hebrew people go. Moses immediately made excuses that he was too old and tired to do such a thing as he was now eighty years old. The Lord assured Moses that he would not be going alone, as God would be with him.

Moses then made another excuse and said he was slow of speech and couldn't speak very well. The Lord then said his brother Aaron would go with him and speak for him. The Lord told Moses he was going to do many mighty miracles before Pharaoh until he would let the people go. Then the Lord told Moses to throw the rod he was holding to the ground. As he did so, it became a snake. Moses jumped with fright and as he picked it up after being told to do so by God it became a rod again. "Put your hand into your coat," the Lord told him; as he did so it became white with leprosy and when he put it back again it returned to normal.

No matter what excuse Moses made, the Lord was able to make a way possible for him, until finally, Moses was willing to go to free his people.

Sometimes there are things the Lord wants us to do which we don't want to, so we start to make excuses. God will make it possible for you to go to that place or speak to that person, so long as you are willing.

Moses was now ready for the great journey of returning home to his own people and to the Egyptians. The question was, what would happen when he got there?

MOSES 115

Let my People go

Moses then met up with his brother Aaron and together they went to face the Pharaoh of Egypt. Before this, they stopped with the elders of the Hebrew people and told them about how God appeared before Moses in the Burning Bush and told him to free the Hebrew people from bondage and slavery. The elders were delighted to hear this and news soon spread to all the Hebrew people that soon they would be free.

When Moses and Aaron came before Pharaoh, he was furious, as there was no way he was prepared to let the people go. In fact, he was so cross, he made the children of Israel work even harder. Normally they were given straw to help them make the bricks, now they had to gather their own straw yet continue to make the same number of bricks each day. This was an impossible task and because they could not do it, they were beaten and whipped almost to death.

The Hebrews then complained bitterly to Moses and blamed him for making things worse. Moses had talked about deliverance, but they had seen nothing but disaster. Moses became greatly discouraged and was really confused about what God was going to do. The Lord then appeared to Moses and encouraged him with many of His promises. The Lord God of Heaven explained to Moses that Pharaoh would be forced to let His people go.

SOMETIMES IN LIFE everything seems to go wrong, when before it seemed perfectly straightforward. We must remember that our ways are not GOD'S WAY and God's ways are not our ways.

The first nine Plagues

When the Lord reminded Moses that He would set His people free, Moses was encouraged and believed the Lord. However, the Hebrew people were not so sure and felt really discouraged, defeated and disappointed that they could not be free.

When Moses again approached Pharaoh, he continued to refuse to let the people go. God then began to send plagues upon Pharaoh and the people. First, the river Nile turned into a river of blood; it was a terrible sight with a terrible smell. Pharaoh hardened his heart and would not let the people go. The Lord then sent plagues of frogs, lice and flies that completely covered the land. Pharaoh agreed to let the people go each time but when each plague stopped he hardened his heart again and again and refused to let the people go.

Then God sent a plague of murrain when the animals of the Egyptians began to die by the thousand. Horses, cattle, sheep and herds of all the animals in Egypt were affected, but not those of the Hebrews. The Lord was now making a distinction between the children of Israel and the Egyptians. After this plague, there were several more; thunder and hail, locusts and darkness. Time and time again Pharaoh pleaded with Moses to stop the plagues and he would let the people go. Pharaoh again hardened his heart after these nine plagues; he was so stubborn that he would not let the people go, but God would send one more plague that would break Pharaoh's hardened heart once and for all.

Sometimes people can be like Pharaoh. When everything seems to go wrong and problems abound, then they seem to really need the Lord, but when all is well, they somehow no longer think they need the Lord. The Lord is either Lord of all or not Lord at all.

To read all about the ten plagues,
read Exodus Chapters 8-10

MOSES 117

The death Angel comes

After the ninth plague, God told Moses that the time had finally come when he would lead the people out of Egypt. The time for deliverance and the great Exodus had finally come.

Over the years the Hebrews had gathered up lots of gold, silver and great herds of cattle. There would be lots of things to take with them when the time came to leave Egypt, so they were told to begin packing. Moses then instructed the people what was going to happen that night.

The final plague would be sent that night, when the Death Angel would come and kill every firstborn male in every house. The Hebrew people were told to take a lamb that was as pure and perfect as could be, without marks or injury. They were to kill the lamb and with its blood paint the doorpost of their houses and the beam above their doors. They were also to prepare dinner and eat it standing up as if they were ready to go. The lamb was to be eaten with herbs and unleavened bread.

The blood on the door posts was a sign to the Death Angel, that when the Lord saw the blood, He would pass over that house and not bring death. However, if there was no blood on the door posts, then the Death Angel would enter that home and slay the eldest son. How serious this was for the people. If they neglected to cover their home with the blood of the lamb, then death was sure to come to their home.

This is a beautiful picture of Jesus Christ. He is the Perfect Lamb of God who died upon the cross and shed His precious blood for us. If His blood has never been applied to wash away our sins then we are sure to die and be lost forever. The blood of Jesus Christ can wash away your sin if you believe and ask Him to cleanse you from your sin. This is the most important decision you will ever make in your life, but if you can believe, it will change your life and your eternal destiny.

All about the Passover

At midnight, the Death Angel visited the land of Egypt. All over the country, cries of horror were heard as the Death Angel went from house to house, killing the oldest boy in each home. The only families to escape death were those who had applied the blood to the doorposts of their homes. Thousands of homes were visited that night. Eventually, Pharaoh's home also was visited by the Death Angel; no-one escaped. Without wasting time, Pharaoh begged Moses to take the people out of Egypt. Finally, it was time to go.

"When I, the Lord, shall see the blood I will pass over you," was what the Lord had promised the people. When the people of Israel applied the blood to their doorposts, they were saved from physical death. This plan, the Passover, is a wonderfully clear picture of the salvation God has planned for His people. In the same way, everyone who has the blood applied to their heart will be saved from spiritual death.

The Passover Lamb pointed to Jesus Christ, who died on the cross for our sins. In the New Testament Paul wrote, "Christ our Passover is sacrificed for us," (I Cor.5:7). Only Jesus Christ is the perfect, spotless Lamb of God. When the Death Angel went through the streets from home to home, he did not stop to wonder what type of people lived there. Are they black or white, rich or poor, religious or non religious, good or bad, Hebrews or Egyptians? No, he just looked to see if the blood was on the doorposts.

If the blood was on the doorpost then the Death Angel passed by. He did not stop, but rather passed over that home. The blood on the door was a sign that the people there believed in God and accepted God's way of saving them and taking them to safety. It was not the innocent lamb that saved them; it was the death of the lamb and the blood of the lamb that saved them. Likewise it is not the perfect sinless life of the Lord Jesus that saves us; it is His death and the shedding of His blood that washes away our sin. It was the blood of the lamb that saved the firstborn Israelites from death.

The longest Parade ever

The morning after the Passover, all Egypt was in deep mourning. After ten plagues, Pharaoh finally consented to let the children of Israel go. Early in the morning Moses and Aaron led the procession; this was the longest parade ever, with over two million people on a journey.

They had all their bags packed, tents folded and animals herded together as they began to leave Egypt. There was no time to delay in case Pharaoh would change his mind again. This was a wonderful sight, as the children of Israel had been slaves to Pharaoh for over 80 years living in continual bondage. They had dreamed about this day and prayed for it; now it had become a reality. The Lord was answering their prayer.

As the multitude made their way forward they wondered which direction they should go. Then, up in the sky they noticed a cloud. The cloud was a marker for them to follow by day and then it became a pillar of fire by night. God had not forgotten them, for not only had He saved them in the Passover but now He was leading and guiding them. When the cloud stopped, the people stopped and wherever it went, they followed. They just kept walking and walking towards the land of Cannan, the Promised Land which God had promised them. How long the journey would take, they had no idea.

This is like the Christian life. We never really know how long our journey here on earth will last, but every day of that journey God wants us to stay close to Him. He will continue to guide us and protect us until the journey's end.

An angry Man

The children of Israel were now on their way to freedom, to Cannan, the Promised Land. In the meantime Pharaoh was exploding with anger at what was happening. Egypt was completely devastated by the previous nine plagues and now this final one, with the death of his eldest son, was too much for Pharaoh. Thousands of Egyptian sons were killed by the Death Angel the previous night and all over Egypt there was mourning as every family had lost its eldest son. Pharaoh was warned but he paid no attention.

Pharaoh was so angry that he immediately dispatched his soldiers to chase after the children of Israel, to bring them back again. The soldiers were very angry too, as they would have lost sons the previous night. Pharaoh realised he had lost all his slaves who were able to do so much work for him. Not only this, they had taken with them all their cattle, tents, silver and gold. All of the Egyptian's cattle had died; the country was in ruins and Pharaoh was angry.

God had put a cloud in the sky for the children of Israel to follow, this way, they would know exactly where to go. At night time the cloud became a pillar of fire, like a big bright light or beacon. Suddenly the children of Israel heard a noise, was it a thunder storm? As the sound got louder and louder they realised it was the sound of horses and chariots. They screamed with fear as they realised Pharaoh and the Egyptian army were now seeking revenge and was chasing them at full speed.

Pharaoh was bitter and angry because he never got his own way. It seemed to Pharaoh that Moses outwitted him and he became very angry. Sometimes we can be like this and when we don't get our own way we can get angry and take it out on other people. Moses was on the Lord's side and God promised to help him and deliver the people.

> What do you think were going to happen, especially as the cloud was leading them right to the Red Sea?

Walking through the Red Sea

Moses, together with the two million people, walked as fast as they could while Pharaoh's army seemed to be getting closer and closer. Suddenly they realised that they had walked right up to the Red Sea and there were no ships to carry them across.

The people began to complain against Moses and say it would have been better for them to stay as slaves than to die in the wilderness by the sea. They were sure the army would attack and kill them. Then Moses began to pray and as he did so, something extraordinary happened. The cloud went behind them and covered the whole sky with darkness and fog. This slowed down the Egyptians to crawling speed, as they had no idea where they were going because of the fog.

Then the Lord said to Moses, "Go forward." Moses was asked to stretch his rod out over the Red Sea and as he did so, the Lord caused a great wind that started to blow on the sea. As the Israelites stood staring with amazement, the waters began to part and two great walls of water appeared, creating a path right through the sea. Throughout the night, the wind continued to blow until the path through the sea was completely dry.

Without hesitation, Moses and Aaron started to cross the Red Sea, two huge walls of water towering on either side of them. How fearful and exciting that journey must have been! Then they heard the sound of the horses and chariots once again. They walked as quickly as they could, trying to keep calm. With the Egyptians now almost caught up with them, what was going to happen? Would God deliver them or would they be attacked with no hope at the bottom of the sea?

> God had made a promise that He would deliver them and His promises are rock solid, for the Bible tells us that "God is not a man, that he should lie." In other words, unlike men, who are sinners by nature, God is perfect. Do you keep the promises you make?

An unbelievable Sight

Eventually, Moses and Aaron were first to make it through the Red Sea and out the other side. As they looked back they saw some two million of their people, exhausted and weary with a look of desperation upon their faces. There were men, women and children, cattle, horses, sheep, donkeys, camels, tents and all their equipment.

Then in the distance, approaching the Red Sea was a whole host of Egyptian soldiers; thousands of them on horses and chariots led by Pharaoh. How Moses must have yelled to the people to move fast and keep walking, as Pharaoh and his army were fast approaching! With horror they all looked back and saw the dust in the air, as the Egyptian army moved closer and closer, making their way into the path in the Red Sea.

Then things began to go wrong for the Egyptians. The wheels on their chariots began to fall off, horses stumbled and fell. The whole army seemed to be stuck in the sea, as they tried to come along the path. The journey seemed to last forever, but eventually the last of the Israelites made their way out of the Red Sea.

Then God instructed Moses to put his rod out over the sea again and as he did so, the walls of the Red Sea came crashing down on the Egyptian army. Everyone in the Egyptian army, including Pharaoh, drowned that day.

Isn't it AMAZING how the Lord turned an impossible situation into a perfect solution? Place all your worries and concerns into HIS HANDS and let the Lord sort them out His way in His time.

Giving thanks and praise to God

As the children of Israel stood at the edge of the Red Sea it must have been the most amazing sight ever, watching the walls of the Red Sea falling in on top of the Egyptian army. The people were so filled with excitement as they watched their enemies being defeated. The Bible says they all started singing and worshipping God together.

"Then sang Moses and the children of Israel this song unto the LORD, and spake, saying, I will sing unto the LORD, for he hath triumphed gloriously: the horse and his rider hath he thrown into the sea. The LORD is my strength and song, and he is become my salvation: he is my God, and I will prepare him an habitation; my father's God, and I will exalt him.

The LORD is a man of war: the LORD is his name. Pharaoh's chariots and his host hath he cast into the sea: his chosen captains also are drowned in the Red sea. The depths have covered them: they sank into the bottom as a stone." (Exodus 15:1-5)

How important it is to always give the Lord thanks for absolutely everything in our lives, to continually praise Him for everything. He is such a wonderful God; a most loving and caring Heavenly Father. The Israelites sang praises to God for delivering them out of the hands of their enemies. From the oldest to the youngest they skipped and jumped with joy at the goodness of the Lord.

We are never too young or too old to praise the Lord and to be thankful every day for everything He has done for us and for all He means to us.

> Aim to start each day, by praising the Lord for something He has done for you.

The Journey Continues

Pharaoh's army had been destroyed in trying to catch the children of Israel, as they journeyed through the Red Sea. The slavery in Egypt was now over and the people were so happy.

As they made their journey towards the land of promise, the Promised Land, there would be many trials. Along the way, the great multitude of people had to travel through a great wilderness called Shur.

This would be a long and difficult journey. There was an easier way to travel, but God told them to travel this way to make them stronger and also to rely more on the Lord for their daily needs.

In many ways this can be like the Christian life. Many people assume it will be a nice smooth road to travel to Heaven. This is not the case, for the road can be bumpy and there will be many hurdles along the way. Our faith in God will be tested many times.

All along the way, the Lord is training us to be strong, and teaching us to completely rely on and trust in Him along every step of the way. God will give us the strength for the journey.

The Water that was Bitter

As the people continued their long journey into the wilderness, they became very thirsty. Very soon they had used up their supply and all longed for fresh water to quench their thirst. For three days, they travelled without water; how they all longed for a drink; men, women, children and animals.

They started to complain to Moses. Everything had been wonderful when things were going well. They had thought to themselves, "this is the life." However, suddenly when something went wrong, they had to blame someone.

Then, in the distance they saw something they couldn't believe. It was water. In the dazzling sun, there appeared some water, so sparkling and reflective. As they ran and dived into it, to their disgust they discovered it was bitter water; impossible to drink. All they could do was spit the water out again; it was so disappointing.

Everyone was so thirsty, and to find bitter water after three days of having no water was such a disappointment. God was trying to teach them the importance of totally relying on Him, even for simple, yet vital things, such as water.

The people mumbled, grumbled and complained against Moses and against God. Do you blame God when things go wrong in your life?

BADWATER

The Story of a Tree

Moses was a wise man because every time the people complained to him about their situation, he went to God in prayer. This is a wonderful lesson for us to learn; to take everything to the Lord in prayer.

The people were so weary and there was a big pool of bitter water before them that was impossible to drink. The people could not possibly face another day's journey in the wilderness without fresh water to drink. As they complained and Moses prayed, something miraculous happened. God told Moses to cut down a certain tree. When he cut down the tree, he threw it into the river and the people wondered what he was doing.

How could putting a tree into the water make the bitter waters sweet? Well it did, for immediately the water was pure, sweet and lovely to drink. The water was purified. One by one, the people crept up to the water and tasted it; it was so refreshing and pure.

This tree reminds us of Calvary's Tree; that is the Cross that Christ hung upon. All our sinful and bitter lives can become sweet. By trusting and believing in Jesus Christ, He can take all our bitterness away. This is why Jesus died on the Cross, to take away all the bitterness of sin.

The Bible says, "O taste and see that the LORD is good: blessed is the man that trusteth in him." (Psalm 34:8)

MOSES 127

An Oasis in the Desert

After leaving Marah, the place where God made the bitter waters sweet, Moses continued the journey through the desert. As the people walked, they would talk about the miracle God had just done for them, in making the bitter waters sweet. They would talk about the tree that made the difference.

The tree at Calvary makes the difference for us. When something goes wrong in our lives, God does not want us to become bitter and blame Him. Rather He wants to take the bitterness away and make our experience sweet.

The wilderness was like a desert and as they walked and walked, eventually they came upon a place called Elim. It was like a little forest in the desert and in it were trees and twelve springs of pure water. How refreshing it must have been in the desert, to sit under the palm trees and drink the lovely water. Their stop in Elim was just like an oasis in the desert. They stayed there until they were completely rested and ready to continue their journey.

This reminds us of how God provides for us exactly what we need for our journey along the Christian pathway. He often provides for us, without us even asking Him. All the time the children of Israel were following a cloud in the sky, God was reminding them to follow Him. Today instead of clouds, we have God's Word to direct us and lead us in life.

God leads and provides for many people. He brings opportunities our way to refresh and encourage us. Isn't our God a wonderful, caring God?

There's no more food!

After a lovely rest in the little forest, with seventy Palm trees and fresh water, it was time to move on. God was leading the Israelites by a cloud in the sky but for several weeks it hadn't moved. Now it began to move again so it was time to pack up and continue the journey to the Promised Land.

On their way to Mount Sinai they crossed a huge desert; it was a dry, rocky and sandy desert. There was much grass, very few trees and no animals. The people began to get more hungry and very soon they cried to Moses and told him there was no more food. One by one they began to mumble, grumble and complain. Very soon nearly everyone was complaining of hunger. Had they forgotten about God again? Just a few days ago they were so content with everything they had.

Isn't this the way we are sometimes? When all is going well for us, we are so happy. Then, when things become a little difficult and it's not so easy, we begin to complain; we grumble and moan and blame everybody.

The people here were blaming Moses and his brother Aaron for the lack of food. They were certain they were going to starve to death in the barren desert. They were even wishing they had stayed in Egypt as slaves because at least there, they had food.

Even though the Israelites had seen God do many miracles before, they had not learned to trust Him fully for everything, especially for daily food and water. This is what God wants from us, to completely trust in Him for everything.

Fresh Meat flies in

Moses then began to pray to God concerning the people's hunger. God was so patient with the people even though they were so impatient with Him. We are like this sometimes as we tend to want everything done now, in our time.

God's timing is perfect; He promised Moses that He would send the people meat every night for supper and bread every morning for breakfast. Moses and Aaron then called all the people together and began to explain what God had said He would do. Meat and bread; the people could hardly believe their ears, but where was that going to come from?

Suddenly as they were talking, a wonderful thing happened. As they looked up at the cloud in the sky it began to shine so brightly. It was the glory of the Lord shining for all to see; it was a beautiful sight and it brought an amazing peace upon the people. God was telling them again that He loved them, cared for them and would look after them. Here He was reminding them of His greatness and power.

That evening a most amazing thing happened; suddenly hundreds and thousands of quails came flying by. They were so low the people could catch them and when they landed, the children could run after them and catch them. Quail were very good meat to eat, so they killed the birds, cooked and ate them. They were very tasty, so they ate them until they were full.

God had again supplied their need. The morning would soon come but where would the bread come from?

Bread from Heaven

Waking up early in the morning, the people were very excited, as God had promised them bread. They were so surprised when they went out of their tents for all over the ground were hundreds and thousands of little white things.

Not really knowing what they were looking at they ran to Moses to ask him. Moses explained that just as God promised to send meat in the evening, so he would send bread in the morning. Sure enough that's what it was; it was lovely fresh bread they called 'manna.'

The Israelites were told to gather enough manna to last that day. They were not to store any for the next day. Some people were disobedient and thought no bread would arrive the next day and they kept some over in their tents. The next morning they were shocked as the bread they had kept over was rotten and full of worms. Every morning there was a fresh supply of bread on the ground. It was the freshest bread you could ever taste and God had supplied it.

God was teaching them that His promises are true and that He would take care of their daily needs. It is the same with us today. We should be content with what we have today and leave tomorrow and the future in God's hands. He knows our every need and He can supply it better than we can ever imagine.

Manna today

Just as God supplied manna every morning for the Israelites to eat, so He provides for us today. Not with physical bread, growing on the ground of course, but with His Word, the Bible.

God was again teaching the people that He supplied their basic need for bread, water and rest. Years later when Jesus came to this earth, He was teaching the people and telling them about the manna. He went on to tell them that even though they survived on manna, they all eventually died. Jesus taught the people that He was the Bread of Life; the Living Bread. If we believe in Jesus and receive Him into our hearts we will live forever with Him. When we get saved and trust in the Lord with all our hearts, we become God's children. God wants to speak to us every day. He does this as we read His Word. Just as the manna came fresh every day, so the Word of God feeds our hearts and satisfies our spiritual hunger.

We need to feed every day on this bread so that our souls will become strong enough to live the Christian life. Early morning is the best time to think about God because our minds are fresh; our bodies are refreshed from a good night's sleep. This is the best time to read and pray to the Lord.

"Jesus said, I AM THE BREAD OF LIFE: he that cometh to me shall never hunger; and he that BELIEVETH on me shall never thirst." (John 6:35)

MOSES 132

We're thirsty again

As the children of Israel continued their journey through the desert they began to get thirsty again. Then the cloud which they had been following stopped; this was a sign from the Lord that this was the place they were to stop at and put up camp for the night. The place they arrived at was called Rephidim.

"What about water?" they complained to Moses. "We are so thirsty we are going to die in this desert." Again, they forgot about God and how He had so graciously provided for them before.

God had performed many miracles for the people, yet they still doubted that God was with them. Again, Moses began to pray for the people. They complained to Moses instead of praying to God about the situation. Moses was very discouraged, as the people were almost ready to stone him because he would not give them water to drink. It was God they needed to pray to.

Sometimes in life we forget about God and rely too much on ourselves, or others. Our parents are only human, so we should pray to God about every situation in life. Maybe you have problems at school, or difficulties at home; talk to the Lord about them in prayer. He will help you and He already knows all about it before you talk to Him. God knows everything and He is open to our cry. He loves us to bring our requests to Him.

Water from the Rock

As the people continued to complain about having no water to drink, Moses prayed to God. The Lord told Moses to take the people to Mount Horeb where there was a big rock at the foot of the mountain; "Wait at the rock," God told Moses. There the Lord told Moses to strike the rock with the rod he was holding. This was the same rod that parted the Red Sea and turned into a snake in Pharaoh's Palace. As Moses stood at the rock he told the people that God would give them a daily supply of water. Then Moses lifted his rod high and struck the rock. Immediately a mighty river of water poured from the rock. It flowed for hours until every person and animal had plenty to drink and enough to fill containers. The water was so refreshing to drink and everyone was so thankful.

The rock at Mount Horeb is a beautiful picture of the Lord Jesus Christ. Jesus also was smitten with the rod before He went to the cross (Isaiah 53). God tells us in His Word that 'Christ is the Rock.' "And did all drink the same spiritual drink: for they drank of that spiritual Rock that followed them: and that Rock was Christ." (1 Corinthians 10:4)

Christ was smitten, wounded and bruised on the cross for our sins. By believing in the Lord Jesus as our Saviour, He gives us living water, or everlasting life. That living water gives life and refreshment to a thirsty world. With Christ we will be forever satisfied.

Jesus told the woman of Samaria: "But whosoever drinketh of the water that I shall give him shall never thirst; but the water that I shall give him shall be in him a well of water springing up into everlasting life." (John 4:14)

God's People attacked

In the Christian life there will always be challenges, for even though God is with us, it doesn't mean we will not experience problems and difficulties.

One of the troublesome times Moses and the Israelites had was when they journeyed through the area of Rephidim. The people who lived here were called Amalekites and they were a people who didn't care for God and only thought of themselves.

When they saw the Israelites passing through they decided to attack them from the rear. In the mountains, the Amalekites were hiding and at any moment would attack the people, robbing them of anything they had and even killing some of them to get what they wanted. They seemed to always attack from the rear where it was weakest.

The lesson here is that the devil will always attack us where we are weakest especially when we are not on our guard. When we stop praying and reading the Bible we become weak. Perhaps when people make bad jokes you laugh at them instead of saying, "That's not proper." When people make fun of us we want to attack them, because we are reacting with our natural person instead of the spiritual person that God makes us to be.

In many countries Christians are attacked for their faith. Many people mock and make fun of them; it is good to pray that God would protect these people.

Joshua, a Man of Action

Whenever the Amalekites attacked the Israelites, Moses took immediate action. He called together some of the brave young men, instructing them to fight against the Amalekites and he appointed a young man called Joshua, to be the leader. This is the first time Joshua is mentioned in scripture. Little did he or Moses know that Joshua would one day be the leader of the children of Israel, to lead them into the Promised Land.

Maybe you have great expectations in life; you want to do well and be in a good position in life. This often doesn't come easy, as one must be prepared to first work long and hard at the little things in life. Maybe your mum asked you to help wash the dishes, or tidy your room and you refuse to do such a lowly thing. How do you expect your parents to give you big responsibilities if you are not faithful in the little things? It is the same when you get a job; you may be asked to do all sorts of little jobs. How do you expect to be promoted if you do not prove yourself in the little things in life?

Joshua quickly moved into action and gathered up the young men who would fight in the battle. The next morning it would be time for the battle to begin. God was preparing Joshua for even bigger things in life. This was his opportunity to prove to the Lord that he was willing to do anything, or go anywhere, for Him.

The Secret of Winning the Battle

Early in the morning Moses, Aaron and Hur made their way up into the mountain. In the meantime, Joshua had prepared the army and they were ready to fight the Amalekites, who were attacking the Israelites almost on a daily basis.

When the battle started in the valley, Moses held his rod high in the air. While he did this, Joshua's army were winning the battle, but then Moses' hands became tired and he dropped them, then the Amalekites turned on Joshua's army with a vengeance and started to defeat them. Aaron and Hur realized what had happened and immediately held up Moses's arms for him. When this happened the Israelites started winning the battle and they continued fighting until they finally won. This was the first battle they fought and what a victory it was!

The secret of the victory lay not in the strength of the army but in Moses holding up his hands to God. This was a sign of prayer; real prayer to God is the secret of winning any battle for God. Maybe there are many battles in your life and they seem to be impossible to win. Then learn the lesson early in life, that there is great power in prayer.

The Amalekites in the Bible are a picture of selfishness. The greatest enemy we all have is ourselves. Whenever we get saved we want lives that are pleasing to the Lord, but when God says to do one thing our old nature says, "I want to do my own thing." Until the day we die we will always be fighting against our old nature.

We must fight this battle with prayer and living close to the Lord, and then He will help us have the victory.

At the foot of the Mountain

After winning their first battle against the Amalekites the Israelites travelled on through the wilderness. Their next stop was Mount Sinai. This is the mountain where God gave Moses the Ten Commandments. At Mount Sinai they camped for about a year. God wanted them to stay there for some time, as He wanted to teach them many things.

The Promised Land was in Canaan, where there was a mighty tribe called the Philistines. The Israelites were not prepared to meet such an army yet, which is why God kept them in Sinai for over a year. Sometimes in life God wants to teach us many things. We may be impatient for change, but God may want us to wait for the right time.

Mount Sinai was a quiet, private place, away from the world and all its distractions. There, God was going to reveal Himself before the people to remind them how much He loved and cared for them. He wanted them to focus on Him and not on everything around them.

Sometimes when we try to read the Bible and talk to the Lord, it is difficult. Maybe our phone is near, the television is on, or we can hear others talking.

It is so important to have perfect stillness when being alone with the Lord. Then we must listen, as the Lord speaks in a wonderful way through His Word.

Time to wash our Clothes

While the people waited at the bottom of the mountain, God called Moses to come up and meet with Him. God told Moses to tell the people that He had a special plan for them. If they promised to follow and obey Him, then He would bless them. God was reminding them that they were a special people and that through them He would send forth his Son the Lord Jesus.

The people were slaves in Egypt for a very long time and they had almost forgotten God. That is why they kept sinning over and over again. God wanted them at Sinai for a reason, to teach them more about Himself. God instructed Moses to tell the people to wash their clothes, as many months of travelling had made their clothes very dirty and dusty. God was going to reveal Himself before the people and He wanted them to have a clean appearance. This is why when we go to church and Sunday school we try to look our best, because we are going to worship and meet with the Lord.

But more than this, God was teaching them the importance of having a clean heart before the Lord. The Lord does not communicate with an unclean heart full of sin. God is holy and He hates sin; this is why when we go to church we should always be on our best behaviour showing respect towards a Holy God.

Some people have very little respect for God; they speak about Him in a flippant, joking manner and often mock the things of God's standard that are right, pure and good.

God comes before
all the People

On the morning of the third day, one of the most wonderful events in the history of the world happened. As the people waited for God to reveal Himself; they didn't really know what to expect. Suddenly, there was the mighty sound of a trumpet growing louder and louder until the earth began to shake like an earthquake. God came down from Heaven in a thick black cloud and landed right on top of the mountain.

God manifested Himself before an entire nation, the cloud turned into a fire with thunder and lightning all over the mountain. The people stood silent and amazed at the presence of God Almighty. As the sound of the trumpet increased, the whole mountain began to shake. It was time for the people to witness the presence of God in their midst and to hear the Lord God speak to them in their own language. Can you imagine what it must have been like to see God and hear Him speak?

Then they heard the voice of God. God was explaining to Moses the rules of living in this world; He called them the Ten Commandments. God first began by saying "I am the LORD thy God, which have brought thee out of the land of Egypt, out of the house of bondage." Then God gave the people the Ten Commandments, also known as the Moral Law.

The people were happy to listen to Moses, but when they heard the voice of God with all its power they thought they were going to die, they were so frightened. Moses reminded the people that God had come to them to show them His power and might, so they would learn to fear Him and sin no more.

The People become impatient

It was just a few days after God had revealed Himself to Moses and spoke to him of the Ten Commandments. God had commanded Moses to come up the mountain to meet Him. Moses then left Aaron and Hur in charge of the people; he took Joshua up the mountain with him. Halfway up the mountain Moses told Joshua to wait while he continued to the top to meet with God.

It was a glorious sight to look at, as the Israelites gazed at the top of the mountain they could see a big cloud in what looked like a huge fireball. Here Moses was with God for forty days and forty nights. God was writing the Ten Commandments down in stone so they would never be forgotten.

In the meantime, the people down below were getting very impatient. They thought Moses had forgotten all about them. For days and weeks they waited. Every day they became more and more restless, even though they could see the cloud but they got so impatient as nothing seemed to be happening.

We can be like this, becoming so used to going to church and hearing the Word of God that it no longer has an impact upon us. Only days after the Lord blessed the people with His powerful presence they went to Aaron to complain. They told Aaron to make them another god to lead them through the wilderness. The people were prepared to leave God and go back to Egypt. What was Aaron to do under such pressure from an angry people?

WHAT WOULD YOU have done if you were Aaron?

The Golden Calf

The people were so impatient that Moses hadn't returned to lead them. They went to Aaron and demanded that he make them a new god to lead them through the wilderness.

Instead of telling the people to stop breaking the law of God, especially the second commandment where they were told not to make any graven images, Aaron told the people to gather together all their golden jewellery such as rings etc.

Aaron built a fire, and in it he melted all the gold, making the image of a calf from the gold. This golden calf was going to be their new god. Very quickly they all bowed down to it and worshipped the golden calf. As they bowed down before it they danced and sang and as God looked down from the mountain, the Hebrews broke all the commandments in one day.

Maybe you are given a position of authority at school or at home and your friends tempt you to organize something, or go somewhere, which you know would be wrong. Instead of standing up to them and telling them the consequences of doing such a thing, the real challenge is, would you give in to the pressure as Aaron did? God will not bless you for such a foolish decision. Always take a stand for God and do right before the Lord.

As God looked down from the mountain He was so angry, He said to Moses, "Stand aside, I am going to destroy all the people in an instant." Moses pleaded with God not to do so. What was going to happen to the people now?

God is Angry

Maybe you think God would never get angry. Well the Bible records many times when God was angry. It was nearly always for the same reason. When His people forget about Him and follow after other gods, then this is what makes God angry.

God told Moses to stand aside so He could destroy all the people below. Moses pleaded with God not to do so. "You have promised to send your Son the Saviour of the world through these people. Have mercy on them." Moses pleaded. God realized that Moses was more concerned for others than Himself. It is good to pray for and think about other people even more than ourselves. God then told Moses he would turn His anger away from the people, if they would be sorry for their terrible sin.

When Moses went back down the mountain with Joshua he couldn't believe his eyes. He soon realized why God was so angry. Before him was the golden calf with everyone dancing around and bowing down to it. He was so cross that he threw down the two tablets of stone on which God had written the Ten Commandments. He threw them down with such force, they smashed all over the ground. Just like the tablets were broken, the people had broken the commandments in their hearts. Moses then grabbed the golden calf and threw it into the fire and destroyed it. He challenged the people and said, "Who is on the Lord's side?" This is the challenge which faces everyone today.

Those who were on the Lord's side stood to one side, while those who worshipped the false God went to the other side. ON WHOSE SIDE WOULD YOU BE?

MOSES 143

Whose side are you on?

Moses then divided the people into two groups; those who wanted to follow the true and living God and those who wanted to follow the false gods. All those who stood on the side of the false gods were then killed, as their false gods could do nothing to save them. About three thousand people died that day. This is what happens to those who rebel against God and His law. They will eventually be destroyed.

The next morning Moses went back up the mountain with a very heavy heart, to meet with God. Moses loved the people very much; they were his people and he pleaded with God to forgive them their sin and wickedness. The Lord explained that those who sinned against the Lord must be sorry for their own sin. Moses could not take their punishment for them. Only the Lord Jesus can take our punishment. This is why He died on the cross, to take away our sin and to forgive us.

God then gave the Ten Commandments to Moses for the second time. When we think of the law of God it really does show us our sinful hearts. When we trust in the Lord to save us from our sin and ask Him into our hearts, He then helps us to keep the commandments. When God gave Moses the law it was not to make life boring, but rather for our good, to help us in life and to have the blessing of God upon us.

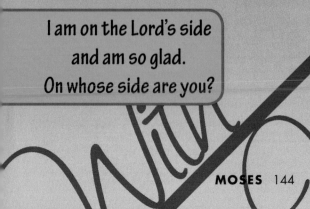

I am on the Lord's side
and am so glad.
On whose side are you?

The Ten Commandments

Moses was the leader of the children of Israel and they were now camped at Mount Sinai. Here Moses carried two tablets of stone up the mountain and while he was up there the Lord descended in a thick cloud to meet with Him. This was the second time, God was giving Moses the Ten Commandments. The first time spoken, the second time broken and now to be kept.

Once again, God wrote the Ten Commandments on two stones. He then instructed Moses to go down the mountain and teach them to the people. The Ten Commandments were passed on from generation to generation; this is why we have them today.

God could have given Moses a thousand commandments or one hundred, but there are only ten. The Lord wants us to learn them, know them and keep them.

The Ten Commandments are divided into two parts; the first four teach us about our duty to God and the last six tell us about our duty to each other. In life, God does not want us just to do as we please but rather, to live our lives pleasing Him.

One of the ways we can please the Lord is by keeping the commandments. The Ten Commandments are also called the Law of God or the Moral Law. Jesus said, "Thou shalt love the Lord thy God with all thy heart, and with all thy soul, and with all thy mind. This is the first and great commandment. And the second is like unto it, Thou shalt love thy neighbour as thyself." (Matthew 22:37-39)

MOSES 145

Do you love God and do you love your neighbours?

1st Commandment

Thou shalt have no other Gods before me

Exodus 20:1-3

One of the things that makes God very angry is when we put other things before Him. God must have first place in our lives, as He is the only true and living God.

If we love any person, place or thing more than God, we have broken the first commandment. We may have a favourite sport or television programme that we prefer more than spending time with the Lord; God is very displeased when this happens.

The danger is we may end up spending so much time with people and things that we enjoy, that very soon there would be no time for God in our lives.

If we love the Lord more than anything else in the whole world then we will want to put Him first in our lives. Maybe there is something you put before the Lord and it has become more important to you than God. Perhaps now is the time to readjust your priorities and start putting the Lord first.

"But seek ye first the kingdom of God, and his righteousness; and all these things shall be added unto you." (Matthew 6:33)

I AM THE LORD THY GOD
THOU SHALT HAVE NO
OTHER GODS BEFORE ME
THOU SHALT NOT MAKE UNTO
THEE ANY GRAVEN IMAGE
THOU SHALT NOT TAKE THE
NAME OF THE LORD THY
GOD IN VAIN
REMEMBER THE SABBATH
TO KEEP IT HOLY

HONOUR THY FATHER
THY MOTHER
THOU SHALT NOT KILL
THOU SHALT NOT COMMIT
ADULTERY
THOU SHALT NOT STEAL
THOU SHALT NOT BEAR
FALSE WITNESS
THOU SHALT NOT COVET

MOSES 146

2nd Commandment

Thou shalt not make unto thee any graven image

Exodus 20:4-6

Whenever we put something in place of God to worship, then this is called an idol. God forbids idols so often in scripture; He wants us to worship only Him in our lives.

Worshipping an idol is called idolatry. In some parts of the world today people worship idols. Idols may be made of stone, clay, wood, silver or gold. Whenever pictures of God or Jesus are used to worship and to bow down to, then this is idolatry.

God clearly commands us not to make images for religious worship. God is a Spirit; Father, Son and Holy Spirit. We are to worship God in Spirit and in Truth.

There may also be idols in our hearts that we worship. Anything that we consider more important than God, can be considered an idol. Even our studies, careers, ambitions, friends or heroes are all examples of idolatry. God clearly warns us not to have idols.

The biggest idol we can have, of course is ourselves. We need to be so careful not to think too highly of ourselves. We need to pray that God, alone, will reign supreme in our lives and hearts.

MOSES 147

Thou shalt not take the name of the Lord thy God in vain

Exodus 20:7

The meaning of this commandment is very important as it is probably the commandment that is broken most often. When people use the name of God, Lord or Jesus it should only be with reverence, whether we are at church, at home or in school.

Many people use the name of God or Jesus as a swear word; this grieves God to the very core. Many films today take the name of God in vain, that is, with irreverence and most disrespectfully. Never be afraid to turn the channel over or the television off when this happens.

God does not like it when we curse. Whenever people curse they often use the name of the Lord in vain. If you have a habit of cursing, God can help you stop. There are so many beautiful words in the English language; we should not need swear words.

God's name is holy and we should use it with the utmost reverence at all times. We would never let anyone speak ill of our parents or friends. It should grieve us when someone takes the Lord's name in vain. It grieves the Lord much more when He hears someone taking His name in vain.

4th Commandment

Remember the Sabbath Day to keep it Holy

Exodus 20:8-11

In the 4th commandment we are required to keep one day of every week special to God. This practice comes from God Himself when He created the world. It took God six days to make the whole world and everything in it; God then rested on the Sabbath Day or the seventh day. As a result, God blessed the seventh day and made it holy unto Himself.

God set this day apart from the rest of the week to make it special for Him. It is a day when we don't go to school and don't have to work. This is the day we should go to church; one day especially to worship the Lord and to give thanks to Him for everything He has done.

Today, we call Sunday the first day of the week and it has become the Sabbath day. The day changed from the seventh to the first because Christ rose from the dead on the first day of the week. From then on, the disciples also met to worship God on the first day of the week.

Even if your friends play sport, shop, or watch television etc on the Lord's day, it doesn't mean you have to. It is a day to reflect on God; all these other things will distract our minds from the Lord and His special day.

God will bless you for making His day special and keeping it holy.

MOSES 149

Honour thy Father and thy Mother

Exodus 20:12

In this commandment we are not only to respect and obey our parents, we are to honour them. This means respecting them for who they are and the position they have over us.

God promises long life and blessing to those who respect, obey and honour their parents. To really honour our parents it also helps to have the right attitude. We should honour our parents because we want to, not because we have to. It was our parents who brought us into this world, fed, loved and cared for us when we were very small and could not look after ourselves. Surely we owe it to them to love, care, respect and honour them.

Maybe you have not been so nice to your parents lately. The Lord teaches us to be sorry and ask for forgiveness. He will forgive us when we sin. Disobeying our parents is not only sinning against our parents, but it is sinning against God.

This commandment also teaches us to honour all those that rule over us. For example school teachers, church leaders and government officials.

"Children, obey your parents in the Lord: for this is right. HONOUR THY FATHER AND MOTHER; that it may be well with thee, and thou mayest live long on the earth."
(Ephesians 6:1-3)

MOSES 150

6th Commandment

Thou shalt not Kill

Exodus 20:13

Sometimes when we don't like someone or they really annoy us we feel like killing them. Have you ever felt like this, or said this? Even though we don't really mean it we still say it.

The Bible teaches us that when we say such a thing it is as bad as doing it. Our thoughts and the words we say often tell us what our heart feels. To kill someone is to murder them; this is the deliberate, unlawful killing of another human being.

When God made man, He made him in the image of God. This makes us different from animals. Humans can think, love, obey, communicate and have fellowship with God. Man has a soul that is precious to God and the soul of every human being will live forever.

Things like anger, jealousy, hatred, envy and murder all come from the same place, a sinful heart. Without God the world would be in total chaos. This is why God has given us the Ten Commandments, in order to have some stability in the land.

It can be easy for us to point out the faults and evil in other people but sometimes we need to be careful we are not guilty of the very sin we are accusing other people of. In Bible times when someone was guilty of murder, then they too lost their life. In some parts of the world this is still the case.

Always remember how we feel about someone is often the way they feel about us. We should always treat other people as we wish to be treated.

MOSES 151

Thou shalt not commit Adultery

Exodus 20:14

Marriage is a wonderful thing. In fact the Bible says, "Whoso findeth a wife findeth a good thing, and obtaineth favour of the LORD." (Proverbs 18:22) When a man and woman meet each other, fall in love and get married it is a wonderful time. This is how God planned it; God's plan is also that when a couple get married, He wants them to stay together.

In the world today more couples than ever are breaking up, going their separate ways and often getting divorced. This makes God sad, as it is not His plan for this to happen. We cannot always change the way other people behave, however when we grow up, we can do what is right in the eyes of God according to His commandments. When a couple get married, one of them should not leave the other to be with someone else and a single person should not break up a married couple.

This leads to all sorts of confusion and problems as marriage carries responsibility. Marriage can have big challenges and pressures, but they must be worked out together. This commandment can show how our heart is. When we have impure and immoral thoughts, when we listen to dirty jokes, watch something on television or on the internet that causes us to blush, this is committing adultery in our heart.

Girls should always be careful how they dress, so they don't cause boys to have lustful feelings. Satan doesn't care, he tells you, everyone else dresses like this and watches what you watch.

Don't listen to him. Obey the Lord and do right in His eyes. The Bible tells us, "As a man thinks in his heart, so is he." We will become what we think about.

MOSES 152

Thou shalt not Steal

Exodus 20:15

Sometimes we often think it is only bank robbers and pirates who are real thieves. Due to our sinful nature, we are all tempted and often break the commandments, especially this one.

If your friend had some sweets with him and you saw one and took it because he is your friend, would this still be stealing? Yes, when you take something that doesn't belong to you without permission, it is stealing. Whenever you start to work and your boss isn't around, if you decide not to work, this is stealing the boss's time because he is paying you to work.

No matter how little an item is, or how many of them there are, never take what doesn't belong to you. You may think nobody knows or has seen you take it. I must remind you that God has seen you because He sees everything. One day He will remind you of everything you have stolen. "For the eyes of the LORD run to and fro throughout the whole earth." (2 Chronicles 16:9)

WE MUST ASK the Lord for forgiveness, give back what we owe and try **NOT** to steal again.

MOSES 153

Thou shalt not bear false witness against thy Neighbour

Exodus 20:16

Bearing false witness is another term for telling lies. One thing God hates is liars; in fact He speaks often about it in the Bible. He says that liars will not inherit the Kingdom of Heaven.

We should always tell the truth no matter the cost or how much it hurts. Sometimes we think that little lies are not so important to God but this is not true. A lie is a lie. There is no difference between a big lie and small lie, or a black lie and a white lie.

Sometimes we may think if we tell half the truth and twist the other half this is alright. This is also telling lies; anything short of the truth is a lie. Covering up a matter and not speaking about it when asked to is also lying.

Satan told the first lie; he deceived Eve in the Garden of Eden. Jesus calls him the "father of liars," and says "there is no truth in him." The Bible says that God will not let those who tell lies stand in His presence. We should always tell the truth from our heart, even if our friends want to tell lies. Do what God would want you to do; He will help you tell the truth.

"And there shall in no wise enter into it any thing that defileth, neither whatsoever worketh abomination, or maketh a lie: but they which are written in the Lamb's Book of Life." (Revelations 21:27)

One lie can often lead to many other lies to cover up the truth. It is better just to tell the truth even if you have to bear the consequences.

10th Commandment

Thou shalt not Covet

Exodus 20:17

To covet something is to want it so badly that it almost controls our entire mind. It is also copying what other people have. We like their ideas, we like what they have and then we want to have exactly the same, or better.

If our friends get a new pair of shoes, a new bike or new toys, suddenly we want just what they have, even though we don't need them. We just want to have them.

This can lead to all sorts of financial problems and put additional pressure on your parents to keep up with others. Lots of people live like this; because their neighbours have something they become jealous and they want it also.

We should always be content with what we have. Be happy for your friends and neighbours who get something new and try not to be jealous of them.

"Godliness with contentment is GREAT gain."
(I Timothy 6:6)

What was the Tabernacle?

Exodus 25:1-9

After God gave the Ten Commandments to Moses on Mount Sinai, He also instructed him to build the Tabernacle. The Lord explained to Moses exactly how it should be built. The Tabernacle was a type of tent where the people could go to meet with God and find forgiveness for sins. From the lessons of the Tabernacle, we see how it is a picture of our relationship with God.

God dwelt in the midst of the Tabernacle. In it was a room called the Holy of Holies, where once a year, only one man could go right into the very presence of Almighty God, bringing with him the blood from an animal sacrifice for the forgiveness of sins.

In order to build the Tabernacle the people were instructed to give an offering towards it, but it had to come from a willing heart.

> "...whosoever is of a willing heart, let him bring it, an offering of the LORD." (Exodus 35:5)

The lesson for us is that anything we do or give to the Lord, must come from a willing heart. The Lord is not interested in half-hearted Christians. He wants us to love and serve Him with all of our hearts and most of all from a willing heart.

> "thou shalt love the LORD thy God with ALL thine heart, and with ALL thy soul, and with ALL thy might." (Deuteronomy 6:5)

Where was the Tabernacle?

The Tabernacle was located in the very centre of the camp because the Lord had told Moses He was going to come and dwell in the midst of them. (Exodus 25:8) Just as the Lord wanted to be in the midst of His people in the Tabernacle in the camp, so today He wants to be in the very centre of our lives. Everything we do, all our plans, actions, conversations, friends, relationships, God wants them all to be centred around Him and His will for our lives.

Around the Tabernacle was a fence, making it impossible to come to the Tabernacle except through the gate. The fence was about seven feet tall, just above eye level; therefore, a person had to go through the gate to get inside. There is only one way to God. Jesus said, "I am the way, the truth, and the life: no man cometh unto the Father, but by me." (John 14:6) Coming to God through Christ alone, is the only way to become a Christian.

On the top of the Tabernacle were badger skins; not very attractive to look at. This is how many people view the Christian life. They see it as not very attractive, nor very interesting. It is only when they come to Christ by faith, aware of their sin before a living God, that they discover how beautiful and wonderful the Christian life really is.

When someone looks at your life, is there something about your life that makes Christianity attractive?

The Brazen Altar

Exodus 27:1-8

When someone came to the gate of the Tabernacle, they would have seen curtains on the gate, made of four different colours; blue, white, red and purple. The four colours of the curtains remind us of Christ. Blue is the colour of the sky, reminding us that Jesus came from heaven. White teaches us about the purity and perfection of Christ, for He is God. Red reminds us that He shed His blood for us at Calvary and purple teaches us of His royalty, for he is King of Kings and Lord of Lords.

When the people came through the gate they came to the Tabernacle courtyard. The reason they would come to the Tabernacle was to have fellowship with God. It was necessary to bring an animal to sacrifice, in order to have their sins forgiven.

The animal was placed on a brazen altar, which looked like a large metal grill. The fire on the brazen altar continually burned, reminding us of hell, where the fire is never quenched. The people then placed their hands on the head of the animal as it became their substitute and was sacrificed and killed. As a result their sins were forgiven.
Jesus became our substitute when He died on the cross. We no longer have to make sacrifices for the forgiveness of sins, as Jesus became the final sacrifice, dying in our place. He became our substitute.

The priest, who assisted the people, would go to the laver, which was a large basin of water made of highly polished brass, like a mirror where he would wash his hands and his feet. The laver was a type of the Word of God, helping the people see their sin spots so they could have them taken away. This is why it is so important to read the Word of God, so that every day we can see our sinfulness in the light of God's holiness. This will lead us to repentance and holiness.

"Thy word have I hid in mine heart, that I might not sin against thee." (Psalm 119:11)

The Holy Place

The Tabernacle itself was not a big stone palace; rather it was a tent, a very special tent were God dwelt amongst His people. From the outside it looked like badger skins, unattractive to look at, just as the Christian life is to unsaved people. Under the badger skins were ram skins dyed red, representing the blood of Christ. Then there was a layer of white goat hair, representing the purity of Christ.

Inside the Holy Place was very beautiful. There were three pieces of furniture: the table of showbread, the candlestick and the golden altar.

The table of showbread contained bread for the priests to eat. Jesus said, "I am the bread of life." (John 6:35) Jesus is the Living Bread. He wants us to study His Word in order to grow as a Christian. Some Christians are content to live in the courtyard, saved but not really going on with God. Pray that God will help you have a real desire to read and learn His Word and have a longing to grow as a Christian.

The second piece of furniture in the Holy Place was a candlestick which was really an oil burning lamp. Oil is a symbol of the Holy Spirit. The candlestick gave light in the Holy Place and never went out. In the Christian life the Holy Spirit wants to fill our lives with His light and to give guidance as our Teacher and Comforter. In this dark and confusing world we need God the Holy Spirit to help us and guide us so much.

> The three pieces of furniture in the Holy Place teach Christians to feed on God's Word, to be filled and guided by the Holy Spirit and to have a daily prayer life.

The third piece of furniture was the golden altar, or altar of incense. This was made of gold and not brass. The golden altar did not have its own fire but rather hot coals were brought from the brazen altar, then sweet incense was sprinkled over the coals causing a sweet fragrance to fill the Holy Place. This represents our prayers before God. The Lord says that our prayers are like sweet incense going up into the nostrils of God. (Revelation 8:4)

> Are you living in the Holy Place or still in the courtyard? Does your life have a real purpose and are you desiring to really know God better?

MOSES 159

The Holy of Holies

Exodus 25:10-22

The Holy of Holies was the second room in the Tabernacle. God only permitted one man, the high priest, once per year to come into the Holy of Holies. All the other priests had to leave the Holy Place before the priest entered. The high priest then pulled the curtain to the side that separated the Holy Place from the Holy of Holies or the Most Holy Place.

In the Most Holy Place there was only one piece of furniture, the Ark of the Covenant, which looked like a golden chest. It contained the Ten Commandments, Aaron's budding rod, and a piece of heavenly manna.

The lid that covered the Ark of the Covenant was called the mercy seat. On either end of the mercy seat engraved in gold, were two cherubim facing each other. In the Most Holy Place there were no windows or candlesticks, but it was not dark. There was light that came from above the mercy seat where the cherubim were looking; this was called the Shekinah Glory. (Exodus 25:22) There was no visible or physical appearance of God because God is invisible, but from this place came a radiance - the Shekinah Glory; the symbol of God's presence.

Once a year the high priest took the blood and sprinkled it on the mercy seat, demonstrating that one day the Lamb of God, the Lord Jesus Christ would come and gave His life for us. Jesus gave His own blood as a once for all sacrifice. When Jesus died on Calvary's hill, the veil (the middle curtain) of the Temple in Jerusalem was torn in two from top to bottom. This happened when Jesus cried, "It is finished." He spiritually broke down the wall of partition that separated sinners from full fellowship with God the Father. Jesus, the true High Priest, then made it possible for us to go right into the presence of God, the Holy of Holies. (Hebrews 4:16)

> When is the last time that you felt the presence of God so real in your life?

MOSES 160

Time to leave the Mountain

The children of Israel were divided into twelve tribes. While they were at Mount Sinai, God instructed them to build a tabernacle. In the tabernacle was the Ark of the Covenant, it was small enough for four people to carry; it was a continual reminder for the people to keep worshipping God wherever they went.

God was still using a cloud in the sky to lead the children of Israel and had been lingering over Mount Sinai for some time. Now it was beginning to move again.

Everyone packed their things together with great excitement now that they were on the move again. Throughout the journey God was teaching them to trust Him fully, as their faith was very weak at times. They had learned many lessons already but there were more to learn.

Their journey is like the Christian today. Every day the Lord is teaching us something new; sometimes we want to learn and other times we don't. Many times when the children of Israel learned something new they would forget what they learned. This is why God kept teaching them so that they would not forget about Him.

Now the cloud was moving and the journey was continuing. They didn't know where they would be tomorrow or what would happen but they were learning to trust the Lord every day.

We know nothing about tomorrow, that is why when tomorrow comes we must ask the Lord to be with us wherever we go and whatever we do.

Grumbling and Complaining

It is hard to believe that so soon after the children of Israel had been blessed by God that they fell away from God so quickly again.

As they walked toward Canaan, the Promised Land, they began murmuring and complaining. Some said the desert was too hot, while others complained there was not enough grass for the cows to eat. Others wondered where the next meal would come from and some were sure their water supply would run out.

As God listened to their grumbling and complaining He became angry again. The more they worried, the less they were trusting completely in the Lord. They remembered all the tasty food they had enjoyed in Egypt, yet seemed to forget all about the slavery and cruelty from which the Lord had delivered them.

Whenever something goes wrong in our lives, we have the habit of being negative. We forget very quickly how the Lord has blessed us so many times before. When things become difficult in life and don't always go our way, it is always good to count our blessings.

COMPLAINING

The heavy load to carry

Has there ever been something on your mind and heart that has caused you to pray? Then when you do pray it seems to be constantly there? That means we just have to keep on praying.

Moses continually prayed for the people and every time he prayed they still kept complaining. It got to the stage that instead of praying, Moses started complaining as well. He asked the Lord why he had to lead the people, "It is too hard to look after all these people. The load is too heavy to carry," he told the Lord. In fact Moses was so discouraged he wished the Lord would let him die. The pressure was almost too much for Moses and the burden too great. Sometimes when we are around complaining people all the time, we start complaining as well.

God told Moses to gather seventy men from the camp and come to the tabernacle. These men were to help Moses lead the people. Moses could tell the seventy men what to do and the seventy men would then explain to the people what was happening next.

Concerning their hunger, God said he would supply a whole month's supply of meat. There would be so much meat they would be sick of it. Suddenly there were so many quails flying by, over two million people had easily enough meat to eat.
God had eased Moses' burden and made the load lighter; this is what God does.

He will not bring into our lives so great a task that we are unable to bare it.

MOSES 163

Moses criticized by his Brother and Sister

It was bad enough when other people complained against Moses, but when his own brother Aaron and sister Miriam began to criticize him he was really upset. One of the things they complained about was that Moses had married a woman from Ethiopia and not from Israel. Aaron and Miriam were both jealous of Moses; they also thought they should be equal leaders with Moses.

This grieved Moses very much, as he loved his brother and sister. After all, it was Miriam who watched over him as he floated down the river among the bulrushes, as a baby. They couldn't bear the fact that Moses was ruling them.

Sometimes in life there may be many things that will make us jealous. These might be friends at school, or even a brother or sister. Maybe parents place them in charge of something and you don't like it because you want to be in charge of it. God is very displeased when we get jealous and cry just to get our way. No doubt it upsets your parents as well.

Be content with what you have and in good time you will be given responsibility over some things.

Miriam turns into a Leper

As God looked down upon the camp He noticed Aaron and Miriam criticizing Moses. Moses was appointed by God to lead the children of Israel into the Promised Land; how dare they criticize Moses. God immediately called for Moses, Aaron and Miriam to come before Him at the tabernacle. God came down in the pillar of cloud to the tabernacle. He told them all to stand at the door of the tabernacle before the camp so that everyone could see what was going on.

God told them that only with prophets would He speak with visions and dreams but with Moses He had chosen to speak face to face. God clearly told them that Moses was a faithful leader and they were not to find fault with him.

Suddenly as they stood there, Miriam became completely white with leprosy. Aaron immediately confessed before the Lord to their sin of jealousy. Aaron then begged Moses to pray for their sister Miriam. God later healed Miriam but not there and then; he wanted to make an example of her before all the people.

Miriam was taken outside the camp before all the people; she had to wait for a whole week before her leprosy was completely healed. During those seven days while the whole camp had to wait for Miriam, she learned a big lesson never to criticize again.

Whenever we criticize other people it can be very hurtful. We don't like to be criticized so why should we do this to other people? Our behaviour is very important as it often affects our friends and family. We should always consider others before we do something selfish that we may regret.

The twelve Spies

After waiting for a whole week until Miriam was completely cleared of her leprosy the Israelites were ready to continue their journey. Travelling through the desert, they came to the wilderness of Paran, just outside the land of Canaan.

Just another day's journey and they would be in the Promised Land; here God had promised them a land flowing with milk and honey. The milk would be all the basic things they needed like food and water and the honey would be all the luxurious things that they would not have had in the desert.

Before entering the Promised Land, Moses chose twelve men to go and spy out the land. They weren't sure what kind of people lived there. Was it a dangerous place to be? Two of the twelve spies were called Joshua and Caleb.

They were told to go and spy out the land, to see if the people were strong or weak and to find out how many people there were, and if they were real cities or just camp sites. They were also to notice the type of land; was it rich or poor? Were there any trees? They were to bring back samples of the fruit that grew in the land.

This was an exciting challenge for the twelve spies. Whenever we go on holiday, it is always good to find out about the place we are going to. Is it safe and what type of food do they eat in that country? These are two of the main questions people ask. Before we do anything for God it is good and important to do careful preparation, just as the spies did before entering the Promised Land.

Always remember to pray that God will keep you safe wherever you go. It is also a good thing to be thankful for whatever food is placed before you to eat.

Two different Reports

After Moses sent the twelve spies into Canaan they remained there for forty days. Whenever they returned, the whole camp was excited to hear how things were in Canaan and they were amazed at the food they brought.

Two of the men brought a massive cluster of grapes which was so big and heavy it took two of them to carry it. They also brought lots of other exotic fruit as well. The people were so excited they wanted to go at once to Canaan, the Promised Land, but whenever the other spies returned, they had two different reports.

Ten of the men brought negative reports; they said the land was full of giants from all sorts of nations. They said the cities had huge walls that were well protected by soldiers and it would be impossible to win a battle against them if war broke out. Two of the spies, Joshua and Caleb, brought a different report. They were very positive in their report. "There may be giants" they said, "but our God is bigger than them all, let us go and possess the land that is ours, as God has given it to us."

In these two reports, one group was looking at the difficulties through the eyes of men, while the other report saw this as another example of how God would lead the people through any difficult situation that would arise.

If you were one of the spies, what type of a report would you bring? Without God we can do nothing. With God we can accomplish anything. I know what side I would be on!

Joshua and Caleb bring a good Report

After hearing the report of the ten spies, the people were very discouraged. They had been looking forward to entering the Promised Land for such a long time and now they were bitterly disappointed.

But Joshua and Caleb reassured the people and helped calm their fears. Even though the city had giants living in it, and had big stone walls surrounding it; even though the people in Canaan seemed to be great and mighty, Joshua was not afraid of them. He was so confident God had it all under control. Joshua wanted to go up at once and possess the land, so convinced was he that they were well able to conquer it.

Was their God not stronger than all the people of Canaan? God, who had defeated the Egyptians, the Amalekites and supplied their every need, could He not do the same here? Again the Israelites had failed to put their trust in the Lord. He promised to be with them, to lead, guide, to take care of them and provide for them and to bring them at last into Canaan, the Land of Promise.

The people believed the negative report of the ten spies rather than that of Joshua and Caleb. Their report was all about trusting God with a heart full of faith; not depending on their own strength but rather on the power of a mighty God.

Joshua was looking beyond the problems with faith, while the unbelief of the others saw nothing but problems.

Doom and Gloom

After hearing the two reports the people were very discouraged. They decided to believe the report of the ten spies that was full of discouragement, gloom and doom. Things were so bad that the people complained bitterly to Moses and Aaron. The people even wished they had been left in Egypt to die for they thought they had come this far to be killed by the giants. They were certain they were going to be made into slaves in Canaan just as they were in Egypt.

They were even planning to elect a new leader to take them back to Egypt. Imagine how Moses felt when he heard what they were planning to do, after all he had done on their behalf. Instead of Moses getting into a confrontation with them, he and Aaron began to pray for them. What a challenge that is for us that when our friends, families or enemies turn against us, we should pray for them.

Joshua reminded the people that this was the Promised Land they had been searching for. God had promised to bring them safely into the land and He would do so. "Nothing will stop the Lord," they told the people. "The Lord is with us; He is on our side. Let us go forward."

This was a great difficulty and a great challenge for the people.

All of us face big decisions and challenges. How much do we trust God when we make our decisions?

Moses appeals to God

The people were so angry with their situation that they were ready to stone Moses and Aaron to death. Suddenly a great light flashed from the tabernacle. The Lord intervened, telling Moses that the people were again making Him angry. Moses was God's chosen leader and they were challenging his leadership. God was willing to destroy them all for their unbelief, but Moses pleaded with God for all the people. God warned Moses that anyone who would not trust and obey the Lord would never see the Promised Land.

The Promised Land reminds me so much of Heaven for we will never be in Heaven unless we put our trust in the Lord and follow and obey Him. The wilderness is like the world in which we live; it is full of all sorts of problems and difficulties. Just as the children of Israel looked forward to entering the Promised Land, so the Christian can look forward to entering Heaven.

God told Moses to take all the people back into the wilderness and to ask them "who is on the Lord's side?" Whoever believed in the Lord would be delivered. In the Christian life we need to continually pray to the Lord and ask Him to forgive us our sin. While we live in the world, sin is all around us and it is in our hearts every day.

Every day we need to ask the Lord to make us clean and to help us live for Him.

The Rebellion of Korah

For many years the children of Israel had been wandering through the wilderness. It had been a much longer journey than they thought, because of their disobedience to the Lord. The people could not find any fault with themselves. They thought they were all good in God's eyes. One of the men called Korah, who was a prince in the land, was one of the chief leaders rebelling against the leadership of Moses.

Korah was of the same tribe as Moses and Aaron; the tribe of Levi. Two other men along with Korah were especially resentful and jealous of Moses; they were Dathan and Abiram, and these two men told Korah that he would be just as good a leader as Moses. In total there were 250 princes who rose up against Moses, challenging his leadership and wanting to overthrow Moses and lead the people themselves.

They told Moses that they were all the children of Israel, God's chosen people and that Moses had no special right to lead the people. What they seemed to forget was that God had appointed Moses to lead the people and they accused Moses and Aaron of appointing themselves as leaders of the people. Moses was so shocked as he had never wanted to be a leader. God chose him for this special task of leading the people through the wilderness, as God also had chosen Aaron to be the High Priest. As usual, Moses did not enter into confrontation, but went immediately to the Lord in prayer.

What a lesson we can learn from Moses. When a crisis occurred in his life, he took it to the Lord in prayer.

MOSES 171

The Choice

Very often in life we have to make choices. Often we must choose between right and wrong and between what is good or bad.

A terrible rebellion was taking place in the camp of the children of Israel as Korah was challenging the leadership of Moses. Moses went to Korah and told him that God would prove who the appointed leader would be, to lead the people into the Promised Land. God would decide who His people were and who were truly following Him. Moses then rebuked Korah as he was doing something very dangerous in questioning the authority of God's appointed person.

Aaron was the High Priest because he had a responsibility and was selected for the special task of doing service in the tabernacle, the place of worship. It was no small thing to minister in the tabernacle and not just anyone could do this, as it was a spiritual duty of the highest kind.

The next morning was to be the time for the people to decide. Either they were to follow Moses whom God had appointed, or they were to follow Korah who was challenging the leadership of Moses. If you were in the camp whose side would you be on?

The people had until the next morning to decide and many were very excited about the prospect of a new leader. Others knew that to challenge God's appointed leader was very rebellious.

The Earth opens up

Korah, Dathan and Abiram were the three men who were challenging Moses for the leadership of the children of Israel. Today was the day that God was going to teach the people a lesson once and for all.

Moses walked to the tents of the three men and announced that if these men and their families died of natural diseases, then they were supposed to lead the people.

However, if an extraordinary thing happens like the earth opening up and swallowing these men, then they would know that God had chosen Moses to lead the people. Moses then warned every one to stand away from these three families. Just as they did, the earth began to open up like an earthquake and in a moment, it swallowed up Korah, Dathan, Abiram and their families, as well as their tents and everything that belonged to them. They immediately went into a pit in the ground and were covered up again. Just as this happened the fire of the Lord came down and killed the 250 men who were self-appointed priests instead of Aaron. What a sight it was for everyone to witness!

However the people never learned their lesson, the very next day many of them were grieving over the three men, as they still believed they were the true leaders. As the people continued to complain against Moses and Aaron, a terrible plague came amongst the people. More than 15000 people died that day because they continued to disobey the Lord.

These were tough lessons to learn. The same thing will happen to all those who do not put their trust in the Lord. They will go to the pit called Hell for ever. It is so important to put our trust in the Lord when we are young.

Aaron's Rod Buds

Aaron was appointed to be the High Priest by the Lord. This was a special job for Aaron, offering incense in the tabernacle to the Lord. It wasn't just for anyone to do this; it was by special appointment only. There were many men who thought they would be the High Priest also. Moses had an idea which would prove to anyone who God had chosen to be the High Priest.

God gave Moses instructions how to carry this out, so he called a leader from each of the twelve tribes to come to the Tabernacle. With them they had to bring a rod in their hand and as they did, Moses told them to write their name on their own rod. The twelve rods were then placed inside the tabernacle, in the inner room. By the next morning, whichever rod blossomed, that would show which man was chosen to be the High Priest of the Tabernacle.

Overnight the rods were left in the Holy Place of the Tabernacle. All these rods were dead pieces of wood, made smooth to be used as rods. The next morning when Moses went to see the rods they were all exactly the same, except for Aaron's. His rod had not only budded but was also blossoming and already had almonds growing on it! This was a miracle from God. Here with this miracle, God was showing the people that Aaron was God's anointed High Priest. Aaron's rod was to remain inside the tabernacle so that everyone would see and know that God's appointed leadership should always be respected.

In the same way Jesus Christ was dead yet came back to life. Every day there is fruit budding and blossoming when people get saved and believe on His name.

MOSES 174

Moses looses his Temper

Sometimes we think that Christians never get angry or cross. Unfortunately while we are in this world, we do have the tendencies to become like the world in many ways. However, when we lose our temper, we should immediately pray to God and ask Him to forgive us and help us to control it better.

Again the people were complaining to Moses and this time they were looking for water. Now that they knew what Canaan, the Promised Land was like, with lots of fresh water and beautiful food they complained even more to Moses. Every time there was a problem they blamed Moses and Aaron, so Moses and Aaron went to the door of the tabernacle to speak with God.

God told Moses to take the people to the rock and when he got there, he was to stand beside it and speak to the rock, so that it would bring forth water. When Moses stood before all the people, he spoke to them with anger and frustration in his voice. Then instead of speaking to the rock, Moses took his rod and stuck the rock twice and water then started to flow from the rock. Moses not only lost his temper with the people, he also disobeyed the Lord. God had asked Moses only to speak to the rock and he beat the rock twice.

The Lord was very displeased with both Moses and Aaron. God told them because of their disobedience, neither of them would see Canaan or enter the Promised Land.

Everyone must pay the price for disobedience. Even Moses and Aaron were answerable to God for their actions. Sometimes our parents punish us for disobeying them; this is often to help us as we grow up and learn the difference between right and wrong.

MOSES 175

Speak to the Rock

Moses was clearly instructed to speak to the rock and not to beat it. He ruined a most important lesson God had for all of mankind. God was teaching the people how the rock was a type of the Lord Jesus Christ. Christ, the Rock of ages was to be struck only once, but never again. He was to be "once offered to bear the sins of many" at Calvary, not many times, over and over again.

Remember the last time Moses brought water from the rock years earlier at Rephidim? There, God told him to strike the rock but this time he was told to speak and not strike the rock.

The Lord teaches us in the New Testament, "For Christ also hath once suffered for sins, the just for the unjust, that he might bring us to God." (1 Peter 3:18) The body of Christ then was offered "once for all." (Hebrews 10:10) As Christ died only once then we need to accept Him only once (not many times) to be our Saviour. We don't need to do this more than once. So many people think they need to do it every day. No, only once do we receive Christ into our hearts for salvation.

Then every time we come to Jesus we speak with Him as our Saviour and friend. We come to Jesus (The Smitten Rock) first of all for salvation and then every other time, to speak to Him about our needs.

The Death of Aaron

After the nice refreshing water at Meribah, where Moses struck the rock twice, it was time to move on. Along the journey they came to a place called Edom; this was to be a shorter route for them to take, however the king of Edom would not give them permission to pass through his land.

This meant a long detour was necessary in order to get to Canaan and the ground they walked on was a wilderness with rocks and mountains. One of the mountains they came to was called Mount Hor and it was here they made camp for the night. While they were making camp God told Moses that this was the place that Aaron his brother, the High Priest would die. Both Moses and Aaron had disobeyed the Lord and because of this none of them would see the Promised Land.

As they walked up the mountain together it was a sad time for the two brothers. They had been very close and had come through all sorts of challenges and trials together. They took Eleazar with them on the mountain. Eleazar was the son of Aaron; he was appointed by God to replace his father as the new High Priest. It would have made his father proud to see his son serving in this way.

Aaron was 123 years old when he died on the mountain top, at Mount Hor. It was a very sad time for all the people; they waited here and mourned the death of Aaron for 30 days. When the people saw Moses and Eleazar coming down the mountain, they knew that Eleazar was the new High Priest.

Such is life with the death of loved ones. We only have each other for such a short time. Life continued for them, as it does for us, and they continued in their search for the Promised Land.

Snakes everywhere

After the death of Aaron on Mount Hor the Israelites continued their journey to the Promised Land. They had been travelling for almost forty years and most of the older generation had died at this stage.

As they made their way through the wilderness they began to murmur and complain again. They started to blame Moses for the long and tiring journey, which seemed to have no end. They even started to doubt God whom they could not see with their own eyes. They blamed Moses for bringing them out of Egypt to die in the wilderness.

God acted immediately to teach them a lesson to stop them complaining and start trusting and following the Lord. All of a sudden, as if from nowhere, the ground was covered with fiery serpents. There were snakes everywhere. Once they bit you, you were certain to die. They crawled into the tents and all over the ground and there were thousands of them. The more they killed the snakes the more snakes there were; it was a terrible plague of snakes. Children and parents were bitten and it seemed as if the whole camp were going to die because of the fiery serpents.

At last the people cried to Moses for mercy; they said they were so sorry for all their complaining. They had complained against God and Moses, and were truly sorry for their sin. Just like every other time, Moses went to the Lord in prayer.

God instantly answered his prayer and told Moses to do something very strange indeed as time was running out. How important prayer is whenever there is a tragedy. God knows all about it before you even pray.

The Brazen Serpent

You may have wondered what happened to all the snakes. Well they were all there; thousands of them everywhere with people being bitten every second. Once they were bitten they began to die, with only a short time to live.

God instructed Moses to make a serpent from brass, which had to look like the lively fiery snakes. Once it was made he had to hang it up on a pole. You may think this was a strange thing to do.

After the serpent was made of brass and put up on a pole, everyone was told if they looked at the brazen serpent after they were bitten, they would live. All they had to do, was look at the serpent high up on the pole and they would be healed and live.

Moses carried out God's command. All the people had to do was look at the serpent and live. Many people died that day, because they refused to look. Those who did look were immediately made clean from the poison that had entered them by the serpents.

They didn't have to crawl to the pole; they didn't have to climb the pole. All they had to do was to look at the serpent on the pole, from wherever they were and they were immediately saved and didn't die. If they looked to the serpent they lived.

The same is true for the sinner today; if we look to Jesus and put our trust completely in Him to save us, we will be saved. Any boy, girl or adult who looks to Jesus for Salvation will be HEALED FROM THEIR SIN forever. If we don't look by faith and trust in Jesus, we will die and be lost forever.

MOSES 179

Time to praise God

The children of Israel were really thankful to the Lord for saving them again. They had all thought they were going to die. Now all they wanted to do was praise the Lord and give thanks to Him. They were learning to understand what it means to trust and obey the Lord. Now when God told them to do something they wanted to obey His Word.

They stopped their murmuring, grumbling and complaining and were full of joy. They were no longer downcast, discouraged or deflated but were ready to march on to victory. The Lord was so pleased with their attitude for they learned that they couldn't complain and rejoice at the same time. It was the first time they had really rejoiced since they had crossed the Red Sea all those years ago. They had wasted years because they had not put the Lord first in everything.

After another long journey the Israelites came to a country belonging to the Amorites. They asked King Sihon for permission to pass through the land. He did not grant them permission but actually attacked Israel with his army. God helped Israel and they easily defeated the Amorites. After this, they were attacked by Og, the king of Bashan and his army. Again, the Lord really helped the Israelites and they defeated the Bashan army.

In the Christian life, the Lord often blesses us while the devil is attacking us. This is why it is so important to stay close to the Lord and He will help you in your battles.

Balaam the false Prophet

After two victories in battle, the Israelites were rejoicing in how God had given them success both times. Now they had made camp in the plains of Moab on the side of Jordan by Jericho. They realised they were very close to the Promised Land.

Little did the children of Israel know that away up high in the mountains above them, was another army, this time it was Balak, the king of the Moabites. He had heard of Israel's recent victories and was afraid of them. He also knew that there was something about the Israelites that was not normal. What he didn't realize was that the secret of Israel's strength in the battle field was the Lord helping them.

Balak the king had a wicked plan. He decided to get a false prophet to come and put a curse on Israel to make them weak. Balak knew of a false prophet called Balaam who lived far away in a place called Mesopotamia. King Balak then sent messengers with a large sum of money to persuade Balaam to come quickly to put a curse on Israel.

Imagine if you were bribed and offered money or nice presents to do something that was wrong, knowing that God would not approve. What would you do in that situation? To give into things like this is wrong and remember, the Bible says "be sure your sin will find you out."

At first Balaam would not go because God warned him not to speak against His people, the Israelites. Then Balaam was persuaded with even more money. He went, but along the way as he journeyed on his donkey a most unusual thing happened.

GOD can use any means to stop people doing wrong, especially when they know it is wrong.

MOSES 181

The Speaking Donkey

Balak finally persuaded Balaam to come and curse Israel with a large sum of money as a bribe. Balaam didn't care what God said but went ahead on the journey to Balak the king. Balaam travelled the long journey. What he was doing was wrong; God had told him not to go and speak against His people, but Balaam was very stubborn and greedy. He took with him two servants and the messengers of Balak.

God sent an angel down to stop Balaam but the angel was invisible to the humans. However, when the donkey saw the angel it ran off the road in fright and into a field. Balaam was so cross he beat the donkey. Further on along the road, by a wall, the donkey saw the angel again with a drawn sword. It stopped and leaned hard against the wall crushing Balaam's foot. Balaam was so sore and frustrated that he beat the donkey again. Further on along the road the donkey saw the angel again with a big sword. This time the donkey fell under Balaam on the road. Balaam was so angry he beat the donkey hard with his stick.

Then Balaam was shocked when he heard the donkey say to him, "Why are you beating me?" Balaam answered "If I had the right weapon, I would kill you, you foolish donkey." He didn't even realise he was talking to the donkey for a moment. He was so cross.

Suddenly the angel became visible before Balaam and he realised that the donkey had stopped so that he wouldn't be killed. Balaam was sorry and was prepared to abandon the journey and return home. The angel told him to continue because he had another plan from God for Balaam to do.

Have you ever suddenly realised why certain things went wrong in life? Maybe you were in a hurry in the car and the traffic lights suddenly turned red and you got upset. Maybe God kept you safe from an accident up ahead.

Curse to Blessing

Balaam continued his journey until he met up with King Balak. Balak wanted Balaam to curse the Israelites and as Balaam was a false prophet he thought he had the power to do this.

Whenever Balaam came to Balak, the king thought that was what was going to happen. Balak took Balaam to the top of the mountain where down in the valley were more than two million Israelites. The Israelites didn't know what the wicked King Balak was planning; the king then told Balaam to curse the children of Israel.

Balak didn't know that the angel had spared Balaam's life and had changed what Balaam planned to do. Instead of cursing the Israelites, Balaam blessed them and told Balak what a great a nation they would become. Again Balak took Balaam to a different part of the mountain and told Balaam to curse the people. Balaam responded by telling Balak that God had told him to bless the people and that what God has promised to do, He will do. For the third time, after building altars and offering sacrifices, Balaam told Balak that God had blessed Israel and these were His people forever. Their land would be rich and beautiful and God would protect them. Israel was saved from harm once again because God had delivered them.

Satan was trying his best to destroy God's people but Satan is no match for God. In the Christian life, Satan and others will try to curse and harm you. God wants to bless you. God has the power to turn cursing into blessing.

Moses writes the Pentateuch

Moses was now 120 years old and the time of his death was very near. There was no one who knew God more intimately than Moses did. God had another special task for Moses to do. It is always good to be busy and available to do the Lord's work until we die. There was no such thing as retirement for Moses.

God wanted Moses to start writing the Bible. God would tell Moses what to write and Moses then recorded it on a scroll. Moses was to write the first five books of the Bible; this is called the Pentateuch, or the books of Moses. The books of Moses are Genesis, Exodus, Leviticus, Numbers and Deuteronomy.

As God told Moses what to write, Moses carefully wrote it down, word for word. The Bible is the written Word of God, God's spoken Word. It was to be preserved so that every generation would have the Word of God. God told Moses to record how the world was created, the fall of man, the flood and the tower of Babel. God's plan to send the Saviour of the world through Abraham, Isaac, and Jacob was also recorded, as well as the great adventures of Joseph and then the life story of Moses.

Moses wrote as he heard God speak. It must have been wonderful to be part of God's plan, to be used of God in this way. Today, God has a plan for all of His children. Like Moses, all we need to do is be willing to be used for God.

We should count it a blessing to be part of God's great plan.

Moses and his final Speech

The life of Moses was divided up into three parts, each lasting forty years. For the first forty years, Moses was a prince in Egypt, the next forty years he worked as a shepherd for his father-in-law and then the last forty years of his life he spent wandering in the wilderness as the leader of the children of Israel.

One of the final things Moses asked God for, was to finally see the Promised Land. He really wanted to go to the Promised Land and see it for himself. For eighty years now Moses had been dreaming about the Promised Land, but when Moses had struck the rock twice out of anger, God had told him he would not go to the Promised Land. Now, a long time later, Moses asked God if he could make the final journey into the Promised Land. Instead, Moses was told to climb up to the top of Mount Pisgah. There he was to make Joshua the new leader of the children of Israel and to encourage Joshua to lead the people into the Promised Land.

Moses was happy to do this as Joshua was a much younger man for the job. Moses gathered the people, for the last time, for his final speech. He began to recall the important events of his life and especially the last forty years. He pleaded with the people not to forget about the Lord. He warned them of the dangers of not following the Lord in their lives and told the people not to be afraid as the Lord was with them and would not fail them. He then passed the new leadership over to Joshua before all the people. He exhorted the people to follow Joshua, who would lead them into the Promised Land. Moses then encouraged Joshua to go and conquer the land which the Lord had given them. Moses then said good-bye and started climbing the mountain, his final earthly journey.

MOSES 185

Moses can see the Promised Land

Moses made his final journey up Mount Nebo to the "top of Pisgah" to meet with God. It was toward evening but still there was a very clear view of everything around.

When he got to the very top, he looked down and saw all his people waiting to cross over into the Promised Land. Then he lifted up his eyes and there, before him was the most beautiful view he had ever seen; it was the Promised Land. For most of his life he had been wondering what it was like.

It truly was a beautiful country and he knew that his people would soon occupy the Promised Land, as God had told them they would. All the battles, difficulties and problems that occurred along the way had been worthwhile. After Moses viewed the Promised Land for the final time, God called him home. Moses died on top of Mount Nebo in the land of Moab. The people mourned the death of Moses for thirty days.

It is quite sad that Moses didn't physically enter the Promised Land, but in many ways he did. The Promised Land reminds me of Heaven, the final home for all of God's children. When we die it is a place that is promised for us. I know for sure that I will be there with Moses. Can you be sure that you will be there as well one day?

Moses talks with Jesus

There is a wonderful thing we read about in the New Testament. Maybe two thousand years later the Lord Jesus took three of his disciples to the top of a high mountain inside the Promised Land. The disciples fell asleep and when they woke up, they saw Jesus talking with two men. One of them was Elijah and the other was Moses. How thrilling and exciting it must have been for Moses to be in the Promised Land.

But how much more special it must have been for Moses to stand and talk face to face with the promised Messiah, the Lord Jesus Christ, the Saviour of the world, the Redeemer that God had promised from the very beginning of history, the One of whom Moses had written about in the Pentateuch.

All the sacrifices that were made in the past had been pointing to the final sacrifice, when Jesus would die on the cross for the sins of mankind. Moses was one of the greatest men who ever lived and he walked close to the Lord.

Moses was now dead; his work was now complete. God's work however must continue. God will always have new workers and preachers to replace the older ones.

Maybe God is going to use you to be a worker for Him. Are you willing to be used? What a privilege that would be, to be used by God to bring His message to the world around us.

MOSES

The Death of Moses

We have now come to the sad end of the wonderful life, of a man of God. Moses is one of the greatest characters in the Bible. While he was a man of God, he still failed the Lord many times as we often do.

Joshua was next to succeed Moses and he would be the one chosen of God to lead the children of Israel into the Promised Land. It is interesting to note that Moses was 120 years old when he died and he still had excellent eye sight. He was also physically strong right up until his death. He did not die from ill health, rather his service for God had come to an end and it was time for the Lord to call him home. How do we know this? The Bible tells us, "Moses was an hundred and twenty years old when he died: his eye was not dim, nor his natural force abated."(Deuteronomy 34:7)

Just like Moses, our lives will one day come to an end. What really is important, is how we live our lives here on earth. Moses lived in touch with God; he spoke to Him every day. Moses himself, humanly speaking, was not much use at anything, as he made so many excuses when God wanted to use him. Then the Lord took him and made him the wonderful man of God he became.

Are you being used of God? Have you given your life over to the Lord to be saved? Are you living every day as if it is your last day here on earth?

Joshua
Here comes Joshua

Today we are going to start learning about another wonderful Bible character. His name is Joshua. Moses had led the children of Israel to the borders of the Promised Land but had died at an old age and never got to see the Promised Land. After that, God raised up Joshua to take over the leadership from Moses.

For a long time God had been preparing Joshua for this important role as leader and Joshua had already proved himself to be one who could lead the people. Often in our lives, situations will arise that will require us to make decisions. How we do this will often determine the type of person we will grow up to be.

At this stage Joshua had enjoyed many victories in battle; he was with Moses up on Mount Sinai when he received the Ten Commandments. He was also chosen as one of the twelve spies who brought back a positive report and wanted to immediately possess the land for God. Before his death, Moses had asked the Lord for a new leader. The Lord told Moses to, "Go and get Joshua, a man filled with the Spirit." Joshua is also described as a "wise man." Often in life we can be tempted to do foolish things that we later regret. Never be afraid to say "no" when tempted to do something foolish.

God had great plans for Joshua; it took a long time before it all happened but he waited patiently. Are you prepared to be patient and wait for God to reveal His plans for you, bit by bit?

Talking with God

Even though Joshua was set apart as the one to succeed Moses, and even though he was an excellent soldier, an experienced leader and a man of great faith, he still needed God. There would have been times when he felt the pressure of responsibility and feared he could never be as good as Moses. It is never a good thing to compare yourself to someone else. It is wiser to thank God for the talents He has given you and ask Him to use them, or even help you see them also!

There were times when the Lord came to Joshua and wonderfully encouraged him in his walk with the Lord. "There shall not any man be able to stand before thee all the days of thy life: as I was with Moses, so I will be with thee: I will not fail thee, nor forsake thee." (Joshua 1:5) The Lord was assuring Joshua of His continued and continual presence with him. With these words the Lord then set Joshua apart as the leader of the Israelite people.

Sometimes we can feel lonely and wonder where God is and sometimes it can be really tough especially when things go wrong for us. Always remember in the Christian life the Lord Jesus is always with us. He promises that He will never leave us; He is always with His children. There will be times when we will feel down and discouraged, but remember the Lord says, "I am the Lord, I change not." He is always near His children. Keep in touch with Him; keep reading the Bible and keep on talking with God; He loves you to talk to Him in prayer.

When is the last time YOU TALKED TO GOD?

JOSHUA 190

Taking responsibility Seriously

As the Lord spoke to Joshua and assured him of his continual presence, the Lord went on to share the secret of being successful and prosperous in this world. This same secret can be shared and known by any child of God anywhere in the world. The secret is knowing the Word of God, thinking about it every day and obeying it by putting it into practice.

> "This book of the law shall not depart out of thy mouth; but thou shalt meditate therein day and night, that thou mayest observe to do according to all that is written therein: for then thou shalt make thy way prosperous, and then thou shalt have good success."
>
> (Joshua 1:8)

The Lord gave Joshua the promise of his continual presence, strength and encouragement along the way. Joshua then knew that he and God's people would have great success. With this came awesome responsibility and Joshua knew that and took it very seriously.

Joshua was now ready for the challenge of leading the people. He really wanted to do everything pleasing to the Lord. We can learn so much from Joshua. When we are doing anything, from our homework, housework or regular work we should do it as unto the Lord as if it was the Lord who asked us to do it for Him. Sometimes we can become careless and slack and not really care anymore. This is a wrong attitude to take and if this is the case, we may need to get re-focused and do everything as unto the Lord. Then we will become much happier within ourselves.

JOSHUA 191

Taking Courage

As we continue with the life of Joshua we will find that this man's life thrills us with some of the most exciting adventures and victories of all time. Most of the people of Moses' generation had all died and a whole new generation of people were on the move. God commanded Joshua to be strong and brave. The land was promised to Joshua and the people, all they had to do was claim it.

Joshua had great faith in God and this is where his courage came from. He would need to be full of courage as there were many battles and struggles ahead of him. Today we may feel blessed but tomorrow or another day all may be different and we need to keep strong and continue to be courageous, even in the difficult times.

The time had now come for Joshua to lead the people over the river Jordan into Canaan, the Promised Land. The Lord promised to be with Joshua, no matter who would come against him, he would have victory. This was a big challenge for Joshua as he was leading some two million people and they were to cross over the river Jordan, which was very wide, deep and pretty turbulent. Also there were no bridges or boats to carry them. When they did get across, there were seven strong nations to face who would not make them welcome. These nations were well skilled in war, and had cities with huge walls around them. It seemed like an impossible task to cross the river and have seven straight victories against these seven strong nations, but God said, "Trust, have faith, be courageous," and He promised to be with Joshua. Joshua was relying completely in God.

Spying out the Land

Canaan was the "Promised Land" that God had promised to Abraham about 400 years earlier. The Canaanites were idol worshippers, and along with their worship of false gods they committed the most horrible, wicked, and evil practices that could be imagined. God commanded Joshua to conquer and destroy these seven evil nations because of their wickedness.

On the other side of the Jordan River, a couple of miles from the Israelite camp, was a large city named Jericho. It was well protected by a very high wall and strong gates which were secured every night. Joshua knew that this was the first city that would resist him, so he must conquer it before going further into Canaan.

Joshua sent two spies over to Jericho to spy out the land. Here they were to gather all the information Israel needed to know before they would proceed. The children of Israel had been travelling for over forty years and they were very excited at the prospect of entering the Promised Land. Joshua told the people to get ready; they were immediately submissive and encouraged Joshua by telling him that whatever he commanded them to do they would do.

In the meantime the spies had crossed the river and entered the city of Jericho. They were surprised to see how thick the walls of the city were; in fact they were so thick there were actually houses built on the walls! They moved in amongst the people and then made their way up to the top of the walls to see how thick they really were. In the meantime they were spotted by guards and immediately the soldiers headed across the city and up to the top of the walls. The spies entered a house of a woman named Rahab and to their surprise she agreed to hide them. This was no accident, as she turned out to be the only believer in the whole city.

Each day we live we should always expect to meet and greet a stranger. They may be one of God's children, in need of help or they may not be saved and perhaps by our actions may want to become a Christian.

JOSHUA 193

A perfect Hiding Place

Whenever the two spies had reached Jericho, they began to look carefully at the walls of the city. On the watch for constant danger they realised they had been spotted and ran for their lives. They made their way into a home of a woman called Rahab. She seemed a really friendly person; but in fact she was a harlot, a person who had lived a very sinful lifestyle.

Whenever the soldiers realised that the two spies were seen going into Rahab's house they made their way to her door. Suddenly Rahab and the two spies heard footsteps coming towards her door. Rahab acted quickly and told the men to climb up onto the rooftop. Here she covered them with stalks of flax that she had spread out onto the roof to dry.

Banging on her door the soldiers shouted angrily for Rahab to open up. She quickly opened the door and the soldiers told her to surrender the two spies. Rahab told the soldiers that the spies had been with her and that she didn't realise they were spies and that they had left and were making their way to the city gate. Quickly the soldiers left and ran towards the city gate to find them.

Isn't it amazing how the Lord was able to direct the spies to Rahab's house, hide them on her roof top and eventually save her entire family from destruction?

When we place our lives in the hands of the living God, He will protect and keep us.

I know your God

Whenever the soldiers left Rahab's house, Rahab quickly ran up onto the rooftop to get the two spies who were hiding under the flax. Rahab then startled the men by telling them that she knew their God and had confidence that God was going to give them the victory in conquering the city of Jericho.

She went on to tell them how her people were afraid of the Israelites and of how they had heard their God dried up the Red Sea and made a path to help them escape from Egypt, and how their God had helped them in so many ways.

Have you ever told anyone how great and powerful God is?

Rahab went on to say that she also believed in their God, the Lord God of Israel, the one true God of heaven and earth. The men were taken by surprise. Rahab had been a very wicked woman, a harlot, a very immoral woman, a worshipper of idols. She had been a liar and had lived a terrible, ungodly lifestyle.

Yet, Rahab was the type of person God loved; a great sinner who now believed in the true God of Israel. She said "I know your God." Realising that the two spies also believed in her God, she was willing to help them. These two spies were so different from the men who would normally come to visit her. Rahab was willing to risk her life by hiding the two spies. Rahab either was already a true believer in the God of Israel or became a true believer that very day.

Can you say with all your heart like Rahab, "I know God in a personal way?" Has there been such a change in your life that others can easily tell that you know God and are a Christian?

JOSHUA 195

The Promise

Before the spies left Rahab's house, they made her a promise. Rahab had really surprised the spies by telling them she believed in their God. Evidence of this was to be found in the fact that she hid the spies from the soldiers, as under normal circumstances this would not have happened. In the New Testament it records this in two separate verses, "By faith the harlot Rahab perished not with them that believed not, when she had received the spies with peace." (Hebrews 11:31) and "Likewise also was not Rahab the harlot justified by works, when she had received the messengers, and had sent them out another way?" (James 2:25)

Ever since Rahab heard of the power of God and the mighty works that He had done and seeing that the men who had come to her were so different from the men who usually came to her, she was convinced that the God of Israel was the one true and living God. As a result, she was willing to risk her life for them and became a true believer in the living God.

Rahab asked the spies to promise her that they would save her family when they came back to fight against Jericho. The two men promised that if Rahab would not betray them and let them escape freely, they would save her and her family alive when they came back to conquer the city. The spies told Rahab to hang a scarlet rope out of her window. When they saw the rope they would know her house and she and her family would not be harmed. The men then escaped down the scarlet rope and went off into the night.

What a story this is of how God can use the most unusual situations to save people we would never expect to be saved!

The Plan comes together

Rahab then helped the two spies escape for their lives, as she let them down the outside of the city wall by a red, or scarlet, rope. "Escape to the mountains," she told them. "Hide there for two or three days until the men who are searching for you have returned; then go on your way." After the spies escaped, Rahab pulled the scarlet cord back into the window and as she looked upon it she realised that this was her only means of escape.

The SCARLET CORD is a picture of the only thing that can save us from eternal death - the blood of Jesus Christ. This is the central message of the Bible; sacrifice after sacrifice pointed the way to the final and ultimate sacrifice, when Jesus would be crucified. "...THE BLOOD OF JESUS CHRIST his Son cleanseth us from all sin." (1 John 1:7)

Rahab both knew and realised that she was a sinner. She also knew that she could do nothing to save herself and that only by trusting in the Lord could she be saved. The only way she could be saved from destruction was if she remembered to put out the scarlet cord.

God would soon destroy Jericho; the plan was in place, and Rahab must now warn her family and bring them to safety. What a lesson for us all, to be concerned for our families and try to win them for the Lord. One day the whole world will be destroyed and only those who have trusted in the Lord and had their sins forgiven will be saved.

Is there someone you can share this story with to help them realise their need of a Saviour?

JOSHUA 197

Crossing the River

After three days the two spies returned to Israel's camp and told Joshua all that had happened. Joshua prayed to the Lord and realised that the time had come to cross the River Jordan. He instructed his men to tell the camp that the time had come to cross the river. They must prepare food, pack their tents and gather up for the journey ahead.

Early in the morning Joshua called the people together and assured them of the Lord's help and guidance along the way. He assured them that the Lord would prepare the way and would give them victory on the other side. "The Ark of the Covenant will lead you across the river," he told the people.

The people must have wondered how Joshua planned to get them all across the river as it was very wide and very deep. Was he going to make a bridge or build a ship? There were over two million Israelites making this journey. The order was given to watch out for the priests carrying the Ark of the Covenant; when they began to move, everyone was to follow them.

Just as their fathers had crossed the Red Sea many years before, so would they cross the River Jordan. As the Ark of the Covenant entered the Jordan River, the water just opened up into a big pathway! A huge dam appeared forming a wall of water. What an amazing and breath taking sight this truly was. Hour by hour passed as all two million Israelites made their way across the River Jordan. After they made their way across, the river closed up again and it just seemed like a dream to everyone watching. Sometimes we have to make the first move by faith to really see the Lord working.

God was directing the paths of His people. Can you remember the last time the Lord clearly directed you in your life?

Difficult Days ahead

When the Israelites made their way out of the River Jordan, Joshua instructed twelve men to put up twelve huge stones as a memorial to how God had brought them across the river. It was forty years since the Lord opened up the Red Sea to bring them through and now the Lord had caused another great miracle by bringing them through the River Jordan.

The stones were a memorial to how the Lord had helped and would continue to help them in the future. That's what the Lord does; He keeps on helping and blessing His people.

Now the challenge had come. The Israelites had left the wilderness for ever after a long journey. They were now in the Promised Land, face to face with all the heathen nations. There was no turning back. They were in the Promised Land and all they had to do was to take possession. At the same time the nations in Canaan had heard that God was with the Israelites and was helping them.

For the past forty years God had been feeding His people with manna from Heaven. Now that they were in the Promised Land, there was more than enough food for everyone. Fruit, vegetables, grain and lots of other good food; it really was a land flowing with milk and honey. This was another sign that God was with them. The real challenge now was how would they conquer the other nations? Jericho had huge thick walls, thousands of armed soldiers, and enough food to last for years if need be. Joshua then began to pray for God to help him.

Sometimes things can become DIFFICULT and from the outside, almost seem IMPOSSIBLE. Have you considered TALKING to God and asking for His HELP?

The Lord visits Joshua

Victory seemed impossible, and Joshua did not know what to do. He felt weak and totally helpless for such a task and he began to pour out his heart to the Lord, asking him for wisdom to know what to do. As Joshua finished praying, he lifted up his head and was startled to see a man with a drawn sword in his hand. Reaching for his own sword, Joshua shouted, "Are you a friend or foe? Are you on our side or are you our enemy?" "Neither," said the other person, "I am captain of the Lord's host." Joshua realised that this visitor was no ordinary soldier and no ordinary visitor, that He really was the captain of the Lord's army.

The commander who appeared before Joshua was Jesus, the Son of God. This was a miraculous appearance. Several times in the Old Testament Jesus appeared in visible form and talked with God's servants. What a joy and privilege it was for Joshua to see and talk with the Lord Jesus Christ. Jesus told Joshua to take off his shoes for reverence before Him, just as Moses was instructed to do before the Burning Bush.

What a lesson this is, every time we come before the Lord we must do so with reverence, whether in church or at home, praying or reading His Word. Joshua was facing huge battles but the Lord was there to help him and He assured him of His help. Today Christian's still face many battles in the world, to conform, backslide, grow cold, give in to temptation and so on. Remember, He is always there to help us, guide and protect us from harm and danger.

Just as JOSHUA listened to the Lord revealing His plan for his life, so we must PATIENTLY PRAY and ask God to HELP US.

The March is on

When the Lord visited Joshua, He told him exactly what plan to follow in order to defeat Jericho. It was the most unusual plan Joshua had ever heard of. Joshua was instructed to take his army and march around the city of Jericho once a day for six days. Then on the seventh day the army was to walk around the city walls seven times. No one was to talk; the only sound was to be the rams' horns blowing.

As they began to march each day, the soldiers in Jericho were probably wondering what was going on. They were expecting an attack, not this type of silent marching. After they marched around for the seventh time on the seventh day, Joshua was to give the order for everyone to shout and as soon as they did, the walls would collapse.

Can you imagine how the enemy felt? They didn't know what to do or what to expect. God always knows what is best, but Joshua was in despair and didn't know what to do. When he sought the Lord in prayer, the Lord then made the way clear for Joshua to follow. Sometimes we can be like this and not really know what to do in a situation. The Lord specialises in helping us in times of great need; all we have to do is ask Him.

Remember, "With God nothing shall be impossible."

(Luke 1:37)

Down come the Walls

The Israelites had marched around the walls of Jericho once a day for the last six days, now on the seventh day they had just marched around for the seventh time. Everyone was ecstatic about what was going to happen next.

The priests were then instructed to blow their trumpets, (the rams' horns) with a long continuous blast. Joshua then called to the people "SHOUT, for the Lord has given you the city! All that is in it belongs to the Lord!" Instantly all the men SHOUTED! Suddenly the walls began to shudder and shake as if an earthquake hit the city.

Then by the power of God the huge, great walls of Jericho began to give way, and down they came as the army of Israel continued shouting. As the walls came down the Israelite army quickly invaded and captured the city of Jericho. The Lord gave Joshua a great victory that day. Only one part of the wall never fell; on top of that part of a wall was a scarlet cord, hanging from a window of a house, the house of Rahab.

The Lord instructed that everything belonged to Him in Jericho and no one was to take anything for themselves. Again the Lord had helped the Israelites in a most impossible situation.

> This is what God does; He helps people along the way in their Christian lives. All we have to do is ask Him for help and guidance and He will give us the victory.

Rahab and her Family are Saved

Do you remember Rahab, the harlot who hid the spies in her home? Remember how she asked the two spies to promise her that they would save her and her family alive. The time had now come; the only way Rahab could be saved was if she remembered to hang the scarlet cord from her window.

Whenever the walls of Jericho fell down, the only part that remained was the part of the wall where Rahab lived. When the soldiers saw the scarlet cord, Rahab and her family were escorted to safety and were brought to the Israelite camp where they started a new life together.

Rahab had completely changed; she had given her life to the Lord and now desired to live for Him. Just as the Lord forgave and saved Rahab, who lived a very wicked lifestyle, He can save the worst of sinners today.

The scarlet cord reminds us of the Precious Blood of the Lord Jesus Christ that was shed for us on Calvary. One day the Lord Jesus will come back to this earth. Just as the scarlet cord had to be visible in order for Rahab to be saved so must the Lord Jesus see that His Blood has washed your sins away. This is why it is so important to be saved; to be rescued from our sins by faith, believing that Jesus Christ is the only one who can save you.

Praise God, His blood is so powerful it can wash away your sins. Have you ever asked Him to do that for you?

JOSHUA 203

The Thief

Joshua and all the Israelite army were celebrating their great victory over Jericho. The Bible tells us that the fame of Joshua was "noised abroad throughout the whole country." The Israelites were so happy with the great victory they had achieved. They were totally amazed at all the beauty there was in Jericho. As the soldiers walked among the ruins of Jericho, they noticed the gold, silver, bronze, precious jewels and so many other beautiful and valuable things.

Every soldier was instructed not to touch or take anything for themselves as everything belonged to the Lord. However there was a soldier called Achan who, when he saw all the gold and silver began to want it. He knew it was wrong to take it, but temptation got the better of him and when no one was looking he took a beautiful robe, two hundred pieces of silver and a bar of gold. No one had noticed, so he quickly made his way to his tent, dug a hole and buried them hoping to get them on a later occasion.

Have you ever felt that when the temptation becomes so strong it can be easy to give in? Giving in is sin. On this occasion, the sin was stealing. Taking something that doesn't belong to us is stealing. "Thou knowest the commandments, Do not commit adultery, Do not kill, Do not steal, Do not bear false witness, Defraud not, Honour thy father and mother." (Mark 10:19) Even when no one else sees us or knows anything about it, God sees everything. "For the eyes of the LORD run to and fro throughout the whole earth."(2 Chronicles 16:9)

In life you will be tempted many times to do something that is wrong. Always try not to give into temptation by asking God to give you the strength to say "no."

Loosing the Battle

After defeating Jericho, Joshua realised there were many more battles ahead. The next one was a town called Ai, which was a few miles north of Jericho. In the Christian life we may have many victories, but there will also be many battles to fight. Not physical battles, but battles against attitudes, personalities, temptations and many kinds of sin.

Joshua was so confident about defeating Ai that, after a confident report from a couple of spies he sent a few thousand soldiers to fight against Ai. The battle however had only just begun when the Israelites realised they had to retreat and come back. Joshua had entered this battle without seeking the Lord in prayer about it and within a short period of time thirty six of his men were killed in battle.

Sometimes we can be over confident and try to do things in our own strength. The Lord wants to help us in every situation and in every battle in life. We can become so confident, or stubborn, that we think we no longer need the Lord to help us.

The Israelite army, who were once so confident, were now gripped by fear and had lost all their courage. Joshua took himself off to be alone; he was so shocked and disappointed about losing this battle. Finally, he began to pray asking the Lord why this had happened. Joshua began to question God, as if it was His fault. The Lord then told Joshua why they had lost the battle; it was because there was sin in the camp. Someone had stolen goods from Jericho. By doing this wicked and evil thing they were disobeying the Lord.

The Lord told Joshua that in the morning he would find out who the thief was. This gave Achan an opportunity to confess his sin, but he didn't. He thought no-one knew anything about it.

Whenever we sin we should immediately confess it to the Lord before it brings terrible consequences upon us, as it did with Achan.

JOSHUA 205

The Wages of Sin is Death

The Word of God clearly teaches us that sin is an offence to God and that sin must be punished. Many times in the Bible we read of how God dealt with sin. Today we will learn about Achan who a few days previously had stolen garments, silver and gold from the ruins in Jericho. God had told the people not to take anything for themselves. The precious metals were to go into the treasury of the house of the Lord and everything else was to be burned.

Joshua now knew that sin had come into the camp and as each tribe and family came before him, God indicated to Joshua that Achan was the thief. Joshua explained to Achan that the reason they had lost the battle and lost thirty six soldiers, was because of his sin. When Achan told Joshua that he had stolen the goods and buried them in the ground under his tent, Joshua sent men to his tent to recover them. As a result of this sin of stealing, Achan, his family and his animals were all taken away and stoned and put to death. They were then buried with a great heap of stones reminding the people of what happened and why they had died.

Achan saw the treasure, he wanted the treasure and then he took (stole) the treasure. This reminds me of Eve in the Garden of Eden; she saw the fruit, wanted the fruit and then she took the fruit and from that moment sin came into the world. God commands us not to steal; we all must die one day as a result of Adam and Eve's disobedience. Praise God, there is a cure, Jesus is the cure and we can be forgiven. The Bible tells us in Philippians 2:8 that the Lord Jesus Christ became obedient unto death, to save us from our sins.

Many times we will be tempted to do something wrong; temptation is not sin, but yielding and giving in to temptation is sin. We must run away from temptation when it comes our way.

"For the wages of sin is death; but the gift of God is eternal life through Jesus Christ our Lord." (Romans 6:23)

Joshua is Deceived

God had told Abraham 400 years before Israel came to the borders of Canaan that He would have to destroy all the Canaanites because of their wickedness. God had given Joshua victory after victory, as he went from city to city.

Every town that Joshua went to, lived in fear as they had heard about Joshua's many victories. Most of the other cities united together to fight against Joshua except for one. One day a group of Gibeonites came to the Israelite camp and asked for Joshua. They were very crafty people who matted their hair and beards and wore old clothes to make themselves look old and poor. They brought lame animals to make it look like they had made a very long journey to make peace with Joshua.

These people were Gibeonites and only lived a few miles up the road. Joshua didn't pray to the Lord for advice on the matter, but took pity on the men and signed a peace treaty with them. When Joshua was about to attack the next city the truth came out that he had in fact made a peace treaty with them and could not harm them. Joshua was very upset that he had been tricked; however he had given them his word, so they could not be attacked. Even though God had instructed him to destroy the cities, Joshua made a treaty, so he could not go back on his word.

How easy it is to be fooled, lied to and deceived. This is why it is so important to seek counsel and advice from the Lord in every part of our lives. God hates lies and speaks so often about them in His Word. "And there shall in no wise enter into it any thing that defileth, neither whatsoever worketh abomination, or maketh a lie: but they which are written in the Lamb's book of life." (Revelation 21:27)

"Be sober, be vigilant; because your adversary the devil, as a roaring lion, walketh about, seeking whom he may devour." (1 Peter 5:8)

"For without are dogs, and sorcerers, and whoremongers, and murderers, and idolaters, and whosoever loveth and maketh a lie." (Revelation 22:15) **JOSHUA** 207

The Sun and Moon stand still

Whenever the five neighbouring cities had heard that Gibeon had made a peace treaty with the leaders of Israel they were so angry that they decided to attack Gibeon. Together these five Amorite kings combined their armies for a united invasion of Gibeon.

The Gibeonites quickly sent news to Joshua so that he would come and help them. Joshua, realising he had made a peace treaty with Gibeon felt honour bound to help them. This time Joshua prayed and asked the Lord for help in the situation. How important it is to remember to pray and ask the Lord for help in times of need.

Joshua then headed for Gibeon and started war on the five kings and their armies. Joshua and his army fought hard, but Joshua became concerned that after marching all night and going straight into war, his men might become tired and drop from exhaustion. As the battle intensified Joshua became increasingly concerned, so he began to pray for help and guidance. Always seek the Lord early for help before a situation gets out of control.

Then a wonderful thing happened. Suddenly the sun and the moon stood still, so in one part it never got dark and in the other part it never became light. The atmosphere began to change and a massive hailstorm broke out upon the enemy soldiers, as if heaven itself had opened fire. The hailstorm killed more men than the Israelite soldiers did; the battle was over and again with God's help Joshua had won the day.

The five kings were so afraid they hid themselves in a cave, but Joshua soon found them and put a big stone over the entrance of the cave. One by one they were killed. God had said that these enemy, heathen cities must be utterly and completely destroyed. The Lord had given these cities 400 years to change their ways but they refused and mocked God until God decided they must be punished for their sin.

God hates sin and it must be punished.

Caleb follows the Lord

Joshua and the children of Israel had possessed nearly all the land of Canaan. Joshua now was getting old, so the Lord told Joshua to divide the people into twelve tribes, and divide the land amongst them, then each tribe could drive out the remaining Canaanites.

The Lord then chose where each tribe should go rather than them wander off by themselves. Let the Lord choose whatever path He has for you and do not go through life without the Lord.

A man by the name of Caleb came up to Joshua to talk with him; he was of the tribe of Judah. He was now eighty-five years old and reminded Joshua how he had been with him as a spy some forty years previously. Moses had promised him that the land he had spied out would one day become his, and so it had. Caleb was so happy.

Caleb went on to tell Joshua how the Lord had blessed and kept him these past forty-five years and that how he was as strong now as he had ever been. When Joshua asked Caleb where he wanted to live, he did not say in a nice quiet, fertile place. Rather he said, "Give me this mountain." He knew up in the mountain there were giants, opposition, battles and many, many challenges but he also knew the Lord would help him. Caleb was the only one who succeeded in completely driving out the enemy.

What was Caleb's secret? It was that he wholly followed the Lord in everything he did. From battles, to daily living, Caleb put the Lord first in everything. What a lesson for us to learn, to put the Lord first in every aspect of our lives. When things are good or when things are bad, always put the Lord first.

What a Life

Joshua lived until he was 110 years old. No longer could he lead the Israelite army against their enemies. Just as Moses, Aaron and others had died before him, he knew the time had come and soon he would die. He wanted to gather the people together one final time and encourage them to stay close to God and follow His ways. Isn't this a great thing for us to learn, to encourage our friends to follow the Lord in everything they do?

As Joshua spoke to the people he reminded them how the Lord had blessed, helped and encouraged them along the way. He realised that the people would make up their own mind whether to follow the Lord or not. Joshua reminded the people that if they did not obey the Lord, there would be consequences. God had given them cities, vineyards, land, water and cattle all for nothing and all He wanted in return was for the people to follow Him. Joshua urged the people to love the Lord with all their heart, mind and soul.

Joshua then challenged the people to make a decision, to make up their minds what they were going to do. "Choose you this day whom you will serve, as for me and my house," he said, "We will serve the Lord." Deeply touched by their leader's devotion and love for God, they all replied, "We choose the Lord! Him we will serve, and His voice we will obey."

We have the same choice today, either to accept Christ, or reject Him. There is no middle ground. We are either for the Lord or against Him in everything we do. Will you today be like Joshua and give your life to the Lord and serve Him all the days of your life?

"Choose you this day whom ye will serve...... but as for me and my house, we will serve the LORD." (Joshua 24:15)

JOSHUA 210

Ruth

The Famine

In a small country town called Bethlehem, there was a man named Elimelech. He lived with his wife Naomi and two sons Mahlon and Chilion. Without warning, in Israel where they lived, a terrible famine swept through the land. The crops had failed and soon there would be no more food and the people were starving.

Have you ever experienced a famine, when things are so bad, that the people are dying because there is no food to eat? Have you ever been to a shop where the shelves are completely empty?

Sometimes we take it for granted that we will always have enough food. Many parts of the world are starving today. We should pray for them, that God will help their crops to grow.

Elimelech however, told Naomi that they were going to move to another country, called Moab. God had told them not to go there because the people in Moab did not worship the true and living God of Israel.

Sometimes in life, things can become a little difficult and we can be tempted to make rash decisions to change things. Sometimes we make changes for the right reason and other times we make changes that are not pleasing to God. Whenever we worry about something, it is often because we do not trust in God enough. Maybe we worry about our friends not liking us or about what we will do after we leave school. Whatever it is, learn to trust the Lord for everything in life, the good things and the bad things.

"Trust in the LORD with all thine heart; and lean not unto thine own understanding." (Proverbs 3:5-6)

Three Men Down

Due to the famine in Israel, Elimelech and Naomi moved to Moab with their two sons. After some time, the boys grew up and got married.

They married two girls called Ruth and Orpah. The girls were from Moab, and so were rather ignorant towards God. All their lives they had worshipped idols and false gods and knew nothing of worshipping the true God of Israel. No doubt this bothered Naomi.

After a short time, Elimelech took ill and died. Naomi was now a widow. To make things even worse, a little while after Elimelech died, both of Naomi's sons died also. Naomi had come to Moab with her husband and two sons, and now they were all gone.

What was Naomi going to do? Her plans had completely fallen apart and she wasn't expecting this. While this was going on, Naomi began to think of her home country and the blessed times she knew when worshipping God there.

Complete sadness filled the home of Naomi, and all three women were weeping over their loved ones. No doubt Naomi had wished they had never left Canaan, the land of promise, where she had lived before. One of the ways Naomi would have comforted Ruth and Orpah, would have been by telling them all about God. She would have told them about how He looks after and cares for His people, especially in times of trouble.

Have you ever been in a sad and difficult situation? Has the Lord really helped you through these times? That is the wonderful thing about knowing God. He is forever with us to help and comfort us.

RUTH 212

Three Big Decisions

Ruth and Orpah loved to hear Naomi telling them all about how God had blessed her people in times past, how the Lord had brought them out of Egypt and established them in Canaan. Then she began to tell them of the promised Messiah, and that through some young woman, the Saviour of the World would one day be born.

The more Naomi talked and thought about the Lord, the more she longed to go back home again. One day she heard how the Lord had again blessed His people. The famine was now over and there was lots of food for everyone.

Finally she made her decision. She spoke to Ruth and Orpah and told them she was going back to Canaan, to her home country. At first they wanted to go with her, as Naomi had been so kind to them.

Naomi explained to them that to come to Israel would mean leaving their comfort, country, parents and friends and most of all, their idols. Orpah decided to stay, as she did not want to give up her way of life. This is the reason many people today do not trust in Christ as their Saviour, because they do not want to give up their old way of life.

Ruth had made up her mind. Even though Naomi was poor and had nothing to offer her, Ruth still wanted to go with her. Naomi had spoken with so much feeling about God that Ruth wanted God in her life more than anything.

Ruth said to Naomi, "Your God will be my God and your people will be my people, and where you go I will go." By these words she was now saying, 'I am a Child of God and I want to live for God.' Ruth was prepared to leave and give up everything for God.

Are you willing to give up an old habit that might hinder you in your walk with God? Ruth was prepared to leave everything for God, even her friends. Maybe you have a friend and they hinder you in your walk with God. Are you willing to let them go and find another who loves God the way you do?

Back home again

Ruth had now started her journey back home with Naomi, her mother-in-law. The choice that Ruth made proved to be the right choice, as we will see later in the story. Sometimes in life we have to make difficult choices. When we put God first, He is pleased with us and will bless us for this.

Ruth and Naomi made the long journey back to Israel and eventually they arrived in her home town of Bethlehem. It was harvest time and all over Bethlehem the reapers were busy gathering in the barley.

When Naomi's family and friends saw her, they were very happy and they inquired about her husband and sons. Broken-hearted, she told them the whole story of what had happened during their ten years apart.

Naomi then changed her name to Mara, which means bitter, whilst Naomi means pleasant. She told them that when she left home ten years earlier, she went away happy and full of joy, and now she felt so empty and sad.

The lesson here is very powerful. When we walk away from God, we become very cold and sad and often bitter. Even when things become difficult in the Christian life, you should never give up. Your friends will tell you they are having so much fun, but when you make friends with people who don't love the Lord and don't live for him, very soon you will become very miserable.

The joy you have when you first get saved is wonderful and very special. It is like a fire that has started in your heart. Don't let the fire go out. Keep burning on for the Lord.

Ruth gets a Job

In Bethlehem it was part of the custom for the reapers to leave some grain lying in the field for the poor people to collect. Most of these poor people were either widows or orphans. The poor would walk behind the reapers and collect whatever they could.

Naomi told Ruth of these customs and she was delighted at the prospect of getting some food for free, and she was happy to go to work. The field that Ruth happened to stop at was owned by a very wealthy man called Boaz.

From a distance, Boaz noticed Ruth and enquired who she was. The other people in the field told him her story. Boaz had heard the story before, but he had never met Ruth. Boaz happened to be related to Naomi. He was very impressed with how hard she worked and how she looked after her mother-in-law.

Boaz then introduced himself to Ruth and told her she could stay in this field as long as she wanted. He told his workers to treat her kindly and be especially kind in leaving her some grain. When Ruth went home to Naomi, she was delighted to hear how Ruth had got on at her first day at work.

Whenever we put the Lord first, He always looks after us and promises to supply our every need. Ruth had trusted in the Lord and now the Lord was providing for her in a wonderful way.

The Bible says "My God shall supply all your need." (Philippians 4v19) It does not say God will supply all our greed, just our need. God will not give us everything that we ask for, but he will give us everything that we need.

RUTH 215

Ruth marries her Boss

Naomi knew the laws of Israel very well. She told Ruth that because her husband had died, it was the duty of her husband's closest relative to marry her, in order to help provide for her. He would then be known as a kinsman redeemer.

Naomi told Ruth that Boaz was a very close relative to her and because Ruth was her daughter-in-law, he was therefore a close relative to Ruth too.

The time now was almost at the end of the harvest. Boaz, along with his servants would stay all night guarding the harvest. Naomi told Ruth to go and lie down beside the feet of Boaz in the field. When Boaz noticed Ruth lying there he was startled. Ruth told him that it was his duty to marry her.

Boaz was all excited as he loved Ruth. "There is only one problem," he said. "There is someone closer to you than me and they must have first choice over you."

The next day at the city gate, Boaz, in front of ten witnesses, met with the man and asked him if he wanted to marry Ruth. However, he said no. As a public act, the man then took off his shoe and threw it away, as a sign that he refused to marry Ruth. This then meant that Boaz was free to marry her. Boaz was to become Ruth's kinsman redeemer.

A very short time later, Ruth was happily married to Boaz. Naomi again was thrilled. She was so happy for Ruth. Isn't this a wonderful love story? The very person who owned the field, was the person who Ruth married. It was just like marrying her boss.

God is so good and continued to look after Ruth in a remarkable way. When we put God first then the Lord will honour us for doing so. By this, He will bless you and show kindness to you and will also reward you in Heaven one day where His children one day will be.

"... them that honour me I will honour..."
(1 Samuel 2:30)

RUTH 216

It gets even better

Ruth was now happily married to Boaz, and Naomi was delighted, because very soon she would become a grandmother. Ruth's baby was called Obed. All the bitterness that Naomi felt before, from the death of her family, was now replaced with the joy of this little boy.

When Obed grew up, he had a son called Jesse. When Jesse grew up he had a son called David; King David, a man after God's own heart. Years later, and even many generations later, we read about another little baby boy born in Bethlehem, that is, Baby Jesus, the Lord Jesus Christ, who was born of David's line.

Isn't it wonderful to think how God was able to bless Ruth so much because she made the right decision to follow him. A woman who was once a heathen, worshiping idols in a far away country, made the decision to follow God, and through doing this, the Lord blessed her greatly.

I wonder what God has planned for your life? Have you made the most important step in your life? Have you decided to follow Jesus? This is more than just a decision. It can mean completely changing your life. Maybe your friends are not Christians? Maybe the books you read, and the films you watch, are not good in God's eyes?

Don't be afraid to do what Ruth did, in order to ensure God's best for your life. It was not easy to follow God at the beginning, but in the end the Lord blessed Ruth more than she could have ever imagined. This could also be the same for you.

The Bible says "And we know that all things work together for good to them that love God, to them who are the called according to his purpose." (Romans 8:28)

RUTH 217

Samuel

Hannah prays for a Son

Hannah was married to Elkanah and every year they would make a journey to Shiloh where they would worship the Lord and make sacrifices. When everyone else was eating and enjoying themselves, Hannah would make her way to the Temple to pray.

More than anything else in the world, Hannah wanted a baby boy. Elkanah had another wife, who would often tease and make fun of Hannah because she had no children. God doesn't like it when we make fun of people; no-one likes to be made fun of.

When Hannah was in the Temple, she prayed to God. When Eli only saw her lips moving and did not hear her speak, Eli, the old priest thought she was drunk and started to tell her off. He realised his mistake when Hannah told him she was praying for a son. Eli was surprised and as Hannah was leaving he wished her well, and said, "May the Lord give you the desire of your heart." She promised God that if He allowed her to have a baby son, she would give Him back to the Lord to be used serving in the Temple.

Hannah had great faith in God. The Lord Jesus tells us, "If ye shall ask any thing in my name, I will do it." (John 14:14) This wonderful story in the Bible has a great ending, because about one year later Hannah had a baby boy and she called him Samuel, which means, 'asked of God.'

Maybe there is something on your mind, or in your HEART today. Be like Hannah; spend some time TALKING TO THE LORD about whatever it is.

Samuel the little Boy

God had heard Hannah's prayer and gave her a baby boy called Samuel. For the next few years Hannah did not make the long journey to Shiloh to worship the Lord.

However, Hannah had promised the Lord, that if she had a son she would give him back to the Lord to serve Him in the Tabernacle. Eli was surprised to see Hannah the day she returned to the Tabernacle. He was delighted when she reminded him of her prayer to the Lord to give her a son. The Lord had answered her prayer.

Every year after that, Hannah visited her son Samuel in the temple. Each year she would make him a new coat as a present. Samuel never complained about where he lived; he was very obedient to Eli and helped out wherever he could. Sometimes we don't like where we live, or the conditions we live in. The Bible tells us to be content with what we have. 1st Timothy 6:6 'godliness with contentment is great gain.'

Samuel was a good boy and very obedient; he honoured and obeyed Eli. God's Word teaches us to respect and obey our parents, as well as those who have authority over us, like our teachers.

When Samuel was living in the Tabernacle, the Bible tells us, 'he did not yet know the Lord'. Even though he was serving the Lord and helping others, he did not yet know the Lord. Do you know the Lord? Was there ever a time in your life when you asked the Lord Jesus into your heart, to save you from your sins? When you do that, you then come to know the Lord.

"For whosoever shall call upon the name of the Lord shall be saved." (Romans 10:13)

SAMUEL 219

God calls Samuel

Every day Samuel would help out in the Tabernacle, by opening the doors every morning, dusting and cleaning. Eli was like a grandfather to him and when Eli asked Samuel to help him, he never complained. Maybe sometimes mum or dad need help around the house; it is always good to be willing to help out where needed and do what you're asked.

One evening after a busy day, it was time for Samuel to go to bed and soon he was fast asleep. While he was sleeping, a voice awoke him, "Samuel, Samuel!" Little Samuel rubbed his eyes, climbed out of bed and ran next door to Eli. Eli was sleeping too. "Eli, Eli, did you call me?" "What's wrong? Who? No, go back to sleep...you were dreaming," Eli replied.

Samuel was sure he had heard a voice calling his name but soon he fell asleep again. Three times he woke up and ran to Eli, sure he had been calling him. The third time Eli realised the voice that was calling Samuel was the voice of God. "The next time you hear the voice say, Speak Lord for thy servant heareth," Eli said. How excited Samuel must have felt as he lay there in bed, waiting for God to call his name.

When God called him that night Samuel gave his heart to the Lord. How about you? Have you ever given your heart to the Lord? Perhaps, just like Samuel, God is calling you. Give your life to God and live for Him. That's why God sent His Son Jesus, to die on the cross to forgive us our sin so that we can come to Him.

God had a message for Samuel to give to Eli that night. The Lord had a wonderful plan for Samuel's life and it all began when he was just a little boy.

SAMUEL 220

1 Samuel 3:11-17

A message for Eli

When the Lord awoke Samuel in the middle of the night, He gave him a message to pass on to Eli the priest. Eli had two sons, Hophni and Phinehas, who were bad. Eli never really scolded them whenever they did wrong, and the Bible says they behaved wickedly. These two men, being the sons of the priest, should have set a good example for all to see. The Word of God tells us, "be sure your sin will find you out." (Numbers 32:23)

A man of God had come to Eli not long before this, telling Eli that God was not very happy with the way his two sons were behaving. Eli tried, but they did not change. When God spoke to Samuel that night, he told Samuel to tell Eli that because of the wickedness of Hophni and Phinehas they would both die on the same day. Also on this day there would no longer be an old man in the house.

The next morning, Samuel was afraid to meet Eli, but Eli called Samuel over to ask what God had said to him, so Samuel told Eli everything. Not long after this, Eli's two sons were fighting in a battle and both of them were killed. When the news was brought to Eli, he was so shocked he fell backwards off the chair he was sitting on, broke his neck and died. Samuel could have told Eli a different message or not all the truth. Always tell the truth no matter the cost.

> God had warned Eli many times. We must not treat sin as a small matter, because God hates it so much. If we are doing something we know is wrong, we must stop doing it immediately. When we tell the Lord we are sorry, He will forgive us.

Living a useful life

The secret of success in Samuel's life was knowing God. Samuel grew up to be a judge of Israel. He was the last of all of Israel's judges as they were replaced by kings. Throughout Samuel's life he sought to follow and obey the Lord, even as a young boy he was obedient. "Samuel grew, and the LORD was with him." (1 Samuel 3:19).

Do you remember when he was called by the Lord as a little boy in the temple? He thought it was Eli. When the voice came, he got up and walked to Eli. There is a lesson in this. When our parents call us, do we yell "What?", or do we stop what we are doing and walk to them to see why they called us? It is good manners to come when you are called and equally bad manners to yell, as if your mother is disturbing your time. How much more important is it to obey the call of God.

God takes note of children who obey their parents and teachers, for the Bible says, "Children, obey your parents in the Lord: for this is right." (Ephesians 6:1)

Your life will only last for a certain length of time; nobody except God knows how long that will be. That is why we should live a useful life before the Lord. Many people miss their opportunity and waste their entire lives living for the pleasures of the world.

A verse to remember "Seeing then that all these things shall be dissolved, what manner of persons ought ye to be in all holy conversation and godliness." (2 Peter 3:11)

The Ark of the Covenant

There was a time when the Israelites and the Philistines were at war and Israel lost four thousand soldiers in this battle. After the battle was over, the leaders of Israel met together to discuss why they had lost the battle and how they could win future battles.

Someone suggested that they take the 'Ark of the Covenant' with them into battle. The Ark of the Covenant was the most sacred piece of furniture in the Tabernacle. It was a wooden box overlaid with gold. The lid of the box, which was called the Mercy Seat, had two large cherubim engraved, whose faces looked down towards the lid.

Inside the Ark were the Ten Commandments, a pot of manna and Aaron's budding rod. The presence of God dwelt above the lid. No-one was allowed to take the Ark of the Covenant away from the Holy of Holies, in the Tabernacle. The Israelites thought that by taking this with them it would bring them victory as they went to battle. This is not the way the Lord intended it to be.

Today we have a direct relationship with God. The Lord Jesus Christ has made this possible, by dying on the cross at Calvary. He has opened up a way to Heaven; a way whereby only through Him we can be saved and brought right into the presence of God. What a joy it is to be a Christian.

As you reflect today, what joys can a Christian enjoy?

SAMUEL

Do you believe in luck?

When the Israelites decided to take the Ark of the Covenant into battle with them, they thought it would be some sort of magic charm that would bring them good luck. They thought if they had the Ark of the Covenant with them they would be all right and they would have victory.

The Ark of the Covenant represented God's presence, but they were now misusing it and were assuming that because it was with them they could do whatever they liked. Some people today believe in luck. They hang images, pictures or medals in their homes or cars for good luck. We must ask the question, is God pleased with that? The answer is no, He most definitely is not. Objects cannot help us and this practice offends God, for He wants us to put our trust in Him.

Whenever we believe in luck we are not trusting in God, who knows all things and is in control of everything. We need to pray to God and ask Him to help us instead of trusting in some sort of superstition. To believe in luck is an offence to God. The Israelites were making another mistake and as you read this chapter in the Bible, you will see that they paid the price for it.

That day Israel not only lost the battle, they lost thirty thousand soldiers at war. Worse than that, the Ark of the Covenant was captured and taken from them. God was showing them that it was no lucky charm.

Do you believe in luck and superstition? God is in control of everything and God knows everything. To believe in luck is like saying, "I don't really believe in God's power."

More bad News

The Children of Israel had just lost one of their greatest battles to the Philistines. Not only had they lost the battle, but Eli's two sons, Hophni and Phinehas, were carrying the Ark of the Covenant when they were killed.

Once the battle was over, a soldier escaped and ran as fast as he could to Eli. Eli was very anxious to hear about his two sons, but he was especially concerned for the Ark of the Covenant.

When Eli heard the bad news about the soldiers, his two sons and the Ark of the Covenant being captured, he was in total shock. Eli was now an old man, blind and very heavy. On hearing the news, he fell backwards off his chair, broke his neck and died.

Eli's daughter-in-law was about to give birth. She was so shocked at the news that she died during childbirth. The baby was called Ichabod, meaning, 'the glory is departed from Israel.' She called him this because the Ark of the Covenant had been taken, and because both her father-in-law and her husband, Phinehas, had died. The whole country was in mourning.

Remember when God spoke to little Samuel? This was the message the Lord brought to Eli through Samuel, and Eli had failed to punish his sons. It was a terrible day for Israel, and especially for Eli, who had failed to discipline his two sons. Sometimes when our parents insist on teaching and training us, they know it is for our own benefit. If we continue going our own way without the discipline of our parents, it can often get us into trouble and we may live to regret it the rest of our lives.

Dagon the fish God

The Philistine army was celebrating its great victory over Israel. Soon the Philistines were chanting about how great their god Dagon, the fish god, was. They thought that their fish god was greater than the God of Israel.

The Ark of the Covenant was placed in the temple of Dagon in Ashdod and when the Israelites heard this they must have felt very sad. Then a most unusual thing happened. The Ark of the Covenant was placed beside Dagon, the fish god, and the next morning when the Philistines came out to worship Dagon, Dagon had fallen over. How embarrassed they must have felt. They quickly set the idol upright again.

The following morning the same thing happened. This time, however, Dagon's head and hands had fallen off and were lying on the floor. The Philistines were shocked to the core. What was happening to their god? Of course Israel understood it, because many times the Bible warns us about false gods.

"I am the LORD: that is my name: and my glory will I not give to another, neither my praise to graven images." (Isaiah 42:8) **and,** *"To whom then will ye liken me, or shall I be equal? saith the Holy One."* (Isaiah 40:25). **We are also commanded in the first commandment not to worship any other gods.**

The Philistines were really concerned. One thing they knew for sure; the Ark of the Covenant belonged to Israel and they better get it back to them as soon as possible. They knew they were provoking the true God and they were on dangerous ground.

Sometimes we can be guilty of doing wrong. When we are aware of it we should put things right before God is forced to deal with our wrong doing.

A job for Cows to do

The Lord was very displeased that the Philistines had stolen the Ark of the Covenant. As a result He caused a great plague to break out in the land. Many people were dying from this deadly disease and the Philistines realised that the Ark of the Covenant had to go back to Israel.

The rulers and wise men of the Philistines came up with an idea. They built a new cart and picked two cows with young calves. These cows had never ploughed or pulled a cart before. Their calves were taken away from them and tied away. The test was if the God of Israel had caused the plague and heartache among the people, the cows would pull the cart straight to Israel without turning back.

On the cart they placed the Ark of the Covenant as well as some gifts. Normally cows with new born calves would turn and run madly to find their young calves. This time, however they walked straight and didn't turn to the right or the left to the amazement of the Philistines. They knew and realised that the true and living God of Israel was in control of even the cows. They were so glad to let the Ark of the Covenant go back to Israel.

In Bible times God had to teach the people many valuable lessons. Can you imagine the amazement of the Israelites when they saw two cows pulling a cart with the Ark of the Covenant in it? God demands our worship. This is one of the reasons He created us; we surely cannot live life without God and without God life is not worth living.

Imagine, if God can use cows to do such a great job, what can He do with humans like you and me?

SAMUEL 227

The big thunderstorm

The Israelites really feared the Philistines. One day they came to Samuel and asked him to help them. Samuel told them that if they were really serious about overcoming their fear of the Philistines then they must turn back to their God.

"You must get rid of all your idols, put away your strange gods, and worship the Lord only. You must repent of all your sins and falling away from the true God of Israel," Samuel told them. "Only then will you be delivered from the Philistines." At once they destroyed all their idols and began to worship God.

Samuel called the whole nation to meet in Mizpeh and together the people poured out their hearts to the Lord. They confessed all their sin before the Lord and the Lord heard them. In the meantime, when the Philistines heard about the big gathering of Israelites in Mizpeh, they thought that they were preparing for war.

As a result, the Philistines prepared for war and started making their way to Israel. Then God sent one of the greatest thunderstorms the Philistines had ever seen. It was so fierce; they fled in horror for they knew that the God of Israel was protecting Israel. They knew that Israel's God controls even the weather. The Lord gave Israel a great victory that day, setting them free from the Philistines. Do you remember when the Lord Jesus stood up and said unto the wind and the waves, "Peace be still?" He is still the same God today.

Isn't it amazing to know the true and living God?

SAMUEL

Do you insist?

As Samuel grew older he appointed his sons to be judges over Israel, but his sons were not like Samuel; they were dishonest and greedy for money. Samuel had made the same mistake as Eli. When his children were growing up he had failed to discipline them in the way he should have.

The leaders of Israel didn't want Samuel's sons to rule over them. They wanted to be like all the other nations and have their own king, but this was not God's plan. The Lord wanted Israel to be different from all the other countries and nations. However, the people insisted that they wanted a king. Samuel was grieved that they wanted an earthly king when they should have been content with a Heavenly King.

Samuel warned the people that when a king ruled over the country, he would make slaves of the people and that all the sons of the people would have to go to war. They would not enjoy the same freedom they presently enjoyed. Samuel told them all this, but they still insisted on having their own king.

Like many today, they were content to have God's second best. By insisting on an earthly king, they no longer wanted God to be king of their lives. Sadly, they would not listen to God's wisdom but preferred to do their own thing. They would have to learn the hard way. God never intended Israel to have any other king than himself, for Israel was God's chosen country and it was to be different. Just like Israel, Christians are to be different from the world. The world should look at Christians and know there is something different about them. They belong to the Lord.

The question is, do we insist on doing our own thing, or are we following in the ways of the Lord? Are we keeping the commandments, do we do what's right and have we the desire to please God with our lives in everything we do?

SAMUEL 229

The lost Donkeys

One day God told Samuel to go the next day to the gate of the city and wait there for a young man, who would stand out from the crowd.

In the meantime, out in the countryside was a young man called Saul. His father had lost all his donkeys and he had sent Saul to find them. Saul had searched everywhere, night and day, for the donkeys. At last, together with his servant, he decided to go the next day into the city to look for the prophet called Samuel. Saul thought he would be able to tell him where the donkeys were.

The Lord had arranged for Saul to look for Samuel and for Samuel to be on the look out for Saul. The next day, Samuel was excited as he stood at the city gate. The young man he was to meet would become the first king of Israel. Then Samuel noticed a handsome young man coming walking towards him. The Bible says, "Saul was without equal among the Israelites."

Can you imagine the surprise Samuel got when Saul asked about the donkeys? Samuel already knew about the donkeys and he told Saul they were safe and would soon be returned to his father. In the meantime, Samuel invited Saul for a big feast because he had some news for him, directly from God.

The Lord can use simple animals like donkeys to get our attention. Saul was obedient to his father while searching for the donkeys. It was while looking for these donkeys that Saul would be told he would be the first king of Israel. By the way, read verse 20 of the above chapter to see what happened to the donkeys.

Donkeys are used and mentioned many times in scripture. If God can use donkeys how much more can He use us?

SAMUEL 230

Israel gets their first King

For the first time in their history, Israel would have a king. After having a meal with Saul and thirty other guests, Samuel took Saul to the side and explained to him that he was to become the first king of Israel.

Saul was completely shocked; he told Samuel that he was a Benjamite, of the smallest tribe of Israel. They were a very poor family and very humble. Taking a small bottle of oil, Samuel asked Saul to get down on his knees, then Samuel poured oil on the head of Saul. This was a sign that he was to become a king. "God has selected you to become king of Israel," Samuel told Saul.

Maybe you think your family is not important or well known in the community. Maybe you think you are the least clever person in your class. Whenever we realise that we are not the most important person in the world, then God takes notice of that. When we become humble in the eyes of the Lord, God says, "Give me your life, because I can do something with it, that you could never do yourself."

The Spirit of the Lord came upon Saul and he was a changed man. Samuel told Saul if he followed the Lord fully, then the Lord would guide and direct him in everything he sought to do, to lead the country. Can you imagine how Saul felt as he made his way home that day?

SAMUEL 231

Do I need God to help me?

One of the greatest lessons we can learn as Christians, is how much we need God in our lives. We need God for absolutely everything.

Saul was enthusiastically chosen by the people and they were delighted with their new king. Saul had so much potential; he was a hard working, energetic young man. Soon after Saul became king he heard news that the Ammonites were preparing for war against one of Israel's cities.

One of the lessons Samuel taught Saul was to seek the Lord's guidance in everything he did. Saul made early mistakes by acting in his own strength. On becoming king, he saw how much everyone looked to him and he soon forgot about God. Saul was to rule under God; it was the Lord who had placed him in position and he should not have forgotten that.

Sometimes in life, everything can be going so well for us that we can easily forget about God. We are not only to look to God in the bad times, but also in the good times. The book of Proverbs tells us to acknowledge God in everything we do. When Saul won his first battle, perhaps he asked the question, "Do I really need the Lord to help me?" We do not read in the Bible that he asked the Lord for help. Saul would soon learn the lesson that he needed the Lord more than God needed him.

> "Trust in the LORD with all thine heart; and lean not unto thine own understanding. In all thy ways acknowledge him, and he shall direct thy paths." (Proverbs 3:5-6)

Do you find it necessary for God to help you in life? By this I mean are you strong enough to live your own life without God or are you honest enough to realise you need God to help you so much?

Having no patience

The prophet Samuel gave instructions to Saul at the beginning of his reign and these instructions were signs that God had chosen him to be king. For example, on his way home one day Samuel told him two men would meet him and tell him they had found his father's donkeys. Also some people would meet him and give him bread. All these things happened. Saul was also told to go to Gilgal and wait there seven days for Samuel. He was not to leave or make any decisions, until Samuel came to him.

The reason Saul had to wait for Samuel was because he was going to offer a sacrifice unto the Lord, before they would go into another battle against the Philistines. Saul's son had already defeated some of the Philistines, but this time the Philistines had an army as thick as the sand on the sea shore.

King Saul was very impatient. He knew he was supposed to wait for Samuel to prepare a sacrifice, but even so he prepared his soldiers and rushed off to war. Instead of trusting in the Lord he went on ahead with his own plans. He had no patience to wait for God to lead him. Samuel was very disappointed because this was a test from God of Saul's patience.

Sometimes God uses simple things in our lives to test our patience. Maybe He has a plan for your life but He cannot use you. He may choose to give your plan to someone else, simply because you have no patience.

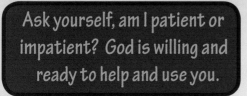

Ask yourself, am I patient or impatient? God is willing and ready to help and use you.

SAMUEL 233

Saul is rebuked

Saul was being taught by Samuel the importance of doing things God's way, especially as he was king of God's chosen people. Saul must look to the Lord to be instructed in how to rule the country, as well as how to prepare for war.

Saul had just failed a major test by not waiting for Samuel to prepare the sacrifice. Samuel explained to Saul that God had planned to use Saul and his descendents to rule over Israel forever. However, Saul must learn to trust the Lord in every area of his life first.

Several years later Saul was put to another test. This time he was told to attack and utterly destroy the wicked, God hating, Amalekites. He was told to destroy all the people and all the animals that belonged to them. The Amalekites had continually rejected God and now it was time for God's judgement to come upon them.

Saul went to war with them and he won the battle easily. God had commanded Saul to destroy everything, but instead Saul spared the king and the best of the animals. When Saul met Samuel he was rebuked for failing to obey the Lord. Saul began to blame the people for keeping the best animals. Samuel sadly told Saul that God had chosen another king, a man after God's own heart, but Saul was so stubborn he didn't care.

Samuel told Saul, "To obey is better than sacrifice, and to hearken than the fat of rams." Giving something of worth to God is fine but God is more interested in our listening and obeying His Word. God wants our total obedience at all times.

People don't care how much we know until they know how much we care.

Saul is rejected by God

By now God had lost patience with Saul. He had been chosen as king, with a great future. All he had to do was to listen and obey the commands of the Lord, but Saul stubbornly and impatiently went his own way and brought disaster on himself.

God gave him chance after chance and still there was no change in him. Samuel rebuked him time after time and still he didn't learn. Now God was preparing another young man to take the throne and his name was called David.

Samuel told Saul that because he had disobeyed the Lord and rejected His Word, then the Lord was rejecting him as king. Samuel mourned for Saul and he never saw him again. He had so much hope for him as he was growing up; now in his adult life, Saul rejected the Lord.

Maybe your parents have great hopes for you. When you grow up will you reject their advice? More importantly, when you get a little bit older will you reject the Lord? No one likes to be rejected. One of the worst imaginable rejections in the whole world is when God rejects a sinner because they have said 'NO' to God for the last time. Friend, I hope this isn't you.

One of the last jobs Samuel had to do was to find David and anoint him as the new king of Israel. As a young boy, Samuel served God in the Tabernacle. He was obedient to God both as a child and as an adult. Throughout Samuel's life, God greatly used and blessed him because he was willing to obey God's commands.

Are you willing to let God use you?

SAMUEL 235

DAVID
A new King is needed

Saul had begun his reign as king of Israel very well, but soon he forgot about God and left God out of all his decisions. Israel was God's special country and the King of Israel must be a man of God. Saul did love the Lord at one time, but now he had drifted far, far away from God. Samuel, the prophet, had told him that because he had neglected the Word of the Lord, the Lord was rejecting him as king of Israel.

Maybe there was a time in your life when you were once close to the Lord. Now everything in your life seems to be going well and you have forgotten about God. Don't make the same mistake that Saul made. Saul forgot about God; he stopped praying to Him, worshipping Him and thought he had made it in life, therefore it was not necessary to keep in touch with the Lord.

Soon Saul was filled with pride, as he thought he had everything this world had to offer. Little did he realise that everything would soon be taken from him and he would become the most miserable man in Israel. The most miserable person in the world is a backslidden Christian. God now needed a new king for Israel, a man of God; a man after God's own heart. Saul must be removed from the throne and replaced with a man of God. The search was on, would there be such a person?

If you were around in those days, would you have made a good candidate as king? What qualities do you think God was looking for in the new king?

The Shepherd Boy

God told Samuel to go to the home of Jesse who was a farmer with eight sons, seven of whom were already grown men. David, the youngest, was still a boy and much younger than his brothers. The prophet Samuel arrived at the home of Jesse and asked to see all his sons. As he looked at them all he thought that any one of these men could be a king, but God said to Samuel, "man looketh on the outward appearance but the Lord looketh on the heart."

Samuel then asked Jesse if he had any more sons, "The youngest is not here, he is out tending to the sheep" Jesse told him. "Bring him to me at once," Samuel requested. Away out in the fields was the young lad called David. He was much smaller and younger than his big brothers. Being a shepherd boy, looking after sheep, does not seem like much of a job. Yet the whole time that David was a shepherd boy, God was preparing him for a mighty task.

Sometimes in life we find ourselves doing things which seem meaningless. Often God will prove us in the little things of life. If we are faithful and try hard in the little things of life then the Lord will open the door to bigger things. David was just a shepherd boy but it was there that he learned to talk to God in prayer and sing to God in praise. That is why he is known as the 'Sweet singer of Israel.'

When David came before Samuel he kneeled down and there Samuel poured oil upon his head. This was a sign that something special was going to happen to him. Can you imagine how David felt when Samuel whispered to him that he was going to be the next king of Israel?

DAVID 237

David fights a Bear and a Lion

While David looked after the sheep, often dangers would come; dangers like snakes in the grass or wild dogs chasing the sheep. David knew his sheep so well, he even knew them by name. Christians are like sheep and the Lord Jesus knows every one of them by name.

One day David noticed that the sheep were frightened. He went closer to see why and couldn't believe his eyes when a big bear seemed to appear from nowhere and attack the sheep. David quickly ran over, jumped on the back of the bear and killed it with his own bare hands. This would be impossible for a boy to do, but God gave David strength to fight the bear.

On another occasion, a lion attacked the sheep and ran off with a little lamb. David ran after the lion, jumped on it and rescued the lamb from the lion's mouth. As the lion turned to attack David, he killed the lion with his own bare hands. Again, the Lord was with David and gave him strength to fight the lion.

The lion reminds us of the devil who loves to attack the sheep, God's people. He will frighten them and even hurt them. The Bible says the devil is like a roaring lion, "Be sober, be vigilant; because your adversary the devil, as a roaring lion, walketh about, seeking whom he may devour." (1 Peter 5:8)

"Submit yourselves therefore to God. Resist the devil, and he will flee from you." (James 4:7) Every time you are tempted to do something wrong, this often comes from the devil. If you keep resisting the devil and don't give in to the temptation then he may leave you alone and start annoying someone else. The secret is not to yield, don't give in to the temptation, whatever it may be.

DAVID 238

1 Samuel 16:14-23

A Musical Talent

While David looked after the sheep he had lots of time on his hands. He could not leave the sheep for fear of them being attacked by animals or stolen, but he still used his time wisely. David was a very skilled harp player and he could spend hours every day playing the harp and singing to the Lord.

He was not doing it to be noticed by others but rather to worship the Lord. Sometimes we can be afraid to sing or play an instrument because we are not good enough, but always remember in everything you do, do it as unto the Lord.

David would sing songs about God's creation, His protection and how God helped him and blessed him. Many of these songs are recorded in the Bible as Psalms. They were real situations for David, real prayers and real songs.

Do you have a musical talent? David loved his music to be about God and wanted to worship him alone. Much of the music in the world is not God gloryifying or God honouring.

Be careful what you listen to and ask yourself, 'does my singing, playing or even listening please God?'

Playing before the King

Saul was the King of Israel and he started off his reign well, but soon he fell away from his love for God and as a result, the spirit of the Lord left him. When this happens to a believer they soon become miserable. Saul became very depressed because God's presence had now gone from him. He couldn't sleep well, even his very countenance changed.

His servants wondered what they could do to help him. Then one of them came up with the idea that someone should play music before the king. Music is very relaxing and maybe it would help the king's mood. It was suggested that David could play for him. Saul did not know David, but God had already anointed him as the next king. Even now as he was coming into the Royal Court, God knew one day it would be David's home as he would soon be the king.

David was brought before the king with his harp and there he played the most beautiful music Saul had ever listened to. The king immediately liked David and requested him to stay longer and play more of this beautiful music before him. Saul was troubled by an evil spirit and every time dark moods came to him, he called for David to play his harp and immediately he was refreshed.

Even though David knew one day he would be king, he was still willing to serve King Saul. He was still willing to tend to his father's sheep. David had a willing, cheerful attitude to life because his trust was in the Lord. Saul, on the other hand, was a selfish, rebellious, depressed king who no longer trusted in the Lord.

Which one would you rather be, an unhappy king without God or a simple shepherd with God?

Goliath the Giant

One day when David was busy out in the fields looking after the sheep, a servant came to him with a message from his father. A war had broken out between the Philistines and Israel. David's older brothers were all soldiers, fighting for Israel, but David was too young to go to war.

David's father Jessie, asked David to go to his brothers to find out how they were getting on in the battle. David immediately began the journey. He took along with him some bread and cheese to give to his brothers. As he got closer to the battle scene, he was surprised to see that no-one was fighting. On one side were the Philistines and on the other side were the Israelites.

While David was talking to his brothers, he heard an almighty roar. As he looked over across the valley there was a huge monster of a man. He stood head and shoulders above the rest; he was a giant of a man. He was challenging one individual from the Israelite army to come and fight him, but everyone was afraid of him.

Maybe there are giant people and giant things in your life that you are afraid of. All the soldiers were afraid of this giant. They failed to put their trust in the Lord to defeat this giant. There are many giant temptations in our lives that we give in to because, in our own strength, we cannot overcome them.

When a giant temptation comes our way do we try to fight it in our own strength, or with the strength the Lord gives us?

David fights Goliath

For forty days now, every morning and evening, Goliath the giant had come out and roared at the Israelites. He insulted and mocked the God of Heaven and David was astonished that no-one would take up the challenge and fight him. His brothers began to get annoyed with David as he continually asked them why no-one was taking up the challenge to fight Goliath.

David then said to them, "Is there not a cause? If none of you are willing to fight Goliath the giant, then I will fight him." David was then taken to King Saul, so that Saul could meet him. Saul was surprised to see David. "You are only a boy," Saul told him. David then told him how the Lord had helped him to kill a lion and a bear. He also told Saul he was sure God would help him to kill Goliath too.

When David tried on Saul's armour he could not carry it, as it was much too heavy. David then began walking towards the giant Goliath. Saul and all his soldiers held their heads in shame as this boy David walked towards the giant. Saul had promised that the man who defeated Goliath would have his daughter in marriage. It had also been agreed that the side that lost the fight would have to serve the winning country.

David stopped at a little brook, picked up five smooth stones and ran with his sling towards Goliath. When Goliath saw the boy coming running towards him, he raged and promised to feed David to the birds. David then shouted to Goliath, "You come to me with your sword and spear but I come to you in the name of the Lord God of hosts and this day I will show you who the Lord God is." With this he put a stone in his sling and fired the stone. The stone went straight into Goliath's forehead, the only small part of Goliath that was unprotected, and he fell down dead. Can you imagine the roar of the Israelite army when they saw Goliath fall?

> God can use the little things in this life to overcome big things.
> Never think you are too small to be used by God.

DAVID 242

David becomes a Hero

David became an instant hero all because of his faith in God. As soon as the giant Goliath fell to the ground, David took his sword, chopped off his head and took it back to King Saul. As soon as the Philistines saw their champion was dead, they fled for their lives.

Goliath had been boasting about what he would do with David, but David boasted about what God would do. What a testimony it was before both these great armies that the Lord God of Israel helped David, because he put his trust in Him. David did not boast about his strength and ability, but rather what God was able to do through him.

David was not afraid of this giant. Humanly speaking, it looked impossible, but we must remember that with God nothing is impossible. We may not have giant people mocking us or wanting to fight us but we can all have giant sins in our lives. We must fight against these every day. Giants such as selfishness, anger, jealousy, temptation, greed, hatred, laziness and disobedience are examples of the sins we all face every day in our lives. We must ask God to help us defeat them before they defeat us.

You may wonder to yourself, if you will ever become a hero. Do you ever think that one day you could become a hero of faith?

Jealousy becomes a problem

King Saul was very impressed with David and invited him to come and live with him in the palace. David was also made captain over the king's army and everyone respected and loved him. David also became best friends with Saul's son, Jonathan. The Bible says that David behaved himself wisely in all his ways. This is good advice for us; to always behave ourselves wisely everywhere we go and in everything we do.

David was obedient to the king. Whatever was asked of him, he did it with all his heart. Then one day the soldiers came home, and together with all the people they began to sing, "Saul has slain his thousands but David his tens of thousands." When Saul heard this singing he began to get really jealous, thinking David was better loved than he was.

In fact he became so jealous, he began to hate David. Jealousy is a terrible sin. Sometimes we can be best friends with someone and overnight we can start to feel jealous of them. This jealousy can eventually lead to hatred in the heart towards that other person. The moment we start to feel jealous towards another person we should immediately stop and ask the Lord to help us overcome this problem. If someone does well in life, instead of being jealous of them, we should be happy for them.

Whenever I start to get jealous of my friends what should I do to overcome it?

244

The King hates David

As the king became more and more jealous of David, things began to get worse. One day while David was in the palace playing his harp, Saul looked at him with envy and hatred in his heart. The more he looked at him the more jealous and angry he became. Everywhere he went the people were singing the praises of David, about what a good soldier he was.

Saul could stick it no longer and as David played his harp to try and comfort Saul, he suddenly grabbed his spear and threw it at David, just narrowly missing him. David soon realised that his life was in danger from the king and that he must be very careful from now on. Saul's hatred for David grew so bad that he wanted David to die. The Lord however was with David and God had great plans for his life. The journey from now on would not be easy but God promised to be with him, to guide and help him.

Saul demoted David and gave him charge over only one thousand soldiers. One day, a battle broke out and David took his soldiers and defeated the enemy. Saul again was jealous of David's victory. Again, when David was playing the harp in the palace Saul hurled his spear at David, narrowly missing him again. David then fled from the palace as he realised his life was in serious danger.

Sometimes in the Christian life, there will be people who hate us and will be jealous of us. The secret is to stay very close to the Lord and always be on your guard.

DAVID 245

1 Samuel 19:1-7

Best friends

David and Jonathan became best friends and they had much in common. Jonathan also knew the Lord. He would naturally be supposed to become the next king, being a prince and a son of Saul. However, he recognised David's calling and was willing to stand aside and let the Lord use David as the next king.

Even though Jonathan pleaded with his father Saul to spare the life of David, it made no difference. Saul's hatred towards David was so bad that he would not settle until David was dead. This is how far his jealousy had come. One sin always leads to another.

David and Jonathan were so close that they made a promise to each other to always remain best friends and that they would look after and protect each other from harm and danger. In life, it is very special to have a friend whom we can trust; a friend who remains with us in the good times and the bad times, through thick and thin. The Lord Jesus is that type of friend. The Bible tells us that to those who love Him, He is closer than a brother.

Do you have a friend whom you would call your best friend?

Why is this person your best friend?

"A friend loveth
at all times."
Proverbs 17:17

DAVID 246

I Samuel 20:23

David runs for his Life

David's life was now in complete turmoil because even though the people loved him, Saul the king hated him. Saul was still the king and the people feared the king. Even though David did everything without fault, he was still hated by the king, simply because the king was jealous of David's success.

Jonathan, the king's son, loved David and they were best friends. One day during an important feast, David was invited to sit beside the king. It was a two day event. This was a test to see if Saul really hated David. Now David was in hiding and during the meal on the second day Saul noticed that David was missing, he was furious. He was so cross he even threw his spear at Jonathan.

Jonathan then went out with his bow and arrow. As he shot the arrow, he said to the young lad helping him, "Run, the arrow is far beyond you." This was a sign to David that his life was in danger from the king and that the king would not rest nor sleep until David was killed. Jonathan then met up with David and explained to him the hatred of his father.

They hugged each other and then David began to run for his life. For many weeks, months and even years he would live like a fugitive in a foreign land. Yet the whole time, God was with him, preparing him to be the greatest king ever; in fact, a man after God's own heart.

In what ways do you think David reminds us of the Lord Jesus?

DAVID 247

Helping those in need

David was now on the run from King Saul because the king realised that David would be king after him. Saul thought that if he killed David this would never happen. David, however, was hiding in the mountains in fear of King Saul. David eventually arrived in Nob, where the tabernacle was.

The high priest Ahimelech was there. When he saw David he recognised him as the brave young man who had killed Goliath. He gave him some bread to eat and presented him with Goliath's sword. David then quickly left. However someone had seen him talking with the high priest; it was Doeg, Saul's chief herdsman.

Even though David was on the run, many people came to him for advice and help. David didn't turn them away, instead he helped them in every way he could. He prayed for them and tried to help them out of their trouble. Even David's own brothers came to him as they feared for their lives as well. Soon David had about six hundred men with him whom he began to train as a small army.

Sometimes we can be so full of self pity, we may become selfish and forget about the needs of others. David wasn't like this; instead he took his sorrow to the Lord and used his energy and strength to help others.

We should always be on the lookout to help others in need who are much less fortunate than ourselves.

Accused in the Wrong

Whenever Doeg, Saul's herdsman reported that he had seen David talking with Ahimelech the high priest, Saul was so furious that he sent for Ahimelech. When Saul questioned him about it, the high priest said he had no idea that there was a problem between the king and David. "He is your son-in-law, as well as the nation's hero," the high priest told Saul, "There is no-one as loyal to the king as David. He plays the harp for you, fights for you and will do anything that you request."

Saul was so angry and jealous of David he could no longer think clearly. He accused the high priest of taking David's side even though the priest was completely innocent. Saul ordered his men to kill all the priests, but the soldiers refused as they knew the priests were God's people. Saul then turned to Doeg who initially told him about David and told him to kill all the priests. Doeg took his dagger and killed all eighty five priests who were present. Then he went out in search for their families to kill them too.

Only Abiathar, one of the sons of Ahimelech, escaped and fled to find David to tell him the horrific news. Can you see how bad things can get whenever we are guilty of spreading rumours that are not always true? The high priest was accused of helping David and the whole time he didn't even realise there was a problem between Saul and David.

> Always check out the facts before gossip and rumours spread as they can really destroy a person's reputation.

Telling Tales

Doeg was Saul's herdsman who was responsible for his herds of animals. When he saw David talking with the high priest, he went to report what he had seen to the king.

As a result of Doeg's meddling, many people lost their lives and King Saul became even more angry with David. Sometimes we see things, or even hear about things, that are none of our business. Whenever this happens we can be guilty of idle talk and gossip.

Telling tales is a terrible thing to do. We may want to tell everybody about everything but always ask yourself the question, "Would I like someone talking about me the way I am talking about them?" Telling tales is not healthy; it pollutes the mind with gossip and unnecessary thoughts. Furthermore, some of the things we are saying may not be true.

It really grieved David when he realised what Doeg had done. Doeg was trying to please himself, and as a result he ended up guilty of murder. When someone starts telling tales to you, don't be afraid to rebuke them by telling them it is wrong to talk about other people the way they are doing. The Lord hates idle gossip; rather tell them to stop telling tales about other people.

Instead of telling tales about someone, try to see the good in them. Telling tales often comes from a jealous spirit in our hearts.

DAVID 250

Praying to God

When Abiathar, the son of the high priest brought the news to David that all the priests had been killed, David was deeply grieved. He thought back to the day when he was talking with the high priest in the tabernacle. Then he realised that the person he had seen in the distance was Doeg, the man who had killed the high priest.

David then promised Abiathar that he would protect him with his life. Abiathar was later to become the new high priest. David knew his life was in even more danger than ever, as there was a manhunt for him. Even though he was the nation's hero, he was the most wanted man in Israel.

David really loved the Lord; he made a practice of praying to Him every day and even now, in the midst of danger, he really prayed to the Lord. He wanted the Lord to guide him in every aspect of his life. Every day he would wake up early and seek the Lord in prayer. God was with David and was protecting him. Many of the Psalms we have in our Bibles are the prayers and songs of David as he was hiding from Saul.

Sometimes we think that because the Lord is with us, life will have no problems. This is not true. The Lord is with His children all the time whether there are problems or not. God will allow problems and difficulties to come into our lives to see how close we are to Him or to test how much we really depend on Him to help us.

DAVID

The hiding Place uncovered

The mountains and hills provided David with numerous hiding places. However some people were able to find out where David was, perhaps told by some of his own men. They then began to think that if they told Saul where David was they might be rewarded.

When Saul found out from them where David was, he immediately went with soldiers to capture him. David, however, was warned of Saul's approach and quickly left the cave where he was hiding. Sometimes in life we can be in a comfort zone. The Lord sometimes needs to take us out of our comfort zone for our own benefit. Never be afraid of change; in the long run it may be for your own good. Sometimes hiding wrong things in our heart is not a good idea. When you know they shouldn't be there ask the Lord to take them away or they may haunt you forever.

Time after time David was unsettled and continued to move. The longer it took Saul to find David the more frustrated and angry he became, but David was wise and the Lord was with him. David came across a city called Keilah which was being attacked by the Philistines. He prayed and the Lord instructed him and his men to attack the Philistines, which they did, victoriously. David and his men then settled into the city of Keilah. Saul soon found out and headed out to meet David. As David prayed for guidance, the Lord instructed him to get out of the city, as even the people of Keilah, whom he helped deliver from the Philistines, would turn against him in fear of the king.

In every situation of life always pray to the Lord for guidance.

Who are the enemies of the Christian? What kind of dangers do God's people face?

"Be sober, be vigilant; because your adversary the devil, as a roaring lion, walketh about, seeking whom he may devour." (1st Peter 5:8)

DAVID 252

Two friends

As David lived in the wilderness and wandered about from place to place, he was always wondering what each new day would bring. One day, however, he got the surprise of his life when his best friend Jonathan came to him. How they embraced each other like two little boys!

This meeting really encouraged David as they had so much to talk about. David was completely confused as to how King Saul, Jonathan's father could hate him so much. Jonathan reassured David that he would be the next king, even though Jonathan was next in line to the throne. He knew David was the man God was preparing to be the next king. Jonathan was a true friend; he was loyal to God and his friend David.

As evening approached, Jonathan and David renewed their trust and friendship with one another. As they said goodbye, they little realised that it was the last time they would see each other. Soon another battle would rage and Jonathan would be killed in the battle.

Sometimes we can hold grudges against each other, especially our family or best friends; this is not a good idea, because life is so short. Make the best of your time with your family, as you don't know how long any of us may be here to enjoy life. Not everyone enjoys a good, long life.

Am I holding a grudge against anyone?

What should I do about it?

DAVID 253

The King's life is spared

As David was hiding in one of his special hide-outs, news soon came to Saul of his whereabouts. David and his men fled for their lives and soon they found a cave in which they thought they could hide from Saul and all his soldiers.

David could not believe his eyes, when they were hiding in the cave, Saul come closer and closer to them. They heard him say to his soldiers, "Keep looking for David while I go into this cave and rest a while." Saul could not see into the cave as it was so dark, but David and all his men could see Saul. Saul then lay down just inside the cave and fell asleep.

"Now is your time to kill him," David's soldiers said. David said, "I will not kill him as he is the Lord's anointed king." David then crept up to where the king was lying and took out his knife. He quietly and carefully cut a piece off Saul's robe and crept back into the darkness of the cave. Saul woke up sometime later and began walking down the mountain, seeing no sign of David.

When he was a good way off, David came out of the cave and shouted, "O, King Saul!" As Saul turned around he could hardly believe his eyes. David then shouted, "King Saul, I could have easily killed you." He held up the piece of Saul's robe which he hadn't noticed being taken. "I have no problem with you King Saul; I love you and respect you as king. Why then do you seek to kill me?"

Saul realised that he was seeking David's life because of his own pride and jealousy. He almost wept with shame as he looked on David. Saul then called his troops and began his journey home. Sometimes we are so full of pride, hatred and jealousy, but when we think about it, there is no real reason for it.

> Sometimes we spend years hating someone and maybe they have no ill feelings towards us at all.

Being Ungrateful

As David and his men continued to live in the mountains, they were able to help many of the farmers and shepherds in the area. One such shepherd was Nabal, who had over six thousand sheep and goats. Often the Philistines and Amalekites would invade the land and steal the animals, and so David's men would protect these shepherds.

During sheep shearing time it was customary for the shepherds to give provisions and special treats to the men who protected their animals from thieves. David waited for Nabal to come to him with meat, wool and other sorts of provisions as he had helped to protect him for months. However there was no sign of Nabal so David eventually sent some of his men to ask where his provisions were. When Nabal met them he just laughed and said, "Who does David think he is, to come to me asking for food and provisions? David is just like a slave that ran away from his master." David and his men were only asking for some food; it was a common request. Most shepherds gladly obliged to such a request, but Nabal was selfish and greedy and he took for granted all that David had done for him.

Sometimes there are people who do so much for us, especially our parents and like Nabal we can be so ungrateful. Have you ever thanked the Lord Jesus Christ for giving His life for you? Have you recognised Him as King of Kings, or are you despising Christ, as Nabal despised David?

Do we ever take the time to say, "Thank you, I appreciate everything you have done and are doing for me?"

MANNERS

The death of a fool

After looking after Nabal's sheep for many months, David was very annoyed by his attitude. He immediately got four hundred of his men together and marched off towards Nabal's house, because of his selfish attitude Nabal was going to die.

Of course what David had planned to do was wrong; he hadn't sought the Lord's will in this matter. In the meantime Abigail, Nabal's wife heard about what David was going to do through one of the shepherds. She knew there was no point in talking to Nabal about what she was going to do, so she quickly gathered together bread, meat, wine and raisins and sent them with the servants to meet David along the way.

When David saw these men with all the food he was surprised. When Abigail met David along the way she bowed down to him and explained who she was, apologising for the folly of her husband, Nabal. She was grateful to David and his men for protecting her animals and David was touched by Abigail's actions. He pulled back his men from attacking her household and then returned to the mountains.

In the meantime, when the news was brought to Nabal about what David was going to do, Nabal was so shocked that the Bible tells us his heart died within him. He took a heart attack and died ten days later. David didn't need to take revenge for God had it taken care of in His own appointed way. This wicked and selfish man died from fear because of his own greed.

Always be willing to share what you have with others. How disappointed God must be to see someone who is selfish, greedy and ungrateful. What do you think God expects of us, in return for all His goodness towards us? Read Psalm 51:16-17

DAVID 256

David gets Married

As we read this great and challenging story of David's life, we find him making another major decision. After the death of Nabal, David began to think about Abigail. He was very impressed with the way she had acted previously. She had courage that David greatly admired.

Without wasting any time, David asked Abigail if she would marry him. Delighted with the proposal, Abigail said, "Yes." Abigail knew nothing about David's future. As far as she knew, he had no wealth, no home and even no certain future, as the king still hated him and sought to take his life. There was something about David that Abigail liked; he was a brave, handsome, young man. She knew he would love, protect and look after her. When a man offers a woman protection, it covers love, care and a multitude of other things. Many people do not recognise the Lord Jesus Christ as King of Kings, but to those who do, He is precious. His protection is all we need. (1st Peter 2:7a)

It is wonderful when God brings two people together like this. Sometimes when we go somewhere we have no idea who we will meet or what will happen. Providence is a wonderful thing, when we can see the whole plan and will of God coming together. When two people fall in love it should always be based upon what a person is and not what a person has. The reason for this is that if a person has something he can lose it at any moment, but when a person has a good character, he can be this person for life.

When mutual attraction is based on a shared love for the Lord Jesus Christ, the foundation of their love is solid and lasting. Riches and good looks are not forever.

Always try to be the person God wants you to be, and not the person others want you to be.

Snoring so loud

King Saul still hated David and wanted to capture him. Saul heard where David was staying and gathered together 3,000 soldiers to help him search for and capture David.

David however heard about this plan and was even more careful about his safety. In fact, Saul came very close to where David was hiding and decided to put up camp for the night. As night time came David was high up in the mountain lying in the grass, watching every move Saul was making.

David very bravely started moving down the mountain towards Saul's camp. As he got closer, he soon noticed where Saul was sleeping and that he had guards all around him. Saul was in a deep sleep and probably no longer conscious of what was going on around him.

God caused the guards to fall into a deep sleep too, so David was able to creep over to where Saul was sleeping and take his spear and water bottle. He could have easily taken his life, but did not. God gave David unusual courage to undertake such a task; David was brave because he knew God was with him.

David then ran up the mountain and yelled back to the king, "Abner the King's chief guard," David shouted, "Why don't you protect your king?" Saul woke up and realised David had come right to his side yet again and could have killed him. David was gracious for he knew God had appointed Saul to be King, so never harmed him.

There may be times when we have opportunity to take revenge on someone who has wronged us, but it is better to be forgiving. Our carnal (fleshly) nature would say, "Go on, get your own back," but the spiritual response is to forgive.

"If thine enemy be hungry, give him bread to eat; and if he be thirsty, give him water to drink: for thou shalt heap coals of fire upon his head, and the LORD shall reward thee." (Proverbs 25:21-22)

DAVID 258

Hide and Seek

For many months and years, David was on the run from King Saul. Because of Saul's jealousy towards David, he sought to kill him. David's life had now become a continual game of hide-and-seek, with Saul trying to find David and David hiding from Saul. Sometimes, while Saul was looking for David, David would creep up upon Saul and really surprise him.

David was a man after God's own heart and the Lord was continually with him. David had lots of problems and troubles in his life as he faced constant danger, but he continually put his trust in the Lord and the Lord delivered him out of all his troubles. Just as David put his trust in the Lord, we must do the same. We need to ask the Lord to save us and then to keep us, protect us and look after us every day.

Sometimes people play hide-and-seek with God, as God continues to seek after them. Very often people hide from God when the Lord wants to find and help them. Often people become afraid of what God will say or do to them. Don't be afraid like these people; He wants to help you. Be brave like David and boldly stand up and say, "Here I am, what do you want to do with me Lord?" Give your life completely to the Lord and stop running and hiding and looking over your shoulder everywhere you go. Rather, seek after God with all your heart.

> "Seek ye the LORD while he may be found, call ye upon him while he is near."
> (Isaiah 55:6)

Is God really real?

David became very discouraged because even though Saul promised to stop trying to capture him and the Lord even assured him that his life would be safe from Saul, David still doubted. Sometimes we can doubt God's Word, our faith can become very weak, and it is often a real challenge for the Christian to take God at His Word.

In fact, David became so afraid, he wondered if God was really real. He even made the decision to go to live with the Philistines, Israel's greatest enemy. The Philistine King Achish, had heard all about David fleeing from King Saul and was sure he was now a traitor. He welcomed David and all his men and gave them a city called Ziklag.

David was now far away from God. Eventually Israel made war with the Philistines and before David realised it, he was in amongst the Philistine army going to war against his own people.

Can you see what happens when your faith becomes weak and you drift far away from God? We can so easily fall into sin and before we know it, we become like the world, even taking part in everything that is against God and His Truth. The whole time David was conscious that he was out of God's will. How terrible he must have felt. He really was on dangerous ground. He must do something quickly.

When we realise we are in the wrong crowd, going the wrong way, we must stop immediately and turn back before it's too late.

An unbelievable Sight

As David marched on towards Israel with the Philistine army he realised he was in great danger. He knew he couldn't fight against his own people and he also knew the Philistines would kill him if they thought he still loved Israel. David really needed God to do something.

Suddenly, the officers in the Philistine army became angry and were not convinced David would fight for them. They went to the king and told him it was the mind of the whole army that David and his men should not fight for them. The king could not persuade them to change their minds so he went to David and told him to return to Ziklag with all his 600 men.

How relieved David must have felt as together they began to make the several days journey home. As they approached their city, in the distance they saw smoke and flames. What a sight met their eyes. Their homes were completely burned to the ground and there was no sign of their wives or children.

The soldiers began to weep for their families, and then things became worse for David. Suddenly his own men turned on him. They blamed David for everything. "Death to David!" they cried. They were so angry, David was sure he was going to die. How sad David was now as he lamented his drifting away from God.
He had completely left God out of all his plans and decisions and now things were becoming worse and worse for him.

What a lesson for us to learn. Always talk to God about your plans and decisions.

1 Samuel 30:7-17

David prays to God

When David's own men talked about stoning him to death he was terrified. He had left Israel when he should have stayed; now his family was gone and his home was burned to the ground and he was going to die.

David began to pray; he had lost everything in the world, but the Bible tells us he encouraged himself in the Lord. God was his only hope; he literally cried to God for help. How he needed the Lord; as David prayed he learned to put his trust in the Lord again, he knew God would help him and deliver him from all his problems. How sorry David was, for running away from God.

David then asked the Lord to guide him whether to pursue after those who had burned his home and taken all the women and children. The Lord answered David and told him to pursue after them. The Lord told him that, if he pursued, all would be recovered. When David spoke to the soldiers, they were convinced God was helping him and spoke no longer of stoning him.

David began to march towards where he thought all the children and women had been taken. He was completely trusting in the Lord to guide him again. This is where the Lord wants us to be in our lives; a place of total surrender and trust to Him. God loves it when we share everything with Him and ask for His help and guidance.

Maybe you are in a place now where you are far away from God. Be like David and earnestly seek the Lord in prayer, bringing your troubles to Him.

The lost Goods returned

As David and his men began searching for their families they walked for several days. 200 of David's men could no longer make the journey as they were now so weak. David advised them to wait, rest and guard what they had.

As the others continued the journey they found a man wounded on the ground. He was an Egyptian and he promised to tell David everything if David would spare his life. Looters had burned Ziglag and taken all the women and children. The man then told David where they were.

The young man took them to where everyone else was. They were in another city and the Amalekites were celebrating their victory. They had taken all of David's animals and the wives and children of his soldiers. Completely unaware of David and his 400 men, they were surprised when David attacked them and took over the city. Only 400 of the Amalekites escaped on camels.

How happy were all the men to have their wives and children back again, how happy too were the other 200 soldiers, who had almost given up. Never give up on what God promises to do for you. David was learning many lessons in life; many times, humanly speaking, everything was going wrong for him, yet God in His own perfect way, was turning out everything for good.

The best lesson of all was that David learned to put his trust in the Lord again. Sometimes when many things seem to go wrong in our lives, the Lord is teaching us to put our trust in Him completely.

The wicked Witch

King Saul was now in a desperate situation, for the Philistines had made camp in the borders of Israel. Saul knew his army was not strong enough to beat them in battle. He also knew he was no longer on speaking terms with God. The high priest had been killed and the prophet Samuel had died. Saul really was afraid.

In Bible times God forbade the practice of Witchcraft. In fact all witches were to be put to death. It is still God's will that Christians should have nothing to do with witches, wizards, horoscopes, fortune tellers, astrology, Ouija boards or any of those things that have anything to do with evil spirits.

Saul was so desperate that he went and found a witch in a small town called Endor. He disguised himself and, in the middle of the night, made a long journey to find the witch. Witches were believed to recall the voices of the dead and speak to them. It is really an evil practice, evil spirits that imitate the dead people.

Saul told the witch that he wanted to talk to the prophet Samuel. This time, God overruled and Samuel not only spoke, but appeared before Saul. The witch screamed in horror as she had never seen anything like it. Samuel then told Saul straight that God had finished with him and that David would rule as the next king. Samuel went on to say that, by the same time the next day Saul and his sons would be with him. Saul collapsed with fear. He realised all his life he had been stubborn, jealous and selfish; he had completely left God out of his life and now his life was about to end.

> Don't waste your life by living it for yourself. Live your life for God. It's only what we do for God that really matters.

David loses his best friend

The day after Saul went to visit the witch of Endor, he got ready for war. The Philistines were ready, more than ever, to fight with Israel. This was a terrible battle for Israel, as the Philistines proved to be much stronger than them.

Disaster struck Saul for he was severely wounded by the enemy. Not only this, but Jonathan and his two brothers were killed in the battle. Saul was so badly wounded that he asked his armour bearer to kill him but he refused to do so; Saul, determined not to be killed by the enemy, then fell upon his own sword and died. How true were the words of the prophet Samuel, when he said the next day Saul and his sons would be with him.

The news that Saul and Jonathan were dead was brought to David by one of the soldiers. David wept for Saul when he heard the news, for he loved the king. How he would have served and fought for the king. He would have even died for King Saul.

David wept even more for Jonathan, his beloved and best friend. How he loved Jonathan as a brother! Much of this friendship was thwarted because of Jonathan's angry and jealous father. David mourned for many days over Jonathan, and then God spoke to him. Israel needed a new king, a man after God's own heart and David was that man.

Choose your friends wisely. When you have a good friend, be kind to them and they will be loyal to you.

God's plan for my Life

Every Christian has a special purpose here in this world. When God enters the life of a person the moment they get saved and trust in the Lord Jesus Christ, something happens. The will of God starts to take effect; God's timing is perfect in every situation. Our plans are not always God's plans and God's plans are not always our plans.

Some people spend their whole lives waiting for God's will to happen in their lives. In reality God's will starts the moment we get saved. The danger is that we can be out of God's will and not even realise it. Always pray that in everything you do, you will be in the centre of God's will.

David was told by Samuel many years before that he would be the next king over all of Israel. This did not happen immediately; it took years before he became king. This did not stop God using him; rather, the Lord continually used David on many occasions in his life.

David waited for God's perfect timing for him to become king. Throughout his life he was learning to be patient; instead of acting on impulse, he would pray and seek the Lord about the matter.

God has a plan for every one of His children; early in life ask the Lord about His plan for you.

David becomes King

King Saul was now dead and Israel had no king. When the men of Judah heard that David had returned to Hebron, a city in the South of Judah, they came and anointed him king of Judah. David reigned over the tribe of Judah for over seven years.

In the meantime, Ishbosheth reigned over all the other tribes of Israel. Abner was the general of King Saul's army and he told Ishbosheth to attack King David and the tribe of Judah so that Ishbosheth would be king of all Israel. When they attacked David's army, David was ready for them and defeated them in battle.

David's men were led by Joab, who was a great commander. One day Abner came to speak to David to make a peace deal. David agreed to talk with him and liked the idea that all Israel should be at peace and not war with each other. Joab didn't trust Abner and on his way back home he attacked and killed him. David was extremely sad at the death of Abner and the whole city of Judah mourned for him.

King Ishbosheth was tragically murdered by his own men and as a result, the elders of Israel came to David and anointed him as king over all of Israel. This was the third time that David was anointed as king. First by the prophet Samuel, then as king of Judah and now as king over all of Israel. God was working in David's life.

Sometimes we don't know the future or where we will be, but we need to see where the Lord has brought us from.

DAVID 267

The Ark of the Covenant is returned

The Ark of the Covenant, also known as the Ark of God, was a part of the Tabernacle furniture. In the Old Testament times it represented the presence of God in the midst of His people. The Ark of the Covenant belonged to Israel, but had been taken many years before by the Philistines.

Such strange things happened to the Philistines when they had it that they were afraid of it and returned it to the land of Israel. David now wanted to return it to Jerusalem, Israel's capital city. God had given specific instructions as to how the Ark was to be transported; it was to be lifted on poles and carried by men.

For some twenty years now, the Ark had been in the home of one of the priests called Abinadab. King David announced to the whole country that the Ark was being returned to Jerusalem. A huge parade was then arranged with 30,000 soldiers, as well as all the people, lining the streets along which the Ark of the Covenant would pass by. This was an exciting time, a very happy time for the King and all the people of Israel.

By desiring to return the Ark of the Covenant to Jerusalem, David was saying "God's presence is important to me." The presence of the Lord was not only important for David, but it was real as well. David's priority in life was pleasing God, more than anything else he wanted to do things right and please God with his life.

Sometimes it is good to step back and have a good look at our priorities, to make sure we are putting the Lord first in all things.

Don't touch the Ark

One of the laws God made about transporting the Ark was that under no circumstance should anyone touch the Ark of the Covenant as it represented the Presence of God. God is a Holy God and we must always remember to have reverence whenever we come into his presence.

As the Ark of the Covenant made its way through the streets of Jerusalem and along the bumpy road, suddenly, something happened. The oxen stumbled on the bumpy road and Uzza, one of Abinadab's sons, immediately reached out with his hand to steady the ark. As he did so Uzza died instantly. Shock waves went through the streets at what had happened.

King David, who was dancing and leaping with joy soon stopped as he learned of the death of Uzza. He then realized that the Ark had not to be pulled by oxen but carried by men. As well as this he realized that because the Ark of the Covenant represented the presence of the Lord, no one could touch the ark as sinful man could not come into direct contact with the Holy God.

Since Jesus died on the cross we can now come directly to God through the Lord Jesus Christ. As a result of His death on the cross and His precious blood, the way to God has now been opened up. David soon learned what the Ark of God truly meant and a new reverence before God was quickly learned by all the people.

A lame little Boy

Jonathan had been David's best friend for many, many years. One day David made a promise to Jonathan that he would show kindness to him and all his family. Jonathan was now dead but David never forgot his promise to his friend.

Jonathan had a son called Mephibosheth and on the day that his father, uncles and grandfather, king Saul, were killed on the battlefield, news was brought to the little boy's nurse. She was so afraid of what might happen to the little boy that she picked him up and began to run with him. As a result, she lost her balance and accidently dropped the little boy so that he broke both his ankle bones. From that day Mephibosheth never walked properly again.

Now, as a grown man, Mephibosheth was crippled in his feet. Mephibosheth lived his life hiding from David. Whenever someone new came to the throne, the new king would often kill off any male relatives of the previous king, in case they would challenge and claim the right to the throne. Mephibosheth therefore, hid from David, but David was looking for him to offer his help.

It is always good practice to look after others especially those less fortunate than ourselves. This little boy was lame from a child; many children today, are sick and unable to do many things in life. Be like David and seek to help such little children. David brought Mephibosheth to the palace and asked him to live with him. He also gave him lots of land and many servants to help him.

Mephibosheth was overcome with emotion when he realised that King David, who had power to destroy him, offered him riches and a place at the king's own table.

Isn't it wonderful how many things in life can turn out for good and much better than we could ever expect. God is so good!

DAVID 270

Proverbs 16:18

Prosperity and Popularity can be dangerous

David was now the king of all Israel. He was a great king and greatly respected by all the people. David had put the Lord first in his life and the Lord was blessing him for that. Every battle and war that he fought was successful; he was greatly respected and admired by other nations.

To be successful and popular is very desirable, and it can be a natural desire for most people. However, if we become too self-confident it can often lead to carelessness. In David's popularity, he began to take his eyes off the Lord and he soon stumbled.

God commanded the men that they should have only one wife, but David disobeyed the Lord and took upon himself many wives. We will see how one sin led to another and how disobeying God eventually broke David's heart so that he was never the same man again.

Sometimes in life we can become successful and popular. If this happens to you, never take your eyes off the Lord. The challenge for the Christian is to remain strong in your beliefs and convictions. The world will want us to be like them but we must never give in to the temptations of the world.

David was a very mighty man. He must have thought he could do anything and get away with it, but he seemed to forget that God was watching him.

With the Christian life comes responsibility. We are responsible for our actions, decisions and in everything we do; we should honour and please the Lord.

Looking at someone wrongly

David was now at the stage in his life when he thought he could relax more. Previously, every time there was a battle, David was with his soldiers. Now, he sent his general, Joab, to lead the battle against the Ammonites. David was at home, while all the soldiers were out fighting. Sometimes when we are idle we can get ourselves into trouble.

In many of the houses in eastern parts of the world they have flat roof tops. In the cool of the evening, it would be normal to go up onto the roof to relax and cool down. From the roof of David's house he could see over a lot of Jerusalem.

One day while he was looking over the city, he noticed one house in particular. On the roof top of this house was a woman who was washing herself. This was probably a normal thing to do, but David began to desire this woman for she was beautiful in his eyes. The Bible calls this lust. He wanted her for his own pleasure. David was married and he knew that this woman was also married, but suddenly he forgot all about his morals and convictions. All he wanted was his own pleasure.

David sent for her, this woman was called Bathsheba. David wanted her in the wrong way, in a lustful way. David spent the night with her and sometime after, it was evident that she was pregnant. Because David looked at this woman lustfully, he ended up sinning and breaking many of God's commandments. David would regret what he had done.

This type of thing unfortunately still happens today. It causes families to break up, children to be distressed and suddenly, stable relationships become very unstable. If you ever get into a situation like David's, look away and run for your life and ask God to help you.

Killed for the Wrong Reason

David was now in a desperate situation. He had committed adultery with Bathsheba who was the wife of one of his best soldiers. Furthermore, if she was found out to be expecting a child and with her husband away in battle, everyone would wonder who the child's father could be. Suspicion might fall on David.

David then arranged for Uriah, Bathsheba's husband, to be at the very front line of the battlefield. Joab, the king's commander was ordered to withdraw his men and leave Uriah to be killed on the battlefield by the enemy. This was a wicked thing that David had done; an innocent man lost his life and was killed for the wrong reason. David even gave the letter of instruction into Uriah's own hands, to give to Joab.

David then arranged for Bathsheba to marry him. No one would ever know what had happened and David would look like a hero, taking a widow as his bride. The whole time this was happening, God was watching from heaven. God sees everything, even the wickedness of our hearts. David tried to cover up his sin, but he couldn't, because God was going to point it out to him. Not only was he guilty of adultery, he was also guilty of murder.

This is how we know we sin; we start to feel uncomfortable because we know we have done wrong. All this began with temptation and David gave in to temptation. Whenever we are tempted to sin, it is important to think of the consequences and run away from the temptation, before it is too late.

DAVID 273

2 Samuel 11:13-23

The Baby dies

David was now married to Bathsheba and all seemed to be going smoothly. Sometime after this, she gave birth to a baby boy. As time went by David never repented of his sin to God. Sometimes the Lord gives us time to do this and if not then He will remind us of what we have done wrong. David thought he had covered up his sin very cleverly.

The Lord sent Nathan the prophet to David. Nathan told David a story about a rich man who had many herds of sheep and cattle. Also in the story there was a poor man who had only one little lamb. He loved the lamb so much that he kept it in his house and treated it like one of his own children. The rich man then wanted to make a feast for a friend and was not willing to kill any of his sheep but rather took the poor man's lamb and killed it.

Nathan waited for David's response, David with anger said, "The person who done this shall surely die and repay the poor man." Nathan looked at David with tears in his eyes and said, "You are this man." The rich man in the story was like David and Uriah was the poor man with the little lamb being his wife Bathsheba.

How terrible David felt. He then began to weep and everything he had done come flooding back to him. The little baby that was born to David soon became ill, David cried day and night for the child. He lay on the floor every night weeping and even stopped eating, but the little child never recovered. News was brought to David that the baby boy had died. This is the punishment that God said David would have to suffer.

David said, "The child shall not return to me but I shall go to him." This is a great source of encouragement that all young children and babies who happen to die will go straight to Heaven to be with the Lord Jesus. For the rest of us who are older and know all about sin, we must ask the Lord to forgive us. He will then save us and make us Christians when we trust in Him with all our hearts.

A rebellious Son

Sometimes when we do wrong and sin, it can affect our lives forever. Even though the Lord forgives us, there are always consequences for our sin. David would continue to have many problems within his own family.

David had a very handsome son called Absalom, who was renowned all over Israel for his beauty. Absalom was not on good speaking terms with his father king David, as years before he had quarrelled with his brother Amnon and killed him. David was so annoyed with Absalom that he refused to speak to him.

Absalom desperately wanted to be back in a loving and speaking relationship with his father but David would not come to him. Absalom then sent a message to Joab, David's commander of the army but Joab refused to come to him. Absalom was so angry and bitter at not getting what he wanted, that he set Joab's barley field on fire. This was a terrible thing to do.

When David heard what Absalom had done he sent for him immediately. He then realised all Absalom was doing was trying to get the attention of his father. This is a natural thing for boys to want. Growing up, it is so important that fathers spend time with their sons; they need it so much.

However, deep within Absalom's heart a seed of bitterness was growing. He became jealous of his father and wanted to become king. Over time, Absalom was gradually persuading people to follow him. Maybe because of what happened between David and Bathsheba, people were losing confidence in their king. Absalom even made a journey to Hebron, to set himself up as a new king of Israel. The people believed in him and many of David's loyal followers joined with Absalom. Would David have to have a battle with his own son? How terrible he must have felt. How he must have thought that all these problems had come because he had given in to temptation?

> Even though God forgives us, sin often leaves scars that will be with us for the rest of our lives. Always think of the consequences.

DAVID 275

On the Run

David was really afraid of what Absalom would do, as he had gathered thousands of people behind him. He had started a major rebellion and now he was ready to fight with his father, David, and take over as king of Israel.

David realised the situation was very serious for most people had deserted him. He told the people they had better prepare to leave Jerusalem or they would be killed. They began to walk bare foot, with ashes on their head, which was a sign of true mourning. It was such a sad procession; some of David's closest friends deserted him to follow after Absalom.

David began to pray and seek God's help in the matter; David was now in a close relationship with God after being so far away from him. What Absalom was doing was wrong and He too would soon learn not to mess with God's elected people. David was the chosen king and Absalom would not take the throne from him, no matter how hard he tried.

David fled to the mountains with all those who were left in Jerusalem. Absalom was preparing for war. David knew he could not win against Absalom's army on his own unless the Lord helped him, so he continued to pray and ask the Lord for wisdom.

In every situation in life it is always good to pray and ask the Lord for wisdom. Even when you face what may seem like an impossible situation in life, always ask the Lord to help you. Sometimes we may feel like we're running away from someone or something. David knew who to turn to in time of need; the Lord was there to help him, He can help you too, no matter what you are going through.

"The LORD is my light and my salvation; whom shall I fear? the LORD is the strength of my life; of whom shall I be afraid?" (Psalm 27:1)

DAVID 276

2 Samuel 17:1-14

Ready for War

One of David's trusted counsellors called Ahithophel, deserted him to go with Absalom. He was a very wise man and when he suggested to Absalom how to attack his father, Absalom was ready for war.

In the meantime David had another counsellor who stayed on his side, called Hushai. David told Hushai to stay in Jerusalem and wait until Absalom arrived. David had already fled Jerusalem with all his soldiers and friends. Now, when Absalom arrived in Jerusalem he found Hushai. He assumed he was also on his side; Absalom then sought advice from both Ahithophel and Hushai.

Ahithophel told Absalom to pursue David as they would be getting tired from walking and would be weak, so could easily be attacked. Hushai advised Absalom not to do so, because at night time David would have gone ahead of the others and would probably be hiding in a cave, as David was an expert in war and he would easily know how Absalom was thinking. Whenever Absalom took Hushai's advice Ahithophel realised he had done wrong in deserting David so he went and hanged himself.

David then was advised to wait behind while Joab, the captain of his army, led the army to fight with Absalom. David pleaded with Joab and all the soldiers to deal kindly with Absalom and try to catch him alive. Both sides were ready for war; many people were going to be killed, all because of a selfish son wanting power and greed.

Many families are broken up because of disagreements, jealousy and many other selfish reasons. Brothers and sisters often fall out with each other, sometimes over a father's inheritance. Absalom was going to learn a painful lesson for his rebellion. Sinful actions will eventually catch up with everyone.

Always make sure God is in every decision and action you take.

DAVID 277

Stuck in a Tree

David's army waited for Absalom's army in the forest and when they met, the battle began. God was with David's army and they easily defeated Absalom's army. Absalom escaped on his mule, but as he was riding away something terrible happened.

Absalom was renowned for his beauty and his long hair. As he was galloping off on his mule to bring his troops together, his hair was flowing behind him in the wind. Suddenly as he rode under the branches of a great oak tree, his hair caught in the branches and he got stuck in the tree. His mule continued running, leaving Absalom hanging by his hair.

One of David's men came across him but would not kill him. When Joab, David's commander came across Absalom, he asked the soldier why he hadn't killed him. The soldier replied that David had told them not to harm his son. Joab didn't care. He saw Absalom as a rebel and with no mercy, took three darts and thrust them into the heart of the trapped prince. Absalom died instantly and was buried under the great oak tree.

All that Absalom desired never came to him and he reaped what he sowed. Many years before he had killed his brother and now he had been killed himself because of a family feud and his own selfish desires. David had now lost 3 sons. Even though he is described as a man after God's own heart he certainly had his own grief and pain. Sometimes we can expect so much of people and forget they have their own personal problems as well. No-one was the winner here, as Absalom lost his life and David lost his son. Quite often in family feuds there are no real winners.

That is why it is best to bring every situation before the Lord in prayer, so that difficulties can be avoided.

David loses his Son

When news was brought to David that Absalom was dead, he went into mourning, as any father would for their son. David was stricken with grief because he knew that through his sin with Bathsheba, all these problems had come into his family. Perhaps his own sin had lost him the respect of his sons.

He cried for his son, and mourned his foolishness: "But the king covered his face, and the king cried with a loud voice, O my son Absalom, O Absalom, my son, my son!" (2 Samuel 19:4)

In the meantime all the soldiers from both camps came back to Jerusalem again and formed one army. David then spoke to all the people. They knew the battle had been foolish as they had been fighting with each other and not uniting to fight against their enemies. David then asked the commander of Absalom's army to be his new general instead of Joab. Joab was a vicious leader and very violent and David knew he had deliberately killed Absalom. By changing leadership David was forgiving those who had risen up against him. Very soon, Israel was united as a country under the leadership of King David.

The story of Absalom's rebellion is one of the saddest stories in the Bible. Throughout these lessons we are continually warned of the consequences of sin. After David's sin with Bathsheba, it is interesting to note that David never personally won any great battles. In fact, in one battle he became so weak he had to be carried off. These battles of Israel were won by others and not David. The great events of David's life all happened before he gave in to temptation.

The Bible teaches how serious sin is against a holy God and how awful it can be to reap the consequences of sin. How we need to ask God for help to be strong and stay close to Him, always resisting the temptation that may lead to tragic consequences.

I Chronicles 28:9-21

Building the Temple

For ten years after the death of Absalom Israel was fairly quiet, without many battles. David had a desire in his heart to rebuild the temple. The temple was a place where they would come together to worship, as well as a place to keep the Ark of the Covenant.

However, God spoke to David and told him that he would not be the one who would build the temple, as he had shed too much blood in his time as a king, instead God wanted his son Solomon to be responsible for building the temple. David was happy with this. He now really loved the Lord and wanted to do what was right in His eyes.

In the meantime David got all the plans together for building the temple. He found all the builders, carpenters, stone masons and all the skilled workmen he could, to help build it. He ordered in all the wood, stones, gold, silver and other material required to undertake such a great task.

Building the temple would be an important task; the temple would be the most important building in Israel and the most important place to be.

This reminds us of church, that it should play an important place in our lives. We should always love going to church and every time we go, try to learn something new about God. The more we learn about the Lord the more we will want to learn.

DAVID 280

David speaks to his Son

After David had gathered together all the materials he needed to build the temple, he called for Solomon. Solomon was another of David's sons who would become the next king of Israel. David told Solomon how the Lord had told him he was not to build the temple but that Solomon was to build it instead.

David explained to Solomon that because he had been a man of war, he was not allowed to build the temple. Solomon would be a man of peace and wisdom, so the Lord wanted him to be responsible for building it instead. David not only charged Solomon to build the temple, but also charged all the leaders of Israel to help him to build the temple.

More importantly, David encouraged Solomon to follow the Lord. The Lord had given the land rest from their enemies, now it was time to be thankful and put the Lord first. Sometimes we can have lots of trouble in our lives and we really need the Lord to help us. There are also times of peace and good health in our lives. These are times when we also need the Lord and should thank Him every day for the many blessings He gives to us.

David realised he would soon die. He urged Solomon, more than anything, to follow the Lord God with all his heart and strength. He wanted Solomon to be a good king over Israel and told him from experience, that if he put the Lord first, then the Lord would be with him, to help and bless him.

> How true this is for us as well. If we continually put the Lord first in our lives then the Lord promises to bless us.

1 Chronicles 29:20-25

Solomon the Wise Man

Solomon was known as the wisest man who ever lived. He took instruction from his father to heart. Sometimes when our parents try to tell us how to live our lives we tend to mumble and complain as if they don't know what they are talking about. The reality is, that just a few years ago, your parents were just the same age as you are, and they know exactly what they are talking about.

Solomon was encouraged by his father not to seek for fame and fortune in this world. King David knew that these were not the important things in life. It was more important to teach the people to keep God's laws, to obey the commandments and to walk with God in daily life.

Sometimes we make the mistake of thinking that worldly possessions, popularity and the pleasures of this world are the important things of life. David was explaining to Solomon that they aren't, that the most important thing in life is finding God, trusting completely in Him and following Him all the days of your life.

In a world that is so full of sin and is constantly changing all around us, what a joy it is to be a part of God's family. God gave Solomon wisdom and he became the wisest man in the whole world. While he was never perfect, he did desire to please the Lord with his life. Solomon was ordained the next King of Israel, after his father David. The people loved David, but were equally happy when his throne passed to his son Solomon.

A Man after God's own Heart

We have now come to the end of David's life and what a journey it has been. Once a little shepherd boy looking after his father's sheep, little did he realise how far life would bring him. David is remembered as one of the greatest kings of Israel; a young boy who defeated the giant Goliath and did many other great things.

However, David is chiefly remembered for the special love God had for him and for how he loved the Lord. God describes him as a man after His own heart; this is a beautiful description. Imagine God describing you as a person after God's own heart!

Many, in fact most of the Psalms were written by David. David was also a singer and a lot of these Psalms were songs that David sang. Others were prayers that he made to God. In the Psalms David was very honest when he talked to the Lord. If he was feeling down, he told the Lord all about it. If he was angry, he talked to God about it. Also, when David sinned, he pleaded for the Lord to forgive him and when he was happy, he rejoiced before the Lord.

The Lord loves an honest person. So many people cover up their feelings instead of being open and honest before the Lord.

Always try to be honest before the Lord and before your friends and family too.

Matthew 1:1 & 20

Jesus the Son of David

Throughout the Old Testament God had promised to send His Son Jesus into this world. He said that he would be born of a woman. Generation after generation came and every time the people wondered when the Saviour would come.

Abraham, Isaac, Jacob and many others, including David, were part of this lineage. God promised that through this line, God would bless the world by sending a Saviour to take away the sins of the world. It was many years after David lived that Jesus was born into David's ancestral family.

Jesus, the Son of David, later died on a cross to save us from our sins. He rose again from the dead. He then went back to Heaven and one day He is coming back to earth to take all His children home to Heaven. Jesus is called "the Son of David" because His earthly mother Mary, and step-father Joseph were descendants of David's family. He was born in Bethlehem, the city of David.

When Jesus was crucified it was written "The King of the Jews", but Jesus is in fact the King of the whole world. He is the King of my life. One day the whole world will bow down before His face. At the name of Jesus, every knee shall bow and every tongue will confess that Jesus Christ is Lord.

Have you ever confessed your need as a sinner before Him? Jesus specialises in the salvation of sinners. David sought to follow God in his life, because he knew God. We too, can know God by trusting in His Son Jesus and believing completely in Him and everything He has done for us. What a joy to be a Christian, a child of the living Lord God and King.

ELIJAH
A wicked King called Ahab

The Old Testament in the Bible is full of stories about kings. In God's eyes, they were either good kings or bad kings. Today we are going to start learning about the life of another of God's servants. His name is Elijah. He lived at a time when the king was called Ahab and his wife was called Jezebel.

The Bible says that Ahab did more to provoke the Lord God of Israel to anger, than all the kings that were before him. God had forbidden the people of Israel to marry idol worshippers. It was a lesson from God that those who worship God should marry people who also worship God. Ahab fell in love with and married a woman called Jezebel. She did not worship God.

Jezebel was a beautiful queen who greatly influenced Ahab. Due to her influence he commanded the people to stop worshipping God and start worshipping a false god called Baal.

Sometimes we can be easily influenced by our friends, maybe because they are handsome or beautiful looking. We believe what they say and are afraid to challenge them. Jezebel was very beautiful and she almost destroyed Ahab's life because of her influence.

Was there ever a time when you were afraid to speak up when you knew something was wrong?

ELIJAH 285

Making God angry

Many times in the Bible, people did things that made God angry. King Ahab's wife, Jezebel, persuaded Ahab to build temples in Israel where the people would worship a stone god called Baal. This idol worship was very sinful and Ahab knew that God had forbidden it.

God loved Israel and the people of Israel. More than anything the Lord wanted His people to love and follow Him. When they started to wander away from Him, He was very concerned. When they turned from Him completely and worshipped false gods, then the Lord became angry.

Jezebel used her own money to spread this false religion of idol worship. She hired 450 prophets of Baal, the pagan idol of stone. Ahab and Jezebel made the worship of Baal so popular that almost the whole country turned from worshipping the living God to worshipping the false god, called Baal. Out of all the whole country only 7,000 people remained faithful to the true God of Heaven.

Things became so bad that Jezebel declared that anyone who refused to worship Baal would be killed. As God looked down from Heaven He was very angry with what was going on. Something needed to be done to bring these people to their senses. God would use a man, a follower of His, to deliver a message to this wicked king and queen.

Is there ever anything I have done to make God angry? Am I putting any other thing in my life before God?

ELIJAH 286

Just an ordinary Person

Throughout history, God raised up many prophets who were men of God. Their job was to speak God's words to the people. When the people would sin or wander away from God then the prophet would warn the people of God's judgement that would come upon them.

Elijah was one of the 7,000 Israelites who refused to bow to the false god Baal. Elijah was a fearless prophet who loved God with all his heart. His name means 'Jehovah is my strength.' He was a rough outdoors man from a little mountain village called Gilead.

Elijah was not a wealthy man. His family was not important in the village and he had no education. However, Elijah's hope, assurance and strength were in the God of Heaven. Elijah was grieved when the announcement came that the people were told to worship Baal, the false god.

When the people worshipped Baal there were many terrible things that came with it, for example the performance of ceremonies which included the killing of children and little babies.

Elijah was just an ordinary man who loved God. The Lord was going to use Elijah to speak to the wicked king Ahab who was sinning greatly and needed to be warned about it. Whenever someone sins and makes God angry, we should tell them how much it hurts God.

God uses ordinary people to do extraordinary things.

ELIJAH 287

A strange Prayer

The king had demanded all the people to turn from worshipping God and instead worship Baal, the false god of stone. Elijah was a prophet of God who realised something had to be done about this new law.

A Christian's greatest weapon is prayer. The Bible says, "The prayer of a righteous man availeth much." (James 5:17)

Elijah began to pray that it would stop raining, not just for a few days or months, but for three and a half years.

Elijah knew that since God created the whole world and everything in it, He could control even the very weather all around. In the New Testament, Jesus stood up on a boat and said to the wind and the waves, "Peace be still." (Mark 4:39) Immediately, in the midst of the storm, the wind and the waves became still.

Elijah believed in the power of prayer. He knew that God not only hears but answers prayer and he wanted the people to come to their senses. They had completely forgotten about God and put Him out of their lives. They relied on the rain to water the crops. Without the rain disaster would come to the whole country, so Elijah began to pray and the Lord heard his prayer. Why did Elijah pray for it not to rain? To prove God is faithful to His Word (Deuteronomy 11:16-17).

Is there anything I have ever prayed for, that sounded strange?

ELIJAH 288

No rain for three and a half years

After Elijah had prayed for the rain to stop, he boldly went before King Ahab and declared that it would not rain for three and a half years. King Ahab and Queen Jezebel were sitting on their thrones. Elijah looked at them both straight in the face and told them that as long as the Lord God of Israel lives, there would be no more rain or morning dew for a long time.

Elijah was not afraid of the king or of what might happen to him. He loved the Lord and the Lord was offended by the king's command to stop worshipping God. Both the king, queen and everyone there laughed and mocked at Elijah. They thought he was a mad man who had lost his mind, as Elijah was dressed in ragged old camel skins, telling the king the latest weather forecast. It always rained and who was Elijah to tell them it would stop raining?

Elijah's prayers were answered. Suddenly it stopped raining for days, then weeks. Months passed by and still it did not rain. Animals began to die, crops began to fail and Ahab began to get concerned. Then he remembered the ragged man who told him it would stop raining. A man hunt commenced for Elijah. Ahab wanted him dead or alive.

Would I be bold enough to tell someone that I had prayed against something wrong that they were doing?

ELIJAH 289

On the Run

After Elijah appeared before the king and boldly told him that it would not rain, God told him that he needed to go into hiding. "Get thee hence, and turn thee eastward, and hide thyself by the brook Cherith." These are the words the Lord used to instruct Elijah.

The king became so angry with Elijah that he sent soldiers to look for him, not only in Israel, but throughout all the surrounding countries. He was in great danger, but God promises to look after His people and He would look after Elijah. The people were also angry with Elijah because they were hungry due to the lack of rain. Elijah stood up for God and it made him very unpopular.

Often whenever you take a stand for the Lord, you will not always be popular. People will talk about you, accuse you of many different things, ignore you and make life difficult for you. Always remember that the Lord is with you and will bless you for taking a stand for Him.

Elijah was on the run, but God told him where to go. His life was totally in God's hands and he was awaiting instructions as to what to do next. This is the way God wants us to live, by totally placing our lives in His hands, in His tender loving care.

Has anyone ever laughed at or mocked you for being a Christian?

ELIJAH 290

A perfect hiding Place

God told Elijah to run for his life as the king and all the soldiers would be looking for him. The place where he went to hide was not in a house, a farm, or a forest. Rather it was by a little brook called Cherith. There was plenty of fresh water to drink and there were trees to offer shelter from the sun.

This was to become Elijah's home for the next two years. You might think that it was a very lonely place to be. It probably was, but Elijah was not alone because God was with him. His life was in danger, but by the brook Cherith he was safe and in the centre of God's will. This is where God told Elijah to go; this is where God wanted Elijah to stay.

Every day blackbirds called ravens flew by and brought food for Elijah. Ravens are scavenger birds, they don't even care for their young, yet God ordered the ravens to bring food to Elijah every day. This was easy for God to do as nothing is too hard for the Lord. The God who created the ravens can easily tell them what to do.

Elijah just had to wait by the brook until the Lord told him to go somewhere else. This is a wonderful lesson for us to learn; to be content where we are and to wait until God tells us to move on. The challenge for all of us is to be obedient to God's will for our lives.

Am I content with what I have and where I live?

ELIJAH 291

No more Water

Elijah had now been at the brook Cherith for almost two years. One day he noticed the water was not flowing as fast as it used to. As the days went by there was less and less water flowing along the brook. Elijah began to be concerned. So far there was plenty of water in the brook and now it had almost dried up.

Elijah had to be patient every day. He had to wait until God gave him further instructions as to what to do and where to go next. Often God's children need to learn the vital lesson of patience. God has a perfect plan for us but sometimes we become impatient. We often speak too soon or move too quickly. That's why it's so important to learn the secret of waiting on God.

Suddenly, one morning Elijah noticed the brook had dried up, and then God spoke and told him it was time to move on. Not really knowing where he was going next, Elijah was ready to obey God because God was leading him and telling him where He wanted him to go. As he watched the brook dry up he did not know what was going to happen but still he trusted God.

When was the last time I felt God making it clear to me, that He wanted me to go somewhere, say something or do something for Him?

ELIJAH 292

Time to move on

Elijah had been by the brook for two full years. The moment it dried up, God spoke to Elijah and told him to go to Zarephath. The Lord said to Elijah that when he got to Zarephath there would be a widow woman waiting for him, to help him and feed him.

The interesting thing to note is that Zarephath was the home town of Queen Jezebel. This would have been the last place Elijah would want to go to. Here they worshipped the false god, Baal. The widow woman was probably the poorest person in the whole town and she would have no-one to protect her.

Elijah was to go to this most unexpected place and to be looked after by the most unexpected person. This was God's plan for his life; he didn't doubt God; he was happy to go where God wanted him to be. Sometimes in life we have to go places we don't want to go. Maybe we have to move house or go somewhere that doesn't please us. God has a wonderful plan and quite often we cannot see why God is leading us in this way, but God's ways are not our ways.

Has there ever been a time in your life when you had to go somewhere and you didn't really want to go? However, when you got there it wasn't as bad as you first thought.

Helped by a Widow

As Elijah made his way to Zarephath he noticed the effect of the drought. All around him the crops had failed. The ground was dry, weathered and barren. Dead animals were lying on the ground as they had died of starvation.

God told Elijah a widow would look after him. No doubt there would have been many widows in Zarephath so he might have wondered how he could find her. Elijah continually looked to the Lord as he knew God would guide him and look after him.

When Elijah got closer to Zarephath, he noticed a widow picking up sticks. He asked her for a drink of water. While she was going to get water for Elijah he asked her for something to eat as well. The widow, who lived with her young son, told Elijah that she had only enough oil and flour to bake one more cake. "After that," she said, "we will starve to death." Elijah told her to go ahead and bake the cake first for him. He then said because she was willing, that the flour in the barrel and oil in the jar would never run out. Can you imagine how she felt the next morning as she went over to look in the barrel and the jar? Would there be any more oil or any more flour?

Elijah may have sounded greedy and selfish but God was doing a miracle through him. He was showing His power to the widow woman. It was a lesson for the woman to put God first in her life and plans. It also showed Elijah that God is able to provide for His people in the most unlikely ways. Through Elijah, it was the Lord who would not let the flour or oil run out (1 Kings 17:14).

Do you know any widows you can help?

Endless supply of oil and flour

The next morning the widow woman would have gotten up early. The day before she had used up the last of the flour and oil, she was so poor she couldn't afford any more food. With the drought in the land, things were desperate.

Then she remembered the words of the prophet Elijah. He told her that her oil and flour would never run out. That would be impossible because yesterday she had used the last of both. Can you imagine how she felt as she lifted the lid of the flour pot and noticed some flour in the bottom, just enough for another cake? Then as she looked at the oil she noticed there was also some in the bottom of it. Elijah was right: both of them never ran out! They may have run low but they never ran out.

Every time she made bread there was always enough for Elijah, herself and her son. This was a miracle happening every day. Elijah then stayed with the widow woman. Here in her house she would make his meals while Elijah would wait on God to see what to do and where to go next.

The oil and the flour remind me of God's Word. In it there is an endless supply of spiritual food for us. God wants to feed us everyday from His Word. Have you taken time to feed upon His Word today by reading something from the Bible?

Death of a little Boy

No doubt the widow woman was extremely glad that Elijah passed her way. Before, she was about to starve to death, then Elijah came and caused the miracle of baking continuous bread to happen. Elijah would have taken the opportunity to tell her about God. She knew Elijah worshipped God because she said at the beginning when she met him, "as the Lord your God liveth."

Do our friends ever notice anything different about us?
Would they come to you and ask you to pray for them
because you know God in a personal way?

The widow woman knew about God but didn't know Him personally. The Lord permitted something to happen. One day her little boy became sick, in fact he was so ill and weak that he died. The widow woman became so frantic she began to scream and blame Elijah for the death of her son.

She blamed Elijah for all her trouble and for exposing her as a sinner. Before anyone gets saved they must realize and believe that they are sinners before God. God has a plan and a purpose in all of the happenings and events in our lives. Nothing happens by accident. God was working in the widow's heart through the death of her son.

Has anything ever
happened in your life
that brought you closer
to God?

Elijah prays for the little Boy

The widow's little boy had died and the mother was frantic. She cried in desperation for Elijah to do something. Elijah asked her to give him her son. She would have found it difficult to let go of her dead son but Elijah took him in his arms and carried the boy upstairs.

Elijah laid the boy on his bed and began to pray that the Lord would give his life back to him. Elijah then stretched himself over the boy and prayed earnestly that the Lord would restore the boy's life to him. Then Elijah sat up. The boy was cold, still dead and lying motionless. Elijah then stretched himself over the boy a second time. Still nothing happened. Then the third time Elijah stretched himself over the body of the boy, he cried unto God to have mercy upon the boy's life and to give it back to him.

Suddenly, after the third time, the little boy opened his eyes and began to blink. His body became warm again and he was alive. Can you imagine how his mother felt when she saw her little boy running to her again? How happy she was to see her little boy again. God not only gave her an endless supply of oil and flour, he brought her little boy back to life. Then she began to think. Elijah's faith is real. His God is real.

Little children can and do die. Do I know any sick children I can pray for today?

The Boy's Mother believes

When the widow woman took the little boy into her arms she spoke to Elijah. "Now I know you are a man of God and that the things you say about the Lord are true." The woman now believed with all her heart in Elijah's God. The Lord had caused the calamity to come upon her to bring her to her senses and most of all to bring her to Himself.

When the Lord sent Elijah to Zarephath He was not only planning to provide for the woman and Elijah but ultimately to save her from her sins. God knew what Elijah needed. He also knew what the widow needed and He supplied for the both of them.

So it is with us, either we know God personally or we only know about him. It is good to learn about God and what the Bible teaches us about Him. It is infinitely better to know the Lord, to believe in Him and to completely put our trust in Him. Just as the widow believed and put her trust in God, we can do the same. Maybe you have already done this. If not, you can do it today.

Put your trust in Him completely to take care of all your needs.

Angry King Ahab searches for grass

In the meantime while Elijah was living in Zarephath, King Ahab was furious. His whole world was falling down around him. It hadn't rained for over three years and the country was desperate for rain. God then spoke to Elijah and told him that He wanted him to return to Samaria and take a message to the king.

It hadn't rained now for three and a half years. Elijah had to go and tell Ahab it was going to rain again. Elijah knew that Ahab hated him and wanted to kill him but he wasn't afraid to go to Ahab, just like when he went three years ago.

In the meantime King Ahab was out searching for grass with his servant Obadiah. Obadiah was a true servant of the Lord. Both of them were out looking for grass to feed the king's horses. King Ahab had many horses that he would use in battle and for riding. Ahab seemed to be more concerned for his horses than he was for his people.

Then Ahab and Obadiah split up and went in two different directions to look for grass for the horses. Elijah was still looking for King Ahab to deliver the message from God. Can you imagine how Ahab felt when he saw Elijah walking towards him?

What are the priorities in our life? Is it people or things?

Elijah meets up with the King

Imagine, it hadn't rained now for three and a half years. The country was in complete drought. Elijah was on a mission to find King Ahab to tell him it was going to rain. While Elijah was walking up the road, he met Obadiah. Obadiah couldn't believe his eyes. King Ahab had searched the whole country for Elijah and all the surrounding countries as well. It was God who hid Elijah, first by the brook Cherith and then in the widow's house in Zarephath.

When Elijah met up with the king, Ahab was furious and accused Elijah of bringing on the famine. Elijah quickly replied and told Ahab he was to blame for the famine. Elijah reminded Ahab that in turning away from God and turning the people away from God he had stopped the rain. He had turned the people away from God to worship Baal, the false god of stone. They continued to blame each other for the drought.

Finally Elijah told the king he would prove to him who the true God of Israel was. He told the king to bring the 450 prophets of Baal to Mount Carmel. Here he would prove who the true God really was.

Quite often people blame God for everything, especially when things go wrong. Sometimes when we follow God and live for Him everything seems to go well. There are times in our lives when we maybe forget about God. Sometimes the Lord will allow things to happen in our lives to bring us back to himself.

Was there ever a time when I seemed to be far away from God?

The Challenge

This is probably one of the greatest challenges in the entire Bible. King Ahab brought 450 false prophets to Mount Carmel. Elijah then spoke to all the people. He said that he was going to prove that the Lord God of Heaven was the only true and living God. The challenge was to see whose God could light the fire to burn the sacrifice on an altar.

Elijah must have felt very lonely; only Obadiah was with him. However, Elijah was confident that the Lord was with him and God would prove to all the people that He was the true God of Israel.

Elijah brought two bullocks (young bulls) to be sacrificed. The false prophets built their altar and placed one of the bullocks on it. Elijah built his altar with 12 stones, one for every tribe of the sons of Jacob. To the people it would seem impossible to light but all things are possible to God. This would show His power and that He was the real God.

The challenge was now on. The prophets who followed Baal would pray to him and ask Baal to light their fire. Then Elijah would have a go. He would pray to God and ask Him to light the fire.

God doesn't need to do things like this today to prove who He is. We have the Bible to teach us all about the Lord and all the wonderful things He has done. Elijah's God is exactly the same today as He was then. Just as He helped, cared for, used and blessed Elijah, He can do the same for us.

Have you ever challenged someone to believe in God?

ELIJAH 301

Can false gods hear?

The challenge was now on. There were two sacrifices. The one that would light the fire would be the true God. The first to try were the 450 false prophets of Baal. They began to shout and scream to Baal to light their fire.

Hours passed by and they yelled louder and louder. They even began to cut themselves thinking that their pain and the sight of their blood would get the attention of Baal.

Baal was a false god made of stone. False gods have eyes but cannot see. They have ears but they cannot hear. They have mouths but cannot speak. The prophets of Baal were praying to a god of stone. Elijah began to tell them to shout louder, mocking them, to show them how ridiculous they were.

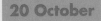

Finally after many hours of dancing around and screaming and shouting they gave up. Now it was Elijah's turn. The false god, Baal, could not light the fire for the sacrifice. The question was could the God of Heaven light the fire? Elijah gathered the people together and told them that they were about to witness the God of Heaven show His power. This would prove to Ahab and all the false prophets that the God of Heaven was the true God of Israel; Elijah's God.

Sometimes we can make gods and idols of things and people. When we think more of them than God in Heaven then they become idols.

ELIJAH 302

Time to Pray

It was now Elijah's turn to call upon his God to light the fire. Before Elijah did so he told the people to bring four barrels of water and pour it on the sacrifice. He then dug out a trench to hold all the water. They then brought another four barrels of water and completely drenched the bullock. It was soaking wet. Then to everyone's surprise, Elijah told them to bring another four barrels of water and pour it on the sacrifice. This made the sacrifice completely wet, making it impossible to light.

Then Elijah told all the people, "Today you will see who the true God of Israel is." Elijah did not begin to yell and shout, nor did he cut himself. Rather he began to pray and talk to the Lord, he wanted the people to turn back to the Lord and wanted to show them just as the Lord could stop the rain, He could send the fire.

Elijah took time to pray, realizing that nothing could be accomplished without prayer. Then Elijah looked up to Heaven and said, "Lord send the fire." Elijah was so confident that God would answer his prayer. Whenever we pray we must pray believing that God will answer our prayers.

Is there something I prayed for and God answered my prayer?

Lord, send the Fire

Elijah had just finished praying. Everyone stood in silence. Elijah then cried, "Lord send the fire." Suddenly the sacrifice seemed to explode with fire. The stones burned and the flames even licked up the water. The wood and the sacrifice were immediately burned with the power of the fire.

As the people stood in complete amazement, they began to say, "The Lord, He is God, The Lord, He is God." The people of Israel immediately repented of their sins. That day they fled from following the false god Baal and began to worship the true God of Israel again. They turned their hearts back to God.

In the meantime all the 450 false prophets of Baal were destroyed by a sword. These were wicked men who killed children and committed terrible sins. There on Mount Carmel they were destroyed. The Israelites turned back to following God; it was a great day for Elijah.

King Ahab was not disturbed about his sin. No doubt, he was impressed with how the fire came down from Heaven, but he did not turn from his sin. Elijah then spoke to the Lord and the Lord told him it was going to rain. After three and a half years it was going to rain.

Some people hate God so much they too one day will die without God. Do you pray for your unbelieving friends and family?

ELIJAH 304

The Rain is coming

What a day it had been for Elijah. He had just witnessed again a mighty act of God's power before all the people. Fire from Heaven had just come down and burned the sacrifice.

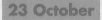

Elijah then began to pray. He prayed specifically for rain to come. It hadn't rained for three and a half years. After he prayed, he sent his servant to the top of a mountain to see if there was any sign of any clouds in the sky.

There was nothing but a clear blue sky. Elijah kept praying that God would send rain. Seven times Elijah sent his servant up to the mountain top to check and see if there was any rain coming. When the servant went to check for the seventh time he noticed in the distance a very small cloud about the size of a man's hand.

Elijah then sent a message to Ahab and told him to go home quickly otherwise he would get caught up with the torrential rain. Ahab had witnessed God working through Elijah so much, first with the stopping of the rain, then with the fire from Heaven and now when Elijah said it was going to rain; he believed him.

Sometimes God answers our prayers immediately, other times we have to pray many times for something to happen. If God answered our prayers the very minute we prayed then we might become proud and think we can order God around. His ways are not our ways.

Is there something I have prayed for that God has answered?

ELIJAH 305

The Man who ran faster than a Horse

God had answered Elijah's prayer, as once the little cloud appeared it began to grow bigger and bigger. The winds picked up and soon there was a sound; the sound of abundance of rain. What a feeling it was when the rain started to fall after three and a half years.

King Ahab was on his way back home to Jezreel to his winter home. He was going full speed ahead in his horse and chariot. Suddenly, as Ahab was riding his chariot the most unbelievable sight appeared before him. There was Elijah running at full speed. He overtook Ahab and ran faster and faster. The journey back to the palace was seventeen miles. Elijah was running faster than the horses. This was a miracle and the sight must have been amazing! He kept running and beat the horses back to Ahab's home.

Elijah was often alone when he was fighting the Lord's battles. Again and again the Lord was helping him. Even when he was hated and despised and when his life was in constant danger, he didn't seem to care what people thought about him. He loved the Lord and he wanted the people to follow Him too. Even today God wants us to be strong in our Christian faith, to be courageous and to trust completely in the Lord concerning every aspect of our lives.

How fast can you run? More importantly how fast can we run for the Lord?

25 October

1 Kings 19:1-2

Threatened to be Killed

When Ahab returned to his home, Queen Jezebel was anxiously waiting for news as to what happened on Mount Carmel. She assumed that her 450 prophets called upon the false god Baal and proved Elijah's God wrong.

How shocked and angry she was when she heard the truth about what happened; first of all to learn that Elijah was still alive and was present at Mount Carmel and secondly to learn that all her prophets had been killed, she must have been furious. When she heard that Baal could not light the fire she was embarrassed and when she heard about how Elijah's God sent the fire she was livid.

Right away she undermined the king and with full authority she sent a message to Elijah. Her messenger was to take a message which was a promise to Elijah. Jezebel told Elijah that because of everything that happened he would be killed before the same time the next day. Within 24 hours he was to die; this was how much Jezebel hated Elijah, this was the promise.

Sometimes everything can be going well for us. God can really use us to do great things for Him. We can be on fire for the Lord and really know His blessing upon our lives. However, suddenly everything can change. The devil can really attack and discourage us. Elijah had two choices. He either faced Jezebel and challenged her promise or else he would run for his life.

Has there ever been a time when someone hated you?

Running Scared

After Jezebel had threatened Elijah's life and told him he was going to be killed, Elijah began to run for his life. He took his servant with him and they fled. They ran and ran. In fact they ran for more than 100 miles. Elijah wanted to get as far away from Jezebel as he possibly could.

This part of Elijah's life is very sad. The powerful mighty man of God was now on the run from a wicked woman. God had used Elijah to speak boldly to Ahab telling him the rain would stop. The Lord then looked after and fed Elijah for three and a half years. God had shown His power on Mount Carmel when He sent the fire. Elijah had faith and had prayed for the rain and was given the strength to run faster than a horse.

This man of God was now running for his life like a coward. When the Israelites needed him he was running away. After running 100 miles with his servant, Elijah left him and continued many more miles alone into the desert to get as far away from Jezebel as he could.

Sometimes we can look at our circumstances and be so concerned and even afraid of what may happen to us. This is the time when we need to really put our trust in the Lord. Just as God was with Elijah on the mountain, so He was also with him in the desert. God hadn't finished with Elijah; He still had more things for him to do.

What is it that frightens me the most?

I'm so discouraged

In the last 24 hours of Elijah's life he had witnessed some amazing events. God had just answered his prayer for fire and rain. He had run faster than a horse. Now his life was in danger and he had just run over 100 miles. He was tired and exhausted, in fact he was so discouraged and depressed he wanted to die.

If you read the life of Elijah it is hard to understand how such a man of God can become so discouraged. Elijah was a human not a super human; he was a man, not superman. We do not always live life on the mountain top. It is special and wonderful when we are up on the mountain, but sometimes there is the valley experience as well. Things don't always go the way we want them. Our whole world can turn upside down beyond our control. Maybe our best friend can fall out with us; maybe someone we know hates us, maybe someone we love is very ill or has even died. There are many things that can discourage us.

Elijah was so discouraged that he sat down under a juniper tree and wanted to die. It was only one day ago that this mighty man defeated all the prophets of Baal and witnessed many of his own people come back to the Lord. Elijah means 'Jehovah is my strength.' Had he taken his eyes off the Lord and was he now relying on his own strength?

When I am discouraged what do I do?

Are you really an Angel?

Elijah was now sitting under a juniper tree completely exhausted and feeling really discouraged. He was starving and very thirsty, especially after running for so many miles. We may wonder, was God angry with Elijah? Was he disappointed with Elijah? The amazing thing about the Lord is His love for us in that it never changes no matter how we feel.

Suddenly, Elijah woke up from a deep sleep. Lying under the tree in the desert, he was awakened by some food and fresh water beside him. Just as God sent the ravens to feed Elijah, the Lord was now using an angel to feed Elijah. The Lord promises to supply all our needs. Elijah needed food and water and God supplied it for him.

After eating, Elijah went back to sleep. The next morning the angel awoke Elijah and told him to rise and eat. In fact the food from the angel was so good it kept him going for the next 40 days. Elijah felt much better after a good rest, but instead of heading back to Israel he kept going in the opposite direction. In fact he kept walking for another 40 days.

God has a plan for every one of His children. It is called God's will for our lives. We can be in God's will or out of God's will. Elijah was now running from God, which was not God's will. God still loved him, wanted him as His messenger and would eventually catch up with him.

How do I know I am in God's will for my life?

ELIJAH 310

Hiding in a Cave

Elijah had done many wonderful things for the Lord. He challenged kings and queens about worshipping idols. He was used to restore a boy's life. He prayed for mighty things and saw God answer his prayers. Now he was running away and God still wanted to use him. So many of God's other children needed Elijah to help them but he wasn't there. He was very discouraged and wanted to be alone.

Elijah eventually found a cave and went in to it to rest for a while. God knew all about Elijah and He didn't want him to be in a cave. God had so much for Elijah to do. Before Elijah was so active, but now he was full of self pity. He thought he would stay in the cave where he would get shelter from the sun by day and would be warm at night.

Elijah once had very strong faith but now he had grown cold. Before he focused on God first and now he was only focused on himself. If we want God's best in our lives we must always put Him first. God needed to speak to Elijah and that is what He did.

Always remember when we focus only on ourselves then we are not focused on God.

ELIJAH

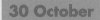
God has a very small voice

When Elijah was hiding in the cave God spoke to him and told him to go and stand at the entrance of the cave. Then God sent a great tornado-like wind. It was so strong it could blow down trees and split rocks. Then God sent a mighty earthquake that shook the mountain. It was so powerful the whole earth began to move. Then God sent a powerful fire.

In all these three events Elijah didn't sense God's presence at all. Then the Lord spoke to Elijah in a still small voice almost like a whisper. This time Elijah felt God's presence and heard His voice. The Lord gently asked Elijah what he was doing in the cave. Today God doesn't speak to us with a voice but through His Word, the Bible.

Feeling full of self pity, Elijah began to tell the Lord that all the people had forsaken God and were following after Baal the false god. He thought he was the only person left who believed in God. He was also hiding because Jezebel was going to kill him.

Then God told Elijah it was time to go. The Lord had plans for Elijah. He had to go and anoint a new king in Syria and a new king in Israel. Also God had already chosen a new man to be the next prophet of Israel. Elijah would have to find him and anoint him. Then God told Elijah something that startled him. Back in Israel there were still 7,000 Israelites who had not bowed to Baal and were worshipping the true God of Israel. They needed Elijah to teach them all about God.

There is always something to do for God. What can I do?

A new Man for the Job

Elijah felt much better after the Lord spoke to him with the still small voice. Now being obedient to the Lord he began to make his way back to Israel to do what the Lord asked him to do.

The first thing he wanted to do was find Elisha. Elisha would be the next prophet of Israel to take over from Elijah. Elisha was a farmer. When Elijah found him he was busy ploughing using 24 cows to pull the plough. With no rain for three and a half years, the ground was very hard. It took this number of cattle to break up the ground.

When Elijah found Elisha he didn't speak to him, rather he took off his coat and put it over the shoulders of Elisha. Elisha new exactly what this meant because when this happened it means that you would one day replace the person who gave you the coat.

Elisha made a big feast for all his family; he broke up his cart and used it for the fire. Then he killed two of his cattle and used them for the meat. This meant he was done with his old life, now he was going to serve God. For ten years Elijah and Elisha would travel and work together. How exciting it must have been for him. Are we willing to give up some of the things maybe even habits we have so that God can use us?

What are some of the habits we have that may hinder God blessing us?

A greedy King

Ahab was the king of Israel. He was very wealthy. All around his beautiful palace were stunning gardens. He loved to walk in them and see their beauty. One day he noticed another beautiful garden beside the palace. It was a vineyard and was used for growing grapes.

A man called Naboth owned the garden. Even though Ahab had lots and lots of gardens he decided he wanted this one too. He began to covet Naboth's vineyard. To covet something is breaking the tenth commandment. Coveting is wanting something you don't really need, like being selfish and it usually involves wanting something which belongs to someone else.

Ahab went to visit Naboth to buy his garden from him but Naboth wasn't interested in selling it. It had been in his family for many generations and he wanted to keep it that way. God's law also taught Naboth not to sell land unless it was absolutely necessary. Naboth was one of the 7,000 Israelites who loved and followed God with all his heart.

Naboth was a strong believer. He wasn't intimidated by King Ahab. To obey the Lord meant more to him than making a greedy king happy. As a result Ahab was very upset because he couldn't get what he wanted.

Is there something I have ever coveted, wanting something for the sake of having it?

An old Sulk

After Naboth told King Ahab that he couldn't have his vineyard, Ahab began to sulk. He was behaving like a spoilt child who was huffing because he couldn't get what he wanted. He went to his bedroom and lay there feeling sorry for himself. When his servants brought food to him he refused to eat.

Soon Jezebel heard about Ahab and went to see what was wrong. Ahab told her that the reason he was sulking was because he wanted Naboth's vineyard and he couldn't get it because Naboth refused to sell it to him. When Jezebel heard this she scolded him. "You are the king," she reminded him, "A king can have and take whatever he wants."

Then Jezebel told Ahab if he wanted the vineyard she would get it for him. Jezebel then came up with a wicked plan that would mean Naboth losing his life and Ahab getting his vineyard. The Bible says, "be sure your sin will find you out," and on this occasion it did.

Maybe we are like Ahab. When we want something and we don't get it then we begin to huff and sulk. Sometimes wanting something for the sake of having it can put an unnecessary financial pressure on our parents. They know you don't need it and it is wrong to continually insist on getting something you don't need. It is also grievous and sinning against God to covet something continually.

It is good to pray and ask the Lord to take away the desire of having something we don't need.

What normally makes me sulk?

ELIJAH 315

Accused in the wrong

Queen Jezebel came up with a wicked plan for Ahab to get Naboth's vineyard. Jezebel organized two men to make up lies about Naboth. They accused him of cursing God and cursing the king.

Naboth was horrified at the accusations that were made against him. Naboth loved God and honoured the king. Jezebel then made a complaint about him to the elders of the town. As a result Naboth was brought before the courts. He was accused of cursing God and cursing the king. The penalty for such crime was death.

Naboth couldn't believe his eyes or ears at what had happened. He was accused in the wrong and he couldn't even defend himself. The elders of the town believed the two men who told lies rather than the innocent Naboth. As a result Naboth was taken outside and stoned to death. When he died the dogs came along and licked his blood as he was bleeding.

This was a horrifying story. People in the Bible were very cruel. People today are just as cruel in some parts of the world. As God looked down from Heaven He saw it all. Ahab thought he would get away with this sin but he wouldn't. His old friend Elijah was on his way back to remind him of his sin.

ELIJAH 316

Terrible sin because of a Vineyard

As soon as Naboth was dead Jezebel was delighted. Her plan had come together and worked brilliantly. She then went to Ahab and told him the vineyard was all his (1 Kings 21:15).

Soon Ahab was walking all around his new vineyard, but he didn't enjoy it the way he thought he would. He maybe thought about Naboth and what happened to him. Naboth died just because of Ahab's greed. His conscience was beginning to bother him.

Ahab first sinned by coveting the vineyard. Now he realized he had been guilty of many sins. One sin led to another. After coveting, there was lying, stealing and murder. A person with a guilty conscience can never be truly happy.

In the meantime God spoke to Elijah and told him all about what happened to Naboth. One day Ahab was walking through his vineyard, feeling much better. He had deceitfully gotten the vineyard and thought no-one knew anything about it. However, walking towards him in the vineyard was Elijah. How shocked Ahab must have felt. Just like that, Elijah said to Ahab, "Have you killed someone and taken possession of this vineyard?" If there was anyone Ahab dreaded walking through his vineyard, it was Elijah, the prophet of God. Elijah had a message from God and it must be delivered.

Is there some sin I have committed, then I must tell the Lord all about it.

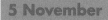

Wicked People can change

Ahab now stood face to face with Elijah the prophet of God. Elijah told Ahab that because of his sin of coveting, lying, stealing and murdering Naboth, the same thing would happen to him and his family.

When Naboth died the dogs came to lick his blood. Elijah told Ahab that he would die with his wife Jezebel and all his family. Not only would the dogs lick up his blood but would eat their bodies. Ahab was horrified and really scared of what might happen.

He then did an unusual thing, he took off all his kingly robes and wore sackcloth, and he even stopped eating. He was very sorry for what happened to Naboth. He began to pray and tell God how sorry he was. When God looked down from Heaven He saw that Ahab was genuinely sorry for his sins. By wearing sackcloth he had humbled himself greatly.

Elijah then told Ahab because he was sorry for his actions and sin that God would not pass His judgment upon him as He had said. Rather, it would be passed on to his children. How merciful God is, even wicked sinners like Ahab and Jezebel He was willing to forgive. However, Ahab didn't change his heart forever, for within a short time he went back to his old ways.

God saves sinners. Even the worst of sinners can be saved if they turn from their sinful ways and give their heart to the Lord Jesus.

When I am truly sorry for something; do I keep going back to the same old habits?

ELIJAH 318

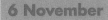

Dividing the River in two

Elijah was now an old man, his time on earth was coming to an end. Elisha had now been with him for ten years following in his footsteps, learning all about being a prophet of God. There were many students learning all about the Lord in Elijah's day. They were called the sons of the prophets.

Elijah wanted to visit them one final time before he would leave this earth. Elisha wanted to be with him everywhere he went. He enjoyed his company so much. He walked so close to God and it was very special. Later that day they came to the banks of the river Jordan. Elijah took off his coat and cast it over the river Jordan. Suddenly the river began to divide in two making a path across the river, Elisha was amazed at this and when they crossed over, the river came back together again.

When they got to the other side, Elijah asked Elisha if there was anything he would like as a present. Elisha could have asked for anything, to be famous, wealthy or rich, but he didn't. He asked for an unusual but wonderful thing. He asked Elijah for a double portion of God's Spirit to be upon him.

In other words, in the way Elijah was a strong man of God and had done many wonderful things in the name of the Lord and had God's power to help him, Elisha was asking to be twice as powerful, to have double the strength as a man of God such as Elijah. God was pleased with what he asked for. Elijah told Elisha that if he would see him as he went away, then his prayer would be answered and if not he could not have what he asked for.

If you could have one thing in this world what would it be?

ELIJAH 319

Straight to Heaven in a Chariot of Fire

Elijah's life on earth had come to an end. One day while he was out walking with Elisha something wonderful happened. Probably one of the most amazing scenes anyone could ever watch.

There was a sudden roar and down from Heaven there came a chariot pulled by horses of fire. Elijah jumped onto the chariot and it soared up to Heaven and out of sight. It must have been a truly marvellous sight for Elisha to see. He was the only one to see Elijah on the chariot of fire in a whirlwind that took him to Heaven.

This means that Elijah went to Heaven without dying. Isn't that a wonderful thought? I look forward to seeing Elijah one day in Heaven. I will be asking him all about that great journey right into the presence of the Lord in Glory.

I wonder will you ever see Elijah in Heaven? Heaven is a real place. Only those who are saved and have put their trust in the Lord Jesus will be in Heaven. Unless the Lord comes back we will have to die before we go to Heaven. The secret is that before we die we must make preparation for Heaven.

Elijah lived his life for God. God loved him and used him mightily here on this earth. God still needs people like Elijah; people who love the Lord and are willing to serve Him with all their heart.

When you think of HEAVEN, what do you think it will be like?

ELIJAH 320

Elijah, Moses and Jesus all meet together

Whenever we read the New Testament we read all about the Lord Jesus and His life here on this earth. One day Jesus took three of His disciples up onto the mountain. The disciples all fell asleep as they were probably tired.

Suddenly they woke up and saw Jesus talking with two other men. Immediately they recognized them as Moses and Elijah. This was almost 1,000 years after Elijah went to Heaven in a chariot of fire. The disciples recognized him as Elijah and the other man as Moses.

They were talking about the Cross and how that very soon Jesus would die on the Cross for the sins of the world and whoever believed in Him would be saved and would also go to heaven. Isn't it amazing that they recognized Moses and Elijah? I believe we will recognise each other in Heaven even though we have never met on earth. "Impossible," some may say but then again is anything impossible with God?

Elijah lived a wonderful life for God. He spoke out boldly for the Lord when he needed to. Life wasn't always easy for him. Sometimes he was greatly encouraged and other times he was greatly discouraged. Nevertheless the Lord was with him and blessed him here on earth.

It is amazing what God can do with one life when a person says, "Here is my life Lord take it and use it for your pleasure, honour and glory."

What have you learned about Elijah?

ELIJAH

Elisha
A Farmer by Trade

Now we are going to study the life of another man. This time it is the life of Elisha. Elisha was the successor of Elijah. He was just an ordinary man with an ordinary job. Like most people of his day he would have lived off the land being a farmer by trade.

God works in exactly the same way today; he uses ordinary people to do extraordinary things for him. Maybe you think you are just an ordinary person and there is nothing special about you. Well I have good news, you are special to God and if you are willing to be used by Him, He will use you for His glory. What an exciting thought!

Elisha had no idea what was in store for him in life, but God knew his heart. Then one day his life changed forever. God said, "Come along and follow me, because I have something else for you to do." You don't have to be grown up to be useful for God; He can use you today, tomorrow and everyday, as long as you are willing to be used by God. The best ability we can have is our availability.

If God were to call you today to do something for Him, would you be willing to do it?

ELISHA 322

Twenty four Cows to plough a Field

Can you imagine seeing twelve yoke or twenty four cows, pulling a plough through a field? Remember it hadn't rained for three and a half years. The ground was so hard and the cattle would have been weak after the lengthy drought.

Today in some parts of the world, cattle are still used to work on farms. In the Western World tractors and all sorts of other machinery are used instead of animals.

Sometimes we can be like the oxen that were used by Elisha. We can become very weak and life can be a constant struggle. The ground which the oxen worked had become so hard it was difficult to turn over the soil. It lacked water. Whenever we stop reading the Bible and praying to God, our Christian lives can become hard and difficult. Life can become frustrating. The secret for the ground to become easy to plough was the rain from heaven. Likewise the secret with our Christian lives is our daily walk and talk with God. We need constant fellowship with Him to really enjoy life.

"But whosoever drinketh of the water that I shall give him shall never thirst; but the water that I shall give him shall be in him a well of water springing up into everlasting life." (John 4:14)

What did you talk to God about today?

ELISHA 323

A new Job

Sometimes changing schools, jobs or even moving home can be very exciting. Although sometimes it can be very daunting as we may not know anybody in our new circumstances.

This is what happened to Elisha. When Elijah put his coat over Elisha's shoulders it was a sign that he was to follow Elijah, take over his job and become the new prophet. Elisha then took his wooden plough and made a fire with it. On the fire he cooked two of his oxen. This was a sign to all his neighbours and friends that he was giving up the old life and was going to serve the Lord full time.

Sometimes in the Christian life we have to give up old habits that may hinder our walk with God. Elisha had been a farmer and was content with doing that. However the moment God called him he was ready to go. God has a plan for every one of his children's lives. When His plan for us is different than ours, are we ready to give in and say, "Lord I want to follow your plan for my life?"

Are you willing to let God decide your future and to follow His plan for your life?

Elisha and Elijah
Work together

For almost ten years Elisha and Elijah worked together. Elijah was a wonderful man of God and was a great inspiration for Elisha. Anything that needed to be done Elisha was there to do it. Elijah watched Elisha very closely to make sure he was the right person for the job.

Sometimes the Lord tests us in the little things of life. Maybe we are asked to help clear the table after dinner or to help with the dishes. Maybe we are asked to hoover the floor. Do we moan and groan or do we do little jobs like this willingly? If we prove ourselves in the little things of life then the Lord may open the way to greater opportunities. If we fail to do the little things in life then the Lord may not give us great things to do for Him.

The time came when Elijah would leave the earth and travel to heaven in a chariot of fire. What an inspiration and example he was to Elisha. We should thank the Lord for the good role models He brings into our lives. It is good to watch and learn from them. It is especially good when the Lord can see us working together. The devil wants us to fight and quarrel, to disagree and complain. We must not let him succeed in this but we should let the Lord see us working well together, just like Elijah and Elisha.

There are people in our lives who can be a great inspiration. Can you think of some Christian people who have been an inspiration to you?

ELISHA 325

A double portion of God's Power

One of the most exciting events in the Bible is when Elijah asked Elisha what he wanted as a present from him. Elisha could have asked for anything, but he didn't. He thought for a moment and then he asked Elijah for a double portion of God's Spirit to be upon him.

Out of all the things in the world, Elisha asked to be twice the man of God that Elijah was. This to me was a wonderful request. Elijah knew that Elisha had asked for a difficult thing, but he also knew that God could give such a gift. Elijah told Elisha that his request would be met if he would be with him when he left this world and went to heaven.

From that moment Elisha never left Elijah's side. Then one day, suddenly from the sky roared a chariot and horses made of fire in a whirlwind. It came like lightning and stopped for Elijah; he jumped on and then it soared up into the sky and straight to heaven. Elisha stood there and gazed into the sky at the wonder of it all. Now his request had been met. He would become twice as powerful as Elijah which was an extraordinary present as Elijah was a mighty man of God. The important thing to remember is that Elisha wanted to be twice as useful for God. He was not asking to be twice as famous as Elijah. Evidence of the double portion can be found in the Bible. The Bible records 7 miracles in the life of Elijah and 14 miracles in the life of Elisha. As you can see this was twice as many.

If there was one thing you could have in the whole world, what would it be and why?

Bitter Waters made Sweet

After Elijah went to heaven Elisha stayed for some time in Jericho. Jericho was the city that Joshua marched around and the walls came tumbling down. It was here that Rahab and her family were rescued. God had done many wonderful things in the city of Jericho.

One day the people came to Elisha and told him that Jericho was a wonderful city, but there was only one thing that bothered them; the water. It was not good to drink as it was very bitter. Elisha immediately told them that God could make the bitter waters sweet to drink.

He asked for a jar of salt and made his way to the spring, which is where the water came out of the ground first. Here he poured all the salt into the spring. The people probably thought he was daft. However, when they tasted the water, it was sweet to drink. This was a miracle. Suddenly all the crops began to grow much better. The people and all the animals were much healthier because of the fresh water. God had used Elisha to make the bitter waters sweet. This miracle occurred over 3000 years ago and the waters in Jericho are still sweet to drink.

Maybe there is something in our lives we are bitter about. We have tried to sweeten it up but it never works.
Ask God to help you sweeten up
your bitterness. It will make you
a much better person to be
around and life will be
much more enjoyable.

What is it that makes you angry and bitter?

Mocking older People

The Bible is full of many wonderful stories. Hidden within these stories are many lessons for us to learn. One day Elisha was walking along the road towards Bethel. Suddenly he heard lots of young people shouting at him and calling him names. They were calling him baldy because they did not believe that Elijah had gone up to Heaven in a chariot of fire as Elisha had told them. "Go up, thou bald head" was what they were shouting. Having no hair of course was the reason they called him bald head.

At first he ignored them but they got louder and louder and continued calling him all sorts of names and making fun of him. Remember lots of people at this time worshipped Baal the false god. Recently King Ahab and Queen Jezebel had almost turned the whole country away from worshipping God. The fact that Elisha was a prophet of God was one of the reasons they were mocking him.

Sometimes Christians suffer name calling because of their belief in God and their love for the Lord Jesus Christ. They were making fun of the fact that Elijah had been taken straight to heaven. They didn't see it, so they didn't believe it. They were committing a terrible sin for they were not just mocking a person, they were mocking God's prophet. The Bible says, "Touch not mine anointed, and do my prophets no harm." (Psalm 105:15) To insult Elisha was an insult upon God himself.

A terrible thing was going to happen to this crowd of young people, over 40 in total. We are taught to respect people older than us. Making fun of people and calling them names is very wrong and sinful before God.

Why do you think it is wrong to mock people?

Chased by two Bears

As Elisha was walking along the road from Jericho a large number of children followed him calling him names. Eventually Elisha turned around and gave them an angry look and told them off in the name of the Lord.

Little did the group of children realise, but there were two large bears in the woods. Normally they would be frightened and run off into the woods, but this time they didn't. Rather, they ran out of the woods towards the large group of children and attacked them. They attacked and tore apart forty-two children that day.

This was a very sad day. God was angry at the boys for mocking Elisha for not believing what he said about Elijah going up to heaven and making fun of his bald head. God allowed the bears to attack and kill the children. Sin must be punished. You might think that this was very cruel; it was, but mocking someone is also very cruel. The parents of these children worshipped idols and possibly encouraged the children to mock Elisha in order to discourage him. What a lesson to learn, sin always has its consequences.

Is there someone you have mocked and made fun of recently?

2 Kings 2:23-24

One Person can change a Nation

Elisha was just an ordinary person willing to serve God. Many people came to him with their problems and he was willing to help them. God had given him power to work in the city of Jericho and many people believed in God as Elisha showed God's kindness and greatness to them.

Not long before this almost the whole country had stopped worshipping God in favour of the false god, Baal. God sent a drought for three and a half years to bring the people to their senses. Now God was using Elisha to witness for Him. God always has a witness. Maybe you are a person who God is using now or will use in the future.

Elisha was able to do many wonderful miracles. It was God of course who performed the miracles but He used Elisha as the human being to teach the people all about His ways. The people of Israel were God's chosen people and He loved them so much. Many times, like lost sheep, they would wander away from Him. "All we like sheep have gone astray; we have turned every one to his own way; and the LORD hath laid on him the iniquity of us all." (Isaiah 53:6) Then God would use His servants like Elisha, to bring the people back.

Today we follow one much greater than Elisha; we follow and serve the lovely Lord Jesus Christ. He not only helps us but He knows all about us. His desire is to keep us very close to Himself. Today He still uses individual boys and girls to do something for Him.

Are you willing to be God's specially chosen witness to do something for Him?

ELISHA 330

Helping a Widow

God's Word, the Bible, tells us we have to be kind and good to everybody, especially to widows. A widow is a woman whose husband has died. They may live alone or with their children.

In the story today, we are told about a widow woman who went to Elisha for some help. Many people went to Elisha for help. Elisha was a godly man and they knew he would pray for them and help them as much as he could. The widow in this story was very poor. In fact, she was so poor she had no money. She also had two young sons.

Her story was very sad, for not only was she poor, but she also owed a lot of money to different people. Things were so bad that the people threatened to take her sons away from her and sell them as slaves. She was in a desperate situation. Of course Elisha listened to the sad story as he wanted to help her in whatever way he could.

If someone came to you for help would you help them? Quite often we can be critical and have a 'serves you right' attitude. To have such an attitude is not very Christian. We are to be like Christ in our Christian living. He is a compassionate Saviour. We are to do unto others as we would like others to do unto us. Elisha was this type of person. He had a plan how to help the widow and he knew it would work.

If someone came to you for help, how would you help them?

ELISHA 331

A House full of Jugs

This seems like a strange story to talk about but we find in our lesson today that a widow had come to Elisha in desperation. The person she owed money to had threatened to take both her young sons and sell them as slaves.

After finding out that the widow had only a little oil in a jar in her home, Elisha told the woman to go around all her neighbours and borrow as many jugs and jars as possible. Together with her two sons she went everywhere, collecting jars and jugs in which to hold oil.

Elisha then told her to start filling them up with the little jar of oil she had in her kitchen. She probably looked at him in shock, as if to say there isn't even enough to fill one other jar. However, she did as he said and the little jar she used to fill the jars never ran out until there were no more jars to fill. Her whole house was filled with jars of oil.

Elisha then told her to sell the oil. Very soon she had enough money to pay her debt and also extra to raise her two sons. God, through Elisha, had performed another miracle. Oil in the Bible reminds us of God's Holy Spirit. We need God's Spirit in us and with us every day. We need to be filled with God's Spirit to witness and live for the Lord. Pray and ask God to fill you with His Spirit.

It is so important that we have God's Spirit to help us live the CHRISTIAN LIFE. Ask God now to help you live your life for Him.

God meets our need

Just as God performed a miracle for the widow woman and provided all the oil for her, so He can do the same for you. He has promised to look after His children. He has promised to take care of our every need.

Remember, it is not our greed, but rather our need He has promised to look after. Sometimes we have a big list of things we want; expectations from God to make our lives perfect. God knows what we need and He decides when, and if, we are to get things. The secret is to be content with our lives, for everything we have comes from God. "But godliness with contentment is great gain." (1 Timothy 6:6)

The Lord had continually provided for Elisha and now He was providing for the widow woman too. Notice she had the responsibility of going out to collect the jugs and jars. Her two sons had to help her as well. Sometimes we have to make an effort. If we are lazy and just sit around and expect God to do everything, then it may never happen.

Whether God gives us what we want or not, a real test of how much we love the Lord is to thank Him for everything anyway. Thank God for listening to your prayers, for knowing your thoughts and tell the Lord whichever way He wants to answer your prayer, you'll be happy.

Just think back over the last 24 hours, how good has God been to you?

Making Room for others

Elisha continued his journey throughout the countryside helping others, making many friends along the way. Mount Carmel was one of Elisha's favourite places as he was able to spend time with God alone. About halfway between Mount Carmel and Samaria there was a place called Shunem.

Along the way there was a godly couple whom Elisha would often stop and visit. The Bible calls the woman "a great woman," probably because of her love for the Lord. They were a wealthy couple with a big house and lots of servants.

One day when Elisha arrived at their home, they surprised him by telling him that they had built a special extension unto their house just for him! Can you imagine how Elisha felt? How thoughtful it was for these people to think of Elisha in such a way. Every time he stopped by he would have his own place and could stay for as long as he wanted.

Do we ever think about others in such a way? The Bible teaches that we should do good to others. When was the last time you surprised someone by doing something for them, or giving something to them? To Christians especially, we are to do good.

"As we have therefore opportunity, let us do good unto all men, especially unto them who are of the household of faith." (Galatians 6:10)

Sometimes we can be guilty of pushing people out of our lives. Does God push you out? Do we like it when our friends push us out?

This couple didn't push Elisha out, rather, they brought him in and made him feel very welcome and the Lord really blessed them for it.

The special Room

The couple that Elisha often visited on his travels made him a special room in which he could stay. It was called "the prophet's chamber." Here in this room he had a bed, a table, a lamp and a chair. This was for Elisha to rest, pray and study God's Word.

No doubt Elisha was deeply touched by the kindness of this couple. Some people also have a spare room in their house which is used to entertain such servants of God as preachers and missionaries. Elisha also had servants that would travel with him from place to place. There was room for them too.

Many people today have a special place or room where they can spend time alone with God. It is a quiet place also known as a "closet" where there are no distractions. It is so important to do this everyday.

"But thou, when thou prayest, enter into thy closet, and when thou hast shut thy door, pray to thy Father which is in secret; and thy Father which seeth in secret shall reward thee openly." (Matthew 6:6)

Have you got a special place in your house where you can talk to God? Have you got a special place in your heart for God? Always make and keep room for the Lord in your life.

You will have a Son

Elisha was so grateful for the generosity of the couple who had made a room for him in their house. One day Elisha asked the woman of the house if there was anything he could do for her. Both she and her husband were very wealthy, so there was nothing she really needed. So she politely said, "no thank you" to Elisha.

However, deep down in her heart she really wanted something. More than anything else in the world, the woman wanted a baby. She had been married for many years and her husband was getting quite old. She thought having a baby at this stage in life would be nearly impossible. That is why she never mentioned it to Elisha.

It is normal to have a family. It is the desire of every woman's heart. As far as she was concerned there was nothing more unfulfilling than not having a baby. Many of the Hebrew women who had children would often laugh and mock those who couldn't have children.

After talking with his servant Gehazi, Elisha called her back and told her that she was going to have a son. At first she thought Elisha was mocking her too. When she realised he was being serious she must have felt very excited. After all these years the God of Heaven would give her what she wanted in her heart.

A sick Boy

Just under a year after the Shunammite woman heard she was going to have a baby, she gave birth to a baby boy. She loved him dearly; he truly was the joy of her heart.

Some years later the little boy was out helping his father in the fields, as little boys do. Suddenly he began to complain of a sore head. As his head became more painful, his father told one of the servants to carry the boy back to his mother. Perhaps he thought he had been out in the sun too long.

When the mother saw the servant carrying her son back she realised something was wrong. She immediately ran to him to see what was the matter with him. He was just not his usual self. She began to panic and worry greatly about what could be wrong with her little boy. In those days they didn't have telephones or cars or even hospitals to help in an emergency.

Sometimes life can be going very well for us. Then suddenly we can become ill and everything changes in a moment. How thankful we must be every day to the Lord for our health. It is good to pray for the doctors and nurses who help people when they are ill. Pray also for all the sick children all over the world. Childrens' hospitals are full of children who are very ill.

Do you know anyone who is ill? Do you pray for them?

ELISHA 337

The little Boy dies

The son of the Shunammite woman was gasping for his life. She didn't know what was wrong with him. Suddenly, while out in the field with his father, he had taken a sore head.

His mother held him in her arms as he got weaker and weaker. She was still holding him when he breathed his last breath and died. His mother then carried him upstairs into the prophet's bedroom and laid him on top of the bed. She didn't tell her husband what happened. Instead, she got a donkey and took a servant with her and told her husband she was going to find Elisha.

Children have accidents and get ill, some may even die. It is not normal, nor is it natural, but it happens. In Bible times it happened and still happens today. Every day somewhere some child will die. This is why it is so important to put your trust in the Lord Jesus Christ when you are young. The Bible tells us and teaches us that we must be saved from our sin if we are to enter Heaven when we die.

There must come a time in our lives when we realise our sin separates us from God forever. This is why we must be born into God's family. When we come to Christ and He saves us He gives us a wonderful peace. Then we don't have to worry about when we will die, because when we do we will go straight home to Heaven to be with Jesus.

If you were to die tonight, do you know where you would be going to?

ELISHA 338

Brought back to Life

When the mother of the boy reached Elisha the prophet of God, she quickly told him what had happened. Elisha told his servant to go on ahead and put his staff on the boy, but the mother insisted that Elisha should come and do something.

The woman had great faith in God. She knew there was something special about Elisha; that he was a man of God. As they walked to the house, Gehazi the servant came running up to Elisha and shouted, "the child is dead." Elisha didn't say anything; he walked into the house and up the stairs to where the boy was.

He went into the room alone and shut the door. There on the bed was the little boy, his body lifeless. Elisha began to pray. He pleaded with God that he would bring the boy back to life. Elisha believed that God not only could, but would, do this miracle. Then Elisha stretched himself upon the child as if to resuscitate him. The heat seemed to pass from Elisha into the child and the boy began to grow warm. He repeated again what he had done. Just then the child sneezed seven times and slowly opened his eyes. Can you imagine the happiness that the mother felt when she walked into the room to see her little boy? Do you think he hugged her?

Mothers love hugs from their children more than anything. Never think you are too big to hug and kiss your mother. The sweetest words you can ever say to your mum are, "I love you." You don't have to shout it; you can even whisper it in her ear. I guarantee you; it will make her smile more than anything. Try it!

A happy Mother

Can you imagine how happy the mother of the little boy felt when she saw him again? Her little boy had died, but now he had come back to life. There is nothing that breaks the heart of a mother more than to see her child suffer. How sad it must have been for her.

Yet, on the other hand, how happy she must have been to see her little boy again. Her faith in God was strong. She was happy to accept whatever happened to her son. When God brought her son back to life her faith grew even stronger. Elisha had encouraged her and she encouraged Elisha. This is what the Christian life is all about, encouraging one another in the Lord.

The Bible doesn't tell us the name of the little boy but his life reminds all those who are Christians, that they were once dead in sins. We were once dead in trespasses and sins but now we are saved because of what Jesus has done for us on the cross. He died to give us life. He died to take away our sin. He rose again from the dead and has gone back to Heaven. One day Jesus Christ, the King of Kings will come back for his children; what a day that will be!

What do you do to make your mother happy?

A Man with everything

Not everyone in the Bible worshipped the Lord God of Heaven. To the north of Israel was Syria. The Syrian army often attacked Israel. The captain of the Syrian army was called Naaman.

Naaman was a mighty man of valour; he was a great soldier and was captain of the king's army. The king loved and respected him and everyone thought he was a brilliant captain. He often led his army to victory. Naaman was a wealthy man who had absolutely everything in this world that he wanted. He had a beautiful wife, a wonderful home, servants and all the money he would ever need. He was second in command to the king.

Yet even though he had everything in the world, he didn't have God. He never believed in God. Sometimes when we have everything and we want and lack nothing, we tend to forget about God. Then when something goes wrong, terribly wrong, we realise how much we need God in our lives.

When God wants to speak to us or to get our attention, He will sometimes upset our daily routine to make us stop and listen to what He has to say.

Are you happy with everything you have or are there other things you would love to have?

A deadly Disease

Even though Captain Naaman had everything he could possibly want there was something that upset him terribly. He had a disease called leprosy. Leprosy was a skin disease. The skin would eventually peel away and the body would begin to rot.

Unfortunately there was no cure for leprosy. Once someone got leprosy it was certain that they were going to die. Leprosy was contagious. If a family member became leprous they had to live apart from everyone else and so they died alone. It was very, very sad for Naaman and his wife. One moment he had everything and the next he had nothing.

Leprosy reminds me of sin. Once a person got leprosy it would eventually kill them. It is the same with sin. Sin will eventually bring death to us. It is because of sin that we all have to die, yet God loves us so much, He sent the Lord Jesus into the world to die for us, to take away our sin. The Blood of the Lord Jesus Christ is the cure for sin today; it can wash away all our sin and make us clean for Heaven. Have you ever asked Him to do that?

Have you ever trusted in the Lord Jesus to take away your sin?

A little Girl speaks up

One day while Naaman's army was attacking Israel they brought home with them lots of gold, silver and things of great value. As well as this they brought with them children and young people, who would become slaves.

One such little girl was brought to Naaman's house where she became a maid for Naaman's wife. She never complained about being away from her home, her country or her family. Deep within her heart this little girl knew the Lord. As a child she was taught all about God and how He loved His people and how those who believed in Him would be cared for and looked after by Him.

One day this little girl heard that Naaman and his wife were very sad because of Naaman's leprosy. She immediately spoke up and told her mistress all about Elisha; how Elisha was a wonderful man of God who was able to do many miracles in God's name. Naaman listened with interest. He had tried everything and nobody could help him. He was desperate and he was willing to try anything to have his leprosy cured. God was able to use a little girl to speak up for Him.

God always gives us opportunities to do something for Him. He will really bless us for doing so. What a joy to know the Saviour and to help others in His name.

Full of Pride

Naaman listened intently when the little girl told him about Elisha; the man who served the true God and who was able to do many miracles in the name of the Lord. The little girl told Naaman he should go to Israel and find Elisha.

Naaman wasted no time and immediately set off with other soldiers to be healed of his leprosy. Instead of looking for Elisha, Naaman went straight to the king of Israel. His own king, the king of Syria, had sent gold and silver with Naaman as a gift to the king of Israel. When the king of Israel saw Naaman, he tore his clothes in anger, as if to say, I cannot do such a thing as heal a man of his leprosy.

In the meantime Elisha heard about Naaman and sent for him as he knew the king could do nothing for him. Elisha wanted to teach the heathen people of Syria that there is only one true God. When Naaman arrived at Elisha's house, Elisha's servant went to meet him. Quite angry that Elisha never came out to meet him, Naaman demanded to see Elisha. Elisha sent a message to Naaman telling him to go and wash in the river Jordan seven times. "Wash in the river Jordan?" said Naaman in disgust, "the dirty old river." If it was a bath he needed, the rivers in his country were much cleaner.

Naaman was in a rage. He thought Elisha would come out and say some kind of prayer and he would be immediately healed. Naaman's problem was that he was full of pride. Before God can work in a person's heart and life they must be humbled. Naaman was so full of self importance he had no time for God. He thought he could get healed the simple way but God had different plans.

God hates pride. He loves humility.

Seven dirty Ducks

After being told to go and wash in the river Jordan, Naaman was angry and very frustrated. He thought, if all he had to do was wash in a river, then the rivers in his own country were much cleaner. Heading for home he was extremely annoyed.

Before making the journey back one of his soldiers spoke to him and said, "If Elisha had asked you to do some great thing, would you not have done it to prove your strength? Why not dip in the river Jordan and see what will happen?"

He realised what the soldier said made sense; after all he came so far and was desperate to have his leprosy healed. After taking off his uniform he waded into the river and dipped himself once, but nothing happened. Time after time he dipped himself in the dirty water and still nothing happened. Then for the seventh time he ducked himself under the water and came back up again.

This time, to his total amazement, he was completely cleansed from his leprosy. It was completely gone. This was a miracle that God had done through Elisha. First He used a little girl and then a soldier to speak up; just a normal soldier spoke up to help him come to his senses.

God uses all sorts of people to speak up for Him. Sometimes we may be shy or afraid to speak up for the Lord. Remember He will help you and even give you the words to say, and most of all He will bless you for doing so.

Please accept my gift

When Naaman came out of the river Jordan he was delighted that his leprosy was all gone. He quickly made his way back to Elisha's house. When Elisha came to the door, Naaman couldn't thank him enough with words so he presented him with lots of gifts. Among these gifts were gold, silver and lovely new clothes.

Naaman was shocked when Elisha refused the gifts. "Please accept my gifts," Naaman pleaded with him. Elisha began to explain to Naaman that it was not him that healed him but God. It was the true God of heaven who healed him from all his leprosy. Elisha refused all the nice presents because he wanted Naaman to see that it was God who healed him and that God should get all the praise and glory.

Elisha then told Naaman to go back home and tell all his soldiers what had happened. "Tell them that it was the true God of heaven who healed you today." Naaman then put his trust in God and said from that moment on he would no longer worship false gods of wood and stone. When Naaman returned home to Syria he told all his soldiers that there was no god like the God of Israel. He encouraged all his soldiers to put their trust in the Lord.

Just like God was able to heal Naaman's leprosy, He was also able to take away all his sin because he had trusted in Him. All Naaman's money and gifts could never buy salvation; it was a gift from God. People today think they can buy their way into heaven, but that is impossible. Salvation is a free gift for whoever will take it.

Have you ever taken the free gift of Salvation from God by trusting in the Lord Jesus Christ?

ELISHA 346

A happy little Girl

Whenever we think of how God cured Naaman of all his leprosy it really was a miracle. Of course, God used all sorts of people to make this happen. He used Elisha, Elisha's servant, the soldier who spoke up and especially He used the little girl.

God often uses little people to do big things for Him. We do not know the name of the little girl but we do know she was not afraid to speak up for God. As a result of her speaking up and telling Naaman to go to Israel to find Elisha, Naaman then became a follower of the Lord. No doubt, through Naaman's influence, many others also became believers too.

Maybe you think you are not important and not many people know your name. Well, God knows your name and He knows all about you. He loves you so much. He wants to use you and bless you. He wants you to be happy, healthy and well. Most of all He wants you to love Him with all your heart. He wants you to tell others that they too can be saved if only they will be like Naaman and put their trust in Him.

"But even the very hairs of your head are all numbered. Fear not therefore: ye are of more value than many sparrows." (Luke 12:7)

The Thief

Naaman was on his way back to Syria rejoicing. The day before he arrived a leper and was expecting to die. Now he was completely healed and he had every reason to be thankful. Most of all he was amazed that Elisha refused to accept any of the gold, silver or lovely clothes that he had offered to him. He realized that Elisha was a true man of God who wanted God to have all the thanks, appreciation and adoration.

In the meantime Elisha's servant Gehazi could not get over the fact that Elisha refused all the lovely gifts. He thought about all the gold and silver and all the lovely clothes. He then thought about doing something very bad. He quickly left the house and ran after Naaman and his soldiers. It soon came to the attention of Naaman that Elisha's servant, Gehazi was following him. Naaman quickly stopped his horse to see what was wrong.

Gehazi told Naaman that soon after he left, two new prophets had arrived and that Elisha would like some of the gold, silver and new clothes to give to them. Without a moment's hesitation Naaman was glad to help. Gehazi had committed much sin in just one day. Firstly he coveted (really wanted something that wasn't his) then secondly he told lies to Naaman. This led him to take (steal) the goods. Can you see how one sin led to another and then another?

He thought nobody knew where he had been. Before he returned home he hid all the stuff he stole and then went back to Elisha. "Where have you been?" Elisha asked him. "Nowhere," Gehazi told him. Elisha being a prophet knew exactly where he had been and told Gehazi that he was there in spirit and saw and heard everything that went on.

The Bible tells us, "be sure your sin will find you out." (Numbers 32:23) Gehazi would have to pay an awful price for his sin.

ELISHA 348

Looking like a Ghost

In just a moment, as a result of Gehazi's sins of coveting, stealing and telling lies, his life was changed forever. The punishment he received when he lied to God's prophet Elisha was that Naaman's disease was now going to be passed unto him. Sin never goes unpunished. Even if you think no-one sees it or knows anything about it, God knows all about it.

Before Elisha had even finished speaking, Gehazi's skin had become leprous. His flesh became white and his skin began to peel off and raw open sores began to appear. His arms, legs and eventually his whole body was covered with leprosy. His skin was now so white that from a distance you would think he was a ghost.

One moment he had everything, with so much potential, yet by yielding to temptation he lost everything in just a moment. Now he was a leper, one of the most despised people in the whole country.

Salvation is the most important thing in the whole world. This is why Elisha refused the gifts from Naaman, to teach Naaman and many others that God's healing, help and salvation is a free gift.

When Gehazi stole these goods and brought them home with him it was like saying these were given for Naaman's salvation. Salvation today is a free gift from Jesus Christ because the Bible says in Romans 10:13 "For whosoever shall call upon the name of the Lord shall be saved."

ELISHA 349

Witnessing for God

Naaman the captain of the king's army returned home again after being healed from his leprosy. He was so happy and so full of joy he wanted to tell everyone about what God had done for him; how God had healed him through the life of Elisha from the terrible disease of leprosy.

Everywhere he went he told all his people and all his soldiers about Elisha, the man of God in Israel. Everyone knew he had leprosy and they knew he was destined to die because of it. In those days there was no cure for this disease. In fact Naaman was the only person to be healed of his leprosy in the days of Elisha.

When he came back again and he was completely healed of his leprosy, people were amazed. "How did it happen?" they wondered. Naaman astounded them all, when he told them that the Lord God of Israel, Elisha's God, had healed him. Naaman told everyone that he now worshipped and believed in the true God of Israel, the God of heaven and earth.

Many people thought seriously about what had happened to Naaman and started following after God and His ways. Naaman's life and testimony became a real witness before the people. Our life can often challenge others to believe in God. The way we behave can have a real impact upon others.

Prayer: -Lord, may my life help make others believe in You.

ELISHA 350

God's Invisible Army

For some time the people of Syria were at peace with Israel. But after a few years they forgot all about what God had done for Naaman. King Benhadad, the King of Syria, wanted to make war with Israel. The king and his army soon came up with many plans on how to attack Israel. In the meantime God was warning Elisha what was going on. Elisha then warned the King of Israel and everytime they were attacked, Israel was well prepared.

The King of Syria was furious, "How did Israel know about all our plans?" he wondered. It soon came to his attention that Elisha the prophet was telling the king of Israel. The King of Syria then sent his army to Dothan where Elisha lived to capture him.

Early the next morning Elisha's servant came running to him to tell him about the massive Syrian army. "Don't worry," Elisha said, "our army is bigger and more powerful than theirs." "We have no army here" replied the servant, "Yes we do," Elisha said. Then he asked the Lord to make the servant see the army. Suddenly before his eyes there was a massive army of horses and chariots of fire. It was an invisible army sent down from heaven. God was protecting Elisha with this invisible army.

This is what God does. He protects His servants from danger. No matter what danger you face, trust in the Lord completely and He will take care of you.

The Syrian army was then made blind and Elisha told them to follow him as he marched them into a city in Israel. When they opened their eyes they realised they had been captured by one man. They could have all been killed but Elisha sent them all home to tell their king that the God of Israel was the one true God and that He looks after His people. Can you imagine how the soldiers and the king felt?

The poisonous Stew

Elisha served God for around sixty-six years. He did many mighty and amazing things in God's name. Elisha, like Elijah, was constantly on the move where God wanted him to be. Very often there were famines in the land and the people had very little to eat.

One day while he was visiting some of his students he sent his servant to make some stew to feed them. Elisha would often visit his students, teaching them the Word of God and lessons on how to live for God. As the servant was out gathering some vegetables for the stew, one of the students accidentally picked up some poisonous wild gourds and mixed them in with the other vegetables in the stew.

Soon the stew was piping hot and they all sat down to eat it. Little did they know they were eating poison. Suddenly one of them shouted, "Death, there is death in the pot." All who had eaten the stew had got food poisoning and would soon die. Even if they spat out or vomited what they had eaten it was too late, the poison would have already entered their bodies.

Elisha quickly asked for some meal and threw it into the stew and stirred it up. Then he told them all to eat up quickly. The stew returned to normal and tasted lovely. None of the students became sick nor did any die from food poisoning. God, through Elisha, had again performed a miracle.

There are a lot of things in life which we see and hear that can poison us, spiritually. There are many things which are good for us and there are lots of things which are sinful and can really harm our relationship with God. What we watch on television or read in magazines is very important. How we need to be so careful about things our friends may offer as they might harm us.

Can you think of anything you can take which would be harmful to you?

ELISHA 352

The flying Hatchet

Elisha would spend quite a lot of time with the students of the Bible College. One day the students came to him and asked him if they could make the college larger. This was a normal request as there were so many students and the building was getting too small for them all.

As they began to chop down trees by the river Jordan they were very excited about their building project. One of the students borrowed a hatchet to help cut down the trees. As he was busy chopping away at the tree suddenly the axe head flew off the shaft and landed in the middle of the river.

The student began to panic, the river was so dirty and deep he would never find it. He was also concerned as he had borrowed it from someone and now he lost it. The student went to Elisha to tell him what had happened. Elisha quite calmly walked over to where he had been cutting the tree. Then he cut down a branch and threw it in the river were the axe head had fallen in. To the student's amazement the axe head began to float!

This was another wonderful miracle that God did again using His prophet Elisha. The student could have covered up the loss of the axe but instead he went to Elisha and asked for his help. This is what we should do when things go wrong for us. The Lord Jesus is our great problem solver. He wants us to take all our problems, difficulties and frustrations to Him.

Problems often happen, even when we are busy working for the Lord. What a lesson, even when we are busy, God is never too busy for us.

Dead man Walking

Elisha had now come to the end of his life. After he died he was buried in a cave; this was the normal custom in Bible times. Many times after this the people of Israel continued to be attacked by different countries. Often there were thieves who attacked people and stole their goods.

One day a man died and his friends and family were carrying him to be buried. In the distance they saw a gang of thieves and robbers coming towards them. They quickly thought about hiding the dead man in a cave and then running for their lives, otherwise they may get beaten up.

They placed him in a cave and intended to go back for him later. Little did they realize, but they placed him in the cave where Elisha was buried. The moment the dead man touched the bones of Elisha he began to move and breathe again. The man stood up and walked out of the cave. He then shouted at his friends and asked them where they were going. If you thought his friends were running fast, they probably ran even faster when they saw their friend who was dead now alive.

God not only used Elisha while he was alive but even in his death he brought life to people. You could call it, 'resurrection power.' This is what Jesus does to us. He brings death to life. We are born dead in our sins, yet by believing and trusting in the Lord Jesus Christ we can be made alive again.

What amazing power God has to save sinners. What a good thing it is to be a Christian.

ELISHA 354

Esther

Esther from Orphan to Queen

There are two books in the Bible named after girls. One is Ruth and the other is Esther. They are both thrilling accounts of how God really blessed and worked in the lives of these two young women.

There is little account given in the Bible of Esther's parents but we do know that when they died she was left in the care of her much older cousin, Mordecai. God loved Esther and her people and had a plan that one day she would be queen over most of the countries of the world.

Sometimes we can take our parents for granted. Some children in the world don't have any parents and have nobody to love them or care for them. Never take for granted your parents' love and care for you. You may not always have them there for you. If you have godly parents, love, respect and obey them and you will be blessed of God.

God's Word tells us to honour our parents; it is the teaching of the fifth commandment. Have you ever imagined what life would be like without your parents there for you? Maybe you know someone who has lost their parents. It is good to pray for them and to help them in whatever way you can.

"Honour thy father and thy mother, as the LORD thy God hath commanded thee; that thy days may be prolonged, and that it may go well with thee, in the land which the LORD thy God giveth thee." (Deuteronomy 5:16)

ESTHER 355

The longest Party ever

The king in the book of Esther was called King Ahasuerus. He was the most powerful king in the whole world ruling some 127 countries. In the third year of his reign he decided to have a huge feast. He would invite lots of important people from all these countries to this party.

In all of human history this was to be the longest party ever, lasting 180 days. Can you imagine all the food and preparation that would be needed for such a party? The king was so proud of his country and his beautiful palace that he wanted to show it to everyone.

The king lived in a place called Shushan. After 6 months of partying everyone went back to their own countries. The people of Shushan had worked very hard to help the king look after all the guests and as a result the king held a small 7 day party for all the local people, both rich and poor. No one was excluded. What a time of celebration that was for all the local people.

In the same way God makes no difference between rich and poor, young and old. He loves and cares for all kinds of people. Do we treat everyone equally and treat our neighbours as ourselves as God desires?

The Queen who lost her Job

After 187 days of the party had past King Ahasuerus asked for his wife, Queen Vashti to come to him. He wanted to show before all the people how beautiful she was. Now at this party the men and women had their own separate parties.

The king had drunk quite a lot of wine and was rather drunk. When Queen Vashti heard that the king wanted her to parade before him, she refused to come. This became extremely embarrassing for the king and he was full of anger. Everyone looked at him to see what he would do. Now she was disobeying him. In Bible times this was completely unheard of. How embarrassing it must have been for the king.

After getting advice from the princes and wise men King Ahasuerus realized that if his wife were to become disobedient to him then all wives may become disobedient to their husbands. It could lead to a national disaster. They advised the king to get a new queen. Queen Vashti was immediately removed from being the queen.

One moment the queen had everything and after one simple act of disobedience she lost everything.
In many ways Queen Vashti was right not to disgrace herself before drunken men, the king was in the wrong morally to ask his wife to do such a thing. Yet this is an account of what is written as fact and is incidental to Esther's story. God however used the incident to bring Esther on the scene.

Often in life we can be put on the spot morally. The decision we make may affect our future and our friends. The challenge is if something is morally wrong then we must resist it at all costs, any thing from dirty jokes, magazines etc.

This is what the Lord wants us to do,
to take a stand for everything pure
and right.

ESTHER 357

The Beauty Competition

Now that the king no longer had a queen to live with, he became very lonely. It was decided that he would find a new queen. No doubt many of the young girls would love to have been queen.

A beauty competition was organised to find a queen for King Ahasuerus. All the girls who were old enough were invited to enter this competition.

There was a man called Mordecai; he was a Jew who lived in Shushan. Mordecai's main responsibility in life was to look after his cousin Esther, so when Mordecai heard about this competition he thought it would be a great idea to have Esther enter. She was a very beautiful young Jewish girl, so when the officials saw Esther they allowed her to enter the competition.

All the girls who qualified for the competition were brought to the palace. For six months they treated themselves with oil to make their skin soft and beautiful. Then for six more months they would add sweet perfumes to help them smell really nice.

Then the time came when one by one the girls would stand before the king. Esther had a quiet confidence in God that if it was His will, then she would win. Do you rely on your outside beauty or do you possess the beauty that Esther had; that inner beauty of being a child of God who lived for Him? Her inner beauty was her strength and her confidence.

> "Favour is deceitful, and beauty is vain:
> but a woman that feareth the LORD,
> she shall be praised." (Proverbs 31:30)

Chosen to be Queen

It was now Esther's turn to stand before the king. She would have been so nervous and her heart beating fast. When Esther appeared before the king, he was astounded by her beauty. Not only for her beautiful appearance and her countenance, but there was something else about Esther.

Esther had an inner beauty as well as an outward beauty which King Ahasuerus liked very much. He made his mind up immediately. Esther had won the beauty competition and she was to be the new queen. Her inner beauty was her relationship with God. The light of God's love was shining through her.

Isn't it amazing how God can turn everything around for our good. Who would ever imagine that a little orphan girl, raised by her older cousin, could be recognised by a king and thought worthy of being a queen! God was in control of the entire competition. He controls the whole world, even the affairs of a king. He had a plan for Esther's life and this was just the beginning.

We don't know what the future is, but we know who holds the future. Put your life in the hands of God. Let Him take you and use you for whatever His plan is for your life.

ESTHER

God's wonderful Plan

There were hundreds of girls who came before the king. Only one would be chosen and this time it was Esther. God had a purpose and a plan for Esther and her people.

Esther was a Jew. The Jewish people were not liked in many parts of the world, but they were God's chosen people and He loved them very much. Esther was now queen over the whole of the Persian Empire.

King Ahasuerus did not know or realize that the new queen was Jewish. No one except Mordecai, her cousin, knew and he told her to keep it a secret. A great calamity was about to enter Esther's life that would test her to the very core of her beliefs.

On the happy day of her wedding, Esther had no idea what the future would hold, but God knew and He worked everything out perfectly. It is so important to completely trust the Lord with our lives and our futures. God has a plan for His children and He works everything out for their good.

His plan is wonderful and absolutely perfect. It is good to be content with God's perfect plan. It can be exciting not knowing what God has in store for us and sometimes we can feel anxious about the future, but we are told in the Bible to trust God.

"And we know that all things work together for good to them that love God, to them who are the called according to his purpose." (Romans 8:28)

ESTHER 360

Being in the right place at the right time

Esther's cousin Mordecai was a small man but he had a big faith in God. His job was to sit at the king's gate. He had a leadership role in the king's palace.

One day while Mordecai was at the gate, he overheard a conversation. Two of the king's guards were planning to kill the king. Mordecai informed Queen Esther immediately and as a result the two guards were found guilty and hanged for plotting to kill the king. This was the custom in these days. Everything that had taken place was written down in the king's log book.

In the meantime the king had a prince called Haman. Haman and all his descendents were Amalekites. They really hated the Jewish people. The king liked Haman and promoted him above every other prince. Haman was of such importance that he told everyone to bow down to him whenever he passed by.

As he walked through the streets everyone would bow down to Haman, everyone except one man, Mordecai. Mordecai was a Jew and the Jews only worshipped one God. They did not bow down to any others. Haman began to hate Mordecai but Mordecai loved the Lord and would not disobey God by bowing to another.

One day God would honour Mordecai just for his faithfulness. The lesson is simple, always stand up for truth and stand against wrong doing.

ESTHER 361

Wicked People seem better off

You might find it strange that on one hand God allowed one of His people to be the queen and yet on the other He allowed a wicked person like Haman to be promoted above all others. However as we read through the book of Esther we will see God's hand in the whole situation.

All around us worldly people seem to prosper and do well, this can be difficult to understand, but remember, God's timing is perfect.

Many times in the Bible wicked people prospered. They often mocked or tempted the Lord but their sinning often came to a sad end. Many times we can see this happening in the Old Testament Scriptures. In Psalm 73, the Psalmist writes of how he often envied the foolish and wicked people around him as they seemed so carefree but when he worshipped God he says, "then understood I their end." (Psalm 73:3-5 & v17)

Haman hated the Jews so much that he wanted to kill Mordecai for not bowing down to him. His family advised him to invent a plan that would not only kill Mordecai but all the Jewish people. Haman loved this idea. Little did he know that Queen Esther was Jewish.

A terrible Law

Haman was the chief of all princes. He was promoted to be second in command to the king. He came up with an idea and brought it to the king.

He told the king that there was a certain group of people who would not respect the king's laws. He said these people have their own laws and do not respect the king's decrees. Haman convinced the king that in order to protect the whole Persian Empire it would be better if these people were destroyed.

Without questioning Haman any further, the king took off his ring and gave it to Haman as a sign that he agreed to destroy these people. Little did he realize that the people Haman was talking about were the Jewish people and that it would include his very wife, Queen Esther. Once the law had the king's seal on it, it could never be changed.

Haman arranged that on the thirteenth day of the twelfth month all the Jews were to be destroyed. A letter was sent out to all Jews in every country. Everything was to be taken from them and they were to be killed on this day. This was a terrible law; history has repeated itself so many times when Satan has tried to destroy God's people.

This can never happen because God will never allow it to happen.

ESTHER 363

A time of Mourning

There comes a time in everyone's life when it is time to mourn over the death of a loved one. Here in this period of Esther's life all her people were doomed to die.

Esther did not know what was going on, for the Jews in the city of Shushan were the first to receive the news. When Mordecai heard the news he tore his clothes and covered his face in ashes, as did all the people. This was to show how sad they were as they thought about their terrible fate.

All around the different countries where the Jewish people lived, there was the sound of weeping and wailing as people received the news. It was now law and nothing could be done to stop the law being changed. Haman, the wicked prince, had agreed to pay the king ten thousand talents of silver to have the Jews destroyed.

Mourning is a natural thing to do. Whenever someone close to you is dying or maybe has died it is normal to shed a tear. Sometimes it can last a few minutes, a few days, or even for years. Everyone has their own way of dealing with their own grief, however, God is the God of all comfort.

Remember He loves you and cares for you and will comfort you in a most wonderful way that no human can.

Whenever Esther received the news that all her people were to die she immediately called her people to fast and pray. Fasting is when a person doesn't eat for some time. On this occasion it was for three days.

Time for Action

When the news came to Esther that her people were to be killed on a certain day she was shocked and called for action. Mordecai sent a message to Esther, urging her to go to the king and plead for the lives of the Jews. Esther was very afraid, but Mordecai was confident that God would not let the Jews be destroyed. One way or another God would preserve His people, "Who knows" said Mordecai, "whether you have come to the kingdom for such a time as this." Esther instructed Mordecai that all the Jews were to fast and pray for three days.

In the meantime Esther called all her maids and friends to do the same thing. Esther needed to go to the king to tell him that what was happening was wrong. However the problem was that anyone who wished to speak to the king needed special permission. The next time Esther was due to visit the king on his throne was in thirty days time. It would be too late then. If anyone walked in on the king without permission and the king did not lift the golden sceptre to accept them they would be put to death. This was a court of law and not even the queen could walk in without permission.

Sometimes in our lives we need to take action to change things. It will not make us popular and could even get us into trouble. Before the Lord, however, when something is not right it is wrong for us to ignore it. Talk to the Lord about it in prayer and if He would have you to change something which isn't right then take the opportunity and correct it while you can. It is important that you are aware of the consequences, as you may have to pay a price.

Prayer is the Answer

When Esther received the message that her people were going to die because of a law that was made, she immediately called her people to pray to God. The challenge that faced Esther now was that she must go before the king without an invitation. This could mean death for her.

Esther was now beginning to understand why God had made her queen. She now found herself in a situation where she was the only one who could make a difference. Sometimes we may wonder why we go to a certain school, class or even place to live; perhaps God has a reason for it. We do not know at the time but one day we will find out.

Esther asked her people to pray for wisdom and that she would be very courageous. It would be easy for the king to end her life and get a new queen. Esther knew this and she realized that God must step into this situation and help them. Throughout the book of Esther you will not find the name of God mentioned. Even though this is the case, you will find the Jews humbling themselves before God, fasting and praying.

Prayer is not only the answer but it is the key to Christian living. Talk to the Lord about every detail of your life. You will find life much more blessed, more enjoyable and extremely refreshing as well as worthwhile.

Prepared to die for her People

The time had come for Esther to approach the King on the throne. Esther realized that the law stated that anyone who approached the king on his throne without permission would die. However, if the king lifted up his hand and held out the golden scepter, this would show he accepted her in his presence and that she was safe.

As Esther approached the throne room of the king her heart was pounding faster and faster. Her body was weak from lack of food and sleep for three days. When she approached the king, Esther was relieved to see him smile and lift up his hand of acceptance. This was the work of the Lord.

Mordecai had told Queen Esther, "Who knows whether you have come to the kingdom for such a time as this." She knew it could mean her death. But she said, "I will go and if I perish, I perish." Esther was prepared to die for her people, for their lives, their freedom and their culture. It meant so much to her.

This is of course what the Lord Jesus has done for us. He paid the ultimate sacrifice for us when He died on the cross to take away all our sins.

We can be saved for evermore by believing and trusting in Him because of what He has done for us on the cross.

ESTHER

Esther before the King

When Esther stood before the king he was so pleased to see her. He asked her what she wanted and proclaimed that she could have anything, even to the half of his kingdom!

As Esther stood before the king she wanted to tell him the terrible news about how all her people were going to die. The king did not know that Esther was a Jew. As she was talking to the king she felt it was not the right time to tell the king about the new law that was going to destroy her people.

Instead Esther invited the king and Haman to a banquet that she would prepare. It must have seemed rather unusual to risk your life coming before the king to invite him for dinner. However, the king readily agreed. Banquets and feasts were important in those days as a way of getting to know one another. Esther was delighted and made her way to prepare the banquet for the wicked Haman and her husband the king.

This is called discernment, knowing when to speak and when not to speak. When a person becomes a Christian, the Holy Spirit lives within them to guide them in their lives. This is a wonderful thing.

It is one of the greatest lessons to learn in life, to let God the Holy Spirit guide you in everything you do.

Esther hosts a Banquet

Can you imagine how excited Esther was to be hosting a banquet for the king? Everything would be prepared to perfection. When the king and the wicked Haman arrived they were delighted at such a beautiful spread.

The king still wanted to know what Esther's request was when she came to the throne. How surprised Haman was to find out that he and the king were invited back the next day for another banquet and there Esther would reveal her request. Again God was leading Esther as to the exact time that she should speak. God's timing is perfect and now was not the right time for Esther to speak. Some things needed to happen, unknown to Esther, to make everything work out.

Haman couldn't believe how fortunate he was. Not only was he the king's right hand man but now the queen thought very highly of him as well. He was so excited because he was invited not only once but twice to a special banquet organized by the queen.

Haman was full of joy and pride, as everything seemed to be going his way but in the background God was organizing everything His way. We will see over the next few days how God turned everything around for good.

In life wicked people seem to prosper and do well but it is only for a short time. If you take notice their prosperity does not last forever.

ESTHER 369

Taking a stand for God

Haman the wicked prince was on his way home from the first banquet. He was so excited. Now he was number one in the king and queen's eyes. As he passed through the gate there was Mordecai standing at the gate. Everyone bowed down to Haman; everyone except Mordecai. This angered him so much.

When he went home he began to tell all his family and friends the good news about the banquets and being invited back the next day, which made him very happy. Then his joy turned to sadness, for everything was going his way except one thing. He began to tell his wife and family about Mordecai and how he refused to bow down to him.

They all suggested that Haman should build a hanging platform (gallows) outside his home on which to hang Mordecai. Haman had such favour with the king that he thought he would easily get permission to do this. That night, workmen built big gallows for hanging people. It was fifteen metres high. How happy Haman felt, as early tomorrow morning he would go to the king and get permission to hang Mordecai. This time tomorrow Haman thought Mordecai would be dead.

Every day we are challenged to take our stand for God, whether it is at school or at home, never give in. Your Christian faith is very precious. Guard it with your life and no matter what, always take a stand for the Lord. This is what Mordecai did. It would have been easy for him to bow to Haman and keep the peace, but this would be wrong and would grieve the Lord.

Am I ever ashamed when other people talk about the Lord or do I get embarrassed when people ask me about my faith?

"For whosoever shall be ashamed of me and of my words, of him shall the Son of man be ashamed….." (Luke 9:26)

The King cannot sleep

After the first banquet Esther arranged, she invited both Haman and the king back the following day for another banquet. Haman was over the moon. His plan of destroying all the Jews would soon be accomplished. Now both the king and the queen thought highly of him, but best of all tomorrow his worst enemy Mordecai would be hanged....so he thought.

That night the king tossed and turned all night and could not sleep. He arranged for his servants to come to him and read out loud the log book of everything that happened in the palace. As the servant read about the men who had planned to kill the king and how the plot was stopped because Mordecai overheard the conversation, the king asked what was done to Mordecai to reward him for saving his life. Nothing had been done for, or given to Mordecai.

Sometimes when we cannot sleep God has a reason for wakening us. Sometimes it is to make us think back in our lives. Maybe the Lord wakens us to make us reflect upon our lives to give thanks for everything He has done, our families and everything we have. We should never take things for granted, especially remembering to thank those who do good towards us.

Falling into your own Trap

Early the next morning the wicked Haman made his way to the palace. Before he could utter his request to kill Mordecai for not bowing down to him, the king asked him a question.

The question was this, "What do you think should be done to the man whom the king wants to honour?" Haman could not believe his ears. Now the king wanted to honour him! "Well," he thought, "I think he should wear the king's robe, the king's crown and be paraded through the city on the king's horse and the whole city should be told that this is the man whom the king delights to honour," suggested Haman.

"That is an excellent idea Haman. You are the very man to walk Mordecai through the streets dressed as a king on my horse and tell everyone I am delighted to honour him," replied the king. Can you imagine how Haman felt?

Shortly after this, Esther met both the king and Haman for her second banquet. When the king asked her to speak she told him all about Haman's wicked plan to kill all her people. The king was horrified. Haman pleaded with Esther for his life but it was all too late.

The very gallows Haman had prepared for Mordecai became his own death trap and that is where he was hanged.

The Bible teaches us, "Be sure your sin will find you out," (Numbers 32:23) and "Be not deceived; God is not mocked: for whatsoever a man soweth, that shall he also reap." (Galatians 6:7)

All things Work together for good

On the thirteenth day of the twelfth month all the Jews were to be killed. This was a law that could not be changed, so something needed to be done quickly to save the lives of the Jewish people.

Together the king and Esther arranged for Mordecai to write a new law. In this law the Jews were told that they could defend themselves. It also stated that the king supported them in their right to life. The law was quickly delivered throughout the 127 provinces all the way from India to Ethiopia.

How happy the Jewish people were to know that they could defend themselves against the enemy. As a result when the day came hardly any Jews were killed. Their lives, possessions and their families all could be spared. The Jews were a very smart people; they would know how to defend themselves.

Everyone wept for joy as this law came sweeping through the land, for now they would not have to die. All this good news could be traced back to one little Jewish girl called Esther who was willing to be used by God and put her life on the line for her own people.

Surely we can learn from this that for those who love God, all things work together for good.
(Romans 8:28)

Esther becomes a Heroine

Have you ever wondered what it is like to be a hero or heroine? Well, Esther became a heroine in her country amongst her own people.

Can you recall at the very beginning of the life of Esther, how she was just a little orphan girl, not having any parents and without any real hope in this world. Yet God looked down from heaven and chose that little girl Esther to be the girl He was going to use to save His people.

Esther knew God in a personal way. This was her secret in life. She knew when to speak up and when not to. Esther realised the importance of prayer when calamity came to her and her people. Many Jews today have special feasts once a year to remember how God delivered their people. They often read through the book of Esther reminding themselves of all that happened.

Even though God's name is never mentioned in this book we can easily see the hand of God in every aspect of Esther's life. The God of Esther and Mordecai is also our God. Just like He helped, guided and protected them, He can do the same for us.

God knows all about us, our lives, our circumstances, our challenges, and the decisions we have to make everyday. Put your life in His hand and let Him guide you. What a blessing it is to be a child of God.

What Children think, say and do!

These are samples of worksheets that children often do at Bible clubs

Children often write very interesting comments as shown in the following pages

What Children think, say and do!

Dear Colin, it is supper to be a christain

Dear Colin, I love God so much and I want to be a christian so much from Jamie

Dear Colin, I am glad I am saved.

Dear Colin, thanks for making me a christian.

Dear Colin, i want to believe in Jesus.

Dear Colin, I want to know what you do to ask Jesus into your heart

What Children think, say and do!

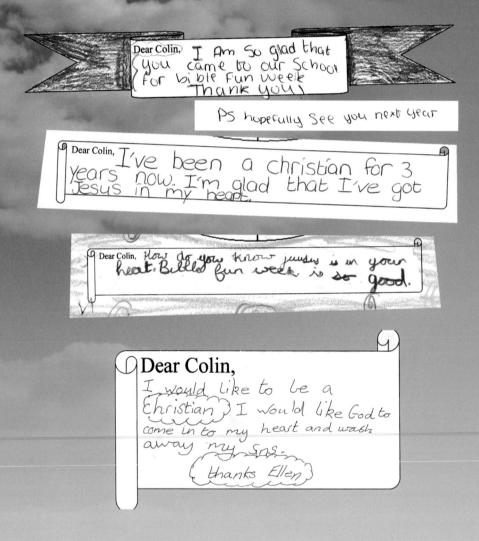

Dear Colin, I Am so glad that you came to our school for bible fun week. Thank you!

PS. hopefully see you next year

Dear Colin, I've been a christian for 3 years now. I'm glad that I've got Jesus in my heart.

Dear Colin, How do you know jesus is in your heat. Bibel fun week is so good.

Dear Colin,

I would like to be a Christian. I would like God to come into my heart and wash away my sins.

thanks Ellen

What Children think, say and do!

Dear Colin, thanks for all the advace and the stepping stones. I want the Bible club to go on and on and on, thanks for learning about Paul, singing, Quizez, compeitions, Memory verses and the whole week. I am now a CHRISTIAN bye and thanks

Dear Colin,
I Love singing your songs. I Love listening to your stories they are so much fun.

Dear Colin, I Was Sevaed today

Dear Colin, I am a christion, I love the bible club.

Dear Colin, I want Jesus to Be my Saviour and save me form my sins.

What Children think, say and do!

What Children think, say and do!

Dear Colin, I also asked God into my Heart. I am clean now

Dear Colin, My name is Jason I just became christian because I asked Jesus into my Heart.

Dear Colin,

I am a christian and I Love God and thank you for teaching me about God.

Ezara xox

Dear Colin, I pray to Jesus and God

Dear Colin, I believe that Jesus died on the cross to take away my many sins. This I am saved because I believed with all my heart

Tracts written by Colin

Books written by Colin